SLIP
one mind, two worlds

By Cristie Yager

 A catalogue record for this book is available from the National Library of Australia

Copyright © 2019 Cristie Yager

All rights reserved worldwide.

No part of the book may be copied or changed in any format, sold, or used in a way other than what is outlined in this book, under any circumstances, without the prior written permission of the publisher.

Publisher:
ASPG (Australian Self Publishing Group)
P.O. Box 159, Calwell, ACT Australia 2905
Email: publishaspg@gmail.com
http://www.inspiringpublishers.com

National Library of Australia Cataloguing-in-Publication entry

Author: *Yager, Cristie*

Title:**SLIP: One Mind, Two Worlds**/*Cristie Yager.*

Designed by Surendra Gupta for Inspiring Publishers

ISBN: 978-0-6484592-7-9 (print)
　　　978-0-6484592-8-6 (eBook)

Chapter 1

She lifted the take-away coffee cup to her lips for a sip, closed her big blue eyes and sighed. The smell of aftershave swirled around her as the tip of her rounded nose pressed against the lid. Fresh aromatic coffee with the residue of a tangy masculine scent, brought Elle closer to being aroused than she had in months.

Especially when she knew the intoxicating smell came from the sexy barista with tattoos up his firm arms. He smiled charmingly at her as she ran her fingers through her dark hair sheepishly.

Elle sat by the window over-looking the beach. She could see the waves crashing up onto the sweeping sands. The ocean was a little violent today. It seemed angry in an-other-worldly shade of turquoise and it met fiercely with a grey sky. She saw lightening crack and split the ash stained clouds. She could hear the dull rumble of the thunder that followed vibrate through the glass.

Rain splattered the window, finally arriving to blur and warp her vision of the world outside into a macabre surreal one. She liked to see it like that. Elle had always felt that there was more to this life than meets the eye. Not everything as it was, but layers upon layers of complex worlds pressed upon one another. She focused on the drops clinging to the glass, watching others higher up speed down towards them like little rivers. They'd merge with the lonely drops below and grow.

Finally, too heavy and pregnant to hold onto their place, they would quiver and fall. She considered if the drops were happier in their secure place despite being alone, or if it were more comforting to be joined and yet spiralling out of control. Elle couldn't answer that question, nor did she find it important enough to ponder for more than a moment.

Storms always gave her a rush. The atmosphere seemed so charged and full of unexpected events in weather like that. She felt alive in this moment. Cosy inside the café as a passionate storm played out, her palms wrapped around a hot cardboard cup; feeling attractive with the undeniably present attention of the dreamy barista. Pretending she was someone else, a sultry stranger.

Once she'd been what people would have called a free spirit. She was artistic and creative and people wanted to be around her, though she'd never felt like she was a part of the crowd. Elle always felt like she was just used as a decoration, just something thrown in to add interest.

She never really wanted to make friends despite the opportunities. She just couldn't commit to the onslaught of events and catch ups. She hated trying to keep a schedule and preferred to make plans as her day progressed. Occasionally she wondered if she was missing out on some special connection that other's felt but she'd made her choice to stick to herself. She thought it best to pack those bags and move on, no need to dwell on decisions made long ago.

Elle thought perhaps that she'd simply grown up. Well decided to lay blame on the fact. She wasn't fun anymore, wasn't as creative and in her own opinion was the most boring person on the face of the Earth. She no longer felt that content peace she once had when she was younger and care fee.

In fact, she was feeling like bits and pieces of her very being were missing. As if along the way little chunks dropped and crumbled off of her. It burned an emptiness inside that seemed to be expanding with each new day. Elle knew that like those falling rain drops, that she too was spiralling out of control within and didn't know how to stop it. This content moment there in the café for Elle was welcome and was very rare.

She'd woken that morning to the comforting sound of rain, a world full of gloom. She'd felt energized, her system buzzing with anticipation of something mysterious playing out. However, it played out almost the same as every other morning.

"Making coffee are you Elle?" Toby asked. "Want to make me one too?"

Elle made an attempt at an agreeing smile. It was weak and she hadn't mastered it, but that didn't matter, Toby walked on past down the hall. He didn't even notice the distasteful look she threw over her shoulder at him.

Sometimes she felt like a naughty teen, rebelling against her parents behind their backs; too afraid to actually stick her tongue out in front of them. She liked to do things for the man in her life, because she cared for him and wanted to show it. Not because it was her job. Not because he thought she should.

She was only making herself an instant coffee, she thought exasperated. A heaped teaspoon of coffee, along with a pinch of sugar, a dash of milk and some hot water, boiled in a cheap plastic, electric kettle. She'd put it in her big soup mug. She liked how it was over-sized and needed two hands to handle. She liked to lift it to her lips, her palms cupped on each side.

It was the perfect mug for her, suited her. Toby always teased, making references about her compensating for other things in her life. She'd smirk at him and tell him he'd be the one to know about all things as such. Toby didn't like her jokes much and would storm off with Elle again rolling her eyes behind his back. He can dish it but he can't take it, she'd think to herself annoyed.

She now wished she'd waited for Toby to have left for work before making her instant coffee. All she'd wanted to do was sit and relax; enjoying the simple things in peace.

Toby on the other hand was what he called cultured. He preferred an espresso coffee, made in his espresso maker. It was much more of a hassle than the uncultured coffee Elle drank. She sighed and pulled the ground coffee beans from the freezer.

His tone of voice as he asked for his daily espresso, made Elle feel as though he'd expected her to have already made that coffee. And that it should have been sitting, steaming on the counter for him to grab on his way past, on route to his little office in the garage.

He made her feel as though; not having it ready was just another inconvenience in his life. She should have already thought of him.

"It'll be ready soon!" Elle called. She wasn't entirely sure if he'd heard her from his little office, but she didn't entirely care. His office, she thought. How I'd burn it down if I were the arsonist type, and if the chances of the rest of the house catching alight were slim to minimal. He practically lived in the small space, glued to his computer.

She wasn't totally aware of exactly what he was working on in there and she didn't really want to know. It kept him busy, kept him out of her hair and kept him from arguing with her about every little thing she chose to do.

Sometimes she considered perhaps she was envious of him spending all his time in that cramped unpleasant room, instead of spending time with her. But on second thoughts she decided not. Maybe once, long ago but not now. They'd grown so far apart, she didn't even want to be near him and his arrogant attitude.

As Elle heaped the freshly ground beans into the stainless-steel pot, she shook her head. She wondered how she'd got to this point, making snide and somewhat violent, internal comments about the man she was meant to love. The man who said he wanted to be with her forever, the man who said he wanted to help her raise her daughter Mai.

Technically they were engaged. He would remind her, as if it was his key to ownership. They spent a whole night sitting together talking about it. Toby had brought it up and was clearly putting his feelers out. By the end of the night he'd declared it was settled.

They were engaged and she could expect a sparkling ring very soon; only that was eight months ago and the only things sparkling in her life right now was his espresso pot. Which she'd have to scrub after making his brew, yet again.

Elle didn't think she'd say yes if he produced a ring at the moment. She'd have to think about it at least. She decided that she did love him in some ways, but he made it hard to do so. Their relationship was a demanding, full time job one in which apparently, she was the only one employed.

They'd met a few years ago in a fancy resort bar. It wasn't the kind of place she'd usually visit but then again it hadn't been her idea. Elle had made sure she looked immaculate. Red figure-hugging dress, the vibrant contrasting colour always made her blue eyes pop when framed by her long, dark hair. She wasn't at the beachside bar to meet Toby.

She was waiting for someone else that night. She and Toby got chatting and laughing. Before noticing she had been stood up, she was in the grips of a tall, dark and handsome stranger.

In the beginning they'd meet at cafes and restaurants, played chess over a wine or two. Until one day she realised they were a couple. He was just always there and she let him. Soon enough, they were house hunting, they picked out a big brick home with a nice garden. She could remember her happiness the day they'd been handed the keys. Elle was holding Mai, who was only two years old at the time, Toby with his arm around her waist beaming down at them both.

Together, a family, just what Elle had always hoped her baby girl would have. Toby was handsome, charming, had a stable job. What any girl would hope for in a man, but Elle concluded she wasn't just any girl anymore. She wanted more, she wanted someone who liked her and showed it.

Soon after they moved in together, they stopped going out and Elle wasn't exactly wearing figure hugging red dresses anymore. Elle quickly learned all of Toby's undesirable traits, like he'd held a breath and now was free to breath. And surely, he'd figured out hers too. They became distant and separate.

Toby liked to socialise with his friends, Elle liked to stay home. Toby was materialistic and motivated by money. Elle just didn't see the sense in accumulating objects and was passionate about art and the environment. They began to argue and disagree. They were very different people. Their relationship quickly became simply real.

The fairy tale certainly had ended as Elle knew it someday would. Toby had become a challenge to handle and Elle had to shut her mind to his ramblings more often than not lately. She couldn't understand his anger and frustration over pointless things and couldn't be bothered engaging in his rants or even putting her opinions forward anymore.

She'd just stare off and interest herself with things worth focusing on; like the small spider weaving its web in the corner of their bedroom window, back and forth, back and forth. So much work for one little creature, so delicate and deadly.

As long as Elle made sure to nod occasionally, Toby was satisfied. She figured he just liked the sound of his own voice rather than sharing and collaborating ideas with her.

She no longer felt attractive, even though deep down she knew she was. She had an alluring innocence about her, she was not a small woman but proportioned well with a natural beauty. She was content within herself, and it was her confidence that enhanced all she had. She knew men were interested but she didn't care.

She'd chosen Toby and he had been enough. And that made things all the more depressing. Not having the one man she'd chosen to have in her life, the only man who was allowed to touch her, allowed to compliment her; not do so? She felt lousy and ugly and hurt. A ball of anxiety. Does he do this on purpose? Is he punishing me? Does he even love me? She'd often find herself asking questions she couldn't answer. He made her feel desperate and hopeless.

Sex was just a vague memory of something she once enjoyed. She couldn't even initiate anything physical with Toby anymore, she was so afraid of rejection it hurt. She felt like he knew that and used it against her. Maybe it's in my head. She didn't know anymore.

Elle felt the problem was hers, she wanted and dreamed of another baby, a passionate relationship and perhaps a rewarding career to top it all off. Of course, she had none of these. People always want what they didn't have, she told herself and tried desperately to appreciate what she had. Sometimes she wanted these things so much that her life and mind began to suffer.

She'd zone out of her present completely. Washing dishes became her favourite day dreaming station. Before she knew it, she'd be finished, all the dishes were sparkling clean and put away and on the odd occasion she couldn't even recall doing any part of this mundane chore.

She'd spent the entire time living out fantasises and feeling emotions, the passions her life just wasn't providing.

The gurgling, bubbling coffee roused Elle from her endless, depressing thoughts. She took the espresso pot from the hot plate and placed it onto the cold one. It sizzled and spat tiny bubbles of scalding coffee and cranky steam from the rim.

The phone rang. Startling Elle who was still wading through the timeline of her rotting relationship, like trying to gasp for breath after swimming the length of a pool. Desperate and ready to surface.

"Ouch!"

She'd burned herself on the hot pot, knocking it as she jumped. Toby's coffee? Fine of course. Her mind informed her grudgingly, so much for your hand.

"Hello?" Elle said into the phone.

She held it with her head tilted against her shoulder, as she grabbed Toby's in proportionate cup and saucer from the cupboard.

"Hey what are you up to?" Nessa questioned.

It was Elle's mum. How thrilled, in a non-interested way, Elle was. Last night Nessa had been going out to meet friends, well that's what she called it. Elle knew she'd hear about it soon enough, but this felt a little too soon.

Nessa was into flings, she didn't like the idea of a long-term relationship, or so she said. She knew the magic left eventually, the thrill would die. Elle wondered if her mother had just never found the one, she'd had plenty of one's though. Surely someone, one day would stick.

Elle had dealt with it her entire life, even as a young girl there would always be a lot of Mummy's good friends come and go, her mind recalled blankly. Elle never had any stable fatherly figure that she could remember. Her father had run off with some woman when she was too small to remember. She wanted something different for Mai, her daughter.

It wasn't really Nessa's choice in men, or even her drinking habits that rubbed Elle the wrong way. The truth of it was that Elle feared turning out just like her. And then to top it off, Elle couldn't let go of her mother's reaction to the birth of Mai.

During pregnancy, she'd been told she was having a boy. Nessa was over the moon, she seemed almost relieved that Elle was carrying a son. She couldn't wait to meet her grandson and Elle relished this happy rare time bonding with her mum. It was such an uplifting feeling knowing that she wasn't going to be alone. Her baby's father had disappeared without a trace before he'd even known she was pregnant.

Nessa and Elle would shop together and lunch together, chatting about the unborn baby boy they'd soon share responsibilities of. Nessa even wanted to be at the birth. Only Max came out into the world and wasn't a Max; he was a she and re-named Mai.

For what should have been the best day of Elle's life, the birth of her first child, it was turned ugly very quickly, by Nessa.

Here was Elle exhausted, sweaty and ragged yet in tears of pure joy at the sight of her newborn. She was beaming in her happiness as she looked up at Nessa.

Nessa appeared distraught at the very sight of Mai being a girl and not the grandson she'd planned for. Elle had been searching for a word that fit her total devastation since. She couldn't decide if she'd ever forgive that move. Over the past two years Nessa had forgiven the sonographers mistake and slowly began to become involved in Mai's life. And still Elle was weary.

"I'm not up to much. Just about to have coffee, though I think mines cold now. Probably just watch Toby drink the one I'd made for him." Elle could hear her own dull meanness in those words. "What about you Mum?" That does it. Get ready Elle, you've done it now, she thought. Yet again rolling her eyes.

"Well...."

Nessa said it in such a way that would make you think she'd just heard it was going to rain gold. Or perhaps that the fountain of youth had just been found and it was only down the street. She said it with too much oomph for one, unworthy little word.

"I went out last night, and I met the nicest guy! His name is Jack, and he is in town for some business thing and he says he just loves kids. And oh god, he's the best kisser, my lips are so swollen! But I haven't heard from him yet, I left my number on the dresser when I left his hotel room this morning. If he doesn't call, I'm going to be so pissed at that prick."

Elle cringed. Her mum always knew how to fill in all the unnecessary blanks.

"Sounds like a great night. But hey, Toby's coffee is going cold, so I have to go..." Elle squeezed in as Nessa drew breath.

"He hates me, doesn't he?" Nessa half yelled.

"Who Mum? This guy Tom?" Elle cringed again.

"No, I don't mean Jack; thanks for listening." She commented snidely. "I meant Toby. Look if he does hate me I don't really care. I just wish he had the balls to say it to my face instead of avoiding me, wearing those fancy clothes with his hair all slicked back. He's going bald, isn't he? That's why he does it. He thinks he's so much better than everyone else. He has no reason not to like me. He has issues." She ranted aimlessly.

"Mum Toby doesn't hate you." Elle sighed, feeling her shoulders dropping and her brain ache. "I really have to go; I'll talk to you later."

"Okay, love you Hun. Call me tomorrow." Nessa hung up.

Elle took the espresso and placed it down next to Toby. By his right hand, so it was in an easy to reach position for him and yet not too close as to get in the way of his mouse using hand. Annoying him. She'd done that before, placed his coffee in the wrong spot.

He'd knocked it over and the hot, dark liquid spilled all over his various papers. He was so angry as the coffee dribbled down onto his expensive pants. He'd yelled at Elle, telling her she was an idiot. She made sure not to make the same mistake again.

She was still a little vague, picking absentmindedly at her bottom lip, deep in thought. Still sorting all her internal stuff as Toby glanced up, pulling his lips up into one of those fake smiles he'd been trying to perfect. Elle returned one and left.

Elle made a frustrated growl sound once she was out of earshot. Shoot me now. Hope Toby's coffee is good enough, too bad if it isn't. She thought sarcastically. Didn't even thank me. Whatever. Call Mum back tomorrow, do I have to?

Though Elle knew she would. She had no friends. She knew a lot of people but didn't want to cross that line between acquaintance and friend, venturing into a place where she'd feel responsible for even more people. She knew she needed to get out of her own head more often than she currently did.

The lack of outlets and human interaction, besides that of her over-excited and often confusing mother; her expectant and demanding partner; her sweet but impatient daughter; had her imagination and curiosity working overtime.

In a lot of ways Elle passed it off as a good thing. It was her unique perspective on things that paused the impending insanity she felt surely was looming. The way she viewed the world helped her occupy herself with things others considered mundane. She could watch the flight of a lone bird for hours, consider its thoughts, dreams and desires, if in fact, they considered such things.

Sit with Mai watching the busy work of ants, living minute lives no-one would ever understand. Poke at the single dewy drops clinging to abandoned webs that looked like jewels made of magic in the mornings.

Elle's mother had always commented on her strange ability to find almost anything and everything fascinating and interesting. She found mystery in it all. With no job to go to, no real hobbies and a complete lack of motivation to pursue her creative interests to pass her time. At least she had a wondering mind to occupy the empty spots between things that needed to be done.

She was imaginative and creative and needed outlets in her waking life or her boredom would build up and invade her dreams. She'd have vivid and colourful dreams, realistic yet fanciful. At other times however, she had the most horrid and terrifyingly bad nightmares, mostly about Toby.

"Toby when something bad happens in a dream it usually means the opposite." Elle would tell him when he'd get mad and defensive after she'd recall a particularly bad dream. "A new beginning or something."

"Why would you be dreaming about me in that way?" He'd demand answers which Elle simply couldn't give.

"It doesn't mean anything." She'd say over and over before chuckling and waving it off. Though Elle didn't think she believed that at all. Some of her dreams were so real she'd be frightened of him when she woke. But she chose not to relive her dreams to Toby anymore. She'd keep them to herself.

Chapter 2

She told herself to stop. Stop dwelling and rehashing things and times and events she could no longer control. Instead she focused. Watching the sexy barista make coffee for an old couple, attempting to delete the morning she'd had from her mind.

She was tired of doing that. Trying to make things right, in her mind's eye after the fact. She knew she needed to take this present moment and move forward from it. Away from what was gone and done. From this café to where? She wondered. She was actually quite amazed that she was even in a café; she'd been so glued to this routine of monotony for so long now.

Perhaps it was meant to be, Toby asking me to make that espresso, mum calling, my coffee going cold. Convincing me of a change, driving by this café with the faded red balloons bobbing in the wind, almost my favourite colour. Calling to me as I drove toward home after dropping Mai at preschool.

Again, over thinking.

She watched from under her lashes, he was dressed in black. His sleeves rolled up, bearing his thick forearms. They were covered in patterns, tattoos in swirling, sweeping shapes. She didn't stare too long to make out specifics but considered taking the time to do so some other day. She glanced at his chest quickly before looking back out to her storm, she couldn't help it. His top buttons undone.

One too many in her opinion not that she minded. The barista was busy throwing in a free warmed muffin for the old couple to share, even cutting it in half. Perhaps I'll make this place a part of my new routine, my moving forward strategy. Elle decided in a husky way she probably shouldn't have, whilst contemplating what the skin of a man who makes coffee all day long, might smell like.

A usual day for Elle had become just repeated steps. An itemised list that passed the time until she decided to create a cosy dark cave in her room. A space to just pull up her blankets and read.

Most of the time, it didn't even matter if it was a good book, just something to stop her constant internal monologue. Something to suck her away from being so very absorbed within her own thoughts. A place away from herself, her life and who she really was. She wanted to be someone else. Everyone else seemed happy and content and she just couldn't grasp it in her own world.

Occasionally, Toby would stroll into the room and dig through the wardrobe for his filing boxes, looking for some paper with an importance she was unaware of.

She'd watch him from behind her book. He was tall and slim. His dark hair in his idea of a smart and classy slick style. It irritated Elle that he spent more time on his appearance than she did. More time on his appearance than with her. He always wore suit pants and dressy shirts.

She wondered in these moments if she found him attractive and thought yes, that sometimes she did. But mostly it was her memories, of when he had pretended as if he liked her, back when he liked her company. When they laughed together and he smiled genuinely at her. These weak memories of who he had once been kept her interested. The false hope that someday he'd be the same man again made him attractive.

But then he'd walk out again. Though before he left, he always made sure. He'd lean over the bed and give her a few pecks on the lips. Always three, she always counted. And then he'd lift his head and pull his lips up into one of those fake smiles at her. Those smiles looked more aggressive than anything. There was no hint of sincerity, no trace of actual happiness in his eyes. Just that odd action of lifting his lips at the corners and squinting.

The only thing those smiles made Elle wonder was why? She didn't have any idea what she'd done to take away his genuine happiness or why she deserved his insincerity. His real smiles which she hadn't seen for quite some time were caring, the kind of smile you could see shinning in his eyes. Loving and warm, but this one was plain careless and slightly hurtful. It doesn't matter, I don't care, she concluded. And gave one back, equally as fake, and surely just as hurtful.

There were times where Toby wasn't working on his computer or out meeting friends, or off enjoying one of his hobbies. When he would decide to sit in the room and read too. At least we're in the same place sharing this time, Elle would think. Trying to appreciate the moment for what it was. She'd continue to read, attempting to pretend he wasn't there in case she annoyed him. She'd quickly remember though, especially when she cleared her throat or coughed.

Every time, she could see Toby grimace as if he were about to catch some incurable disease. Or that Elle had made some ear-piercing sound that would cause him to shrivel and die. He could make her feel so guilty and terrible with the slightest of facial gestures. Elle continually felt she was apologising for some reason or another. Perhaps for simply for being alive.

After all of this time together she began to semi fear some of his habits and reactions. It was easier to just be quiet around him. Her self-esteem was lowering and his seemed to be rising from it. He didn't appear to notice. He didn't appear to notice much, but then again on second thoughts, Elle realised he did notice a lot.

Like the way someone parked their car in a way that was unpleasing to him. The way someone dressed in a way that was incorrect to him. The things they spoke about, basically any small thing that was unpleasing; to him.

Elle kind of felt lucky in a way, that she was neither on nor completely off his radar. More like a smear left behind from a squashed bug on the screen. She wasn't the target of Toby's affections or attacks anymore, and she wasn't that incoming beep either.

Suddenly Toby would rise and declare it was time for work. Relieved, she'd watch him dress and smoke a cigarette.

"I'll miss you. Love you." Toby would say, check his hair and then leave.

Miss me? Love me? Elle sighed. Wondering why they bothered to live in such a way. Grabbed her bag from the fake leather bar stool and head toward the door, time to pick up Mai.

Elle, again, would drive that insanely non-stimulating drive. Make small talk, in which she had no interest, with the bitchy, gossipy mums who stood around competing over their child's qualities. Collect Mai and her things and continued on home. She'd make Mai something to eat. Prop her up on the stool and watch her.

Elle held her chin in her hands as she leaned over the kitchen bench on her elbows. Smiling, she'd watch her little girl's mouth chew ever so slowly. Observing the tiny human, she had helped to create.

Strawberries for afternoon tea, Mai's favourite. Mai would pick up the chopped strawberry and look at it so intently. Turning it around and upside down like she was studying it or searching for a slight imperfection. Her tubby fingers, with her nails painted pink and chipped at the edges, would pop it into her raspberry rimmed mouth. And then she'd begin the process again.

Elle watched in awe, such a perfect creature. Mai was quiet just like Elle. I don't feel quiet within, her mind noted.

"Mai what are you thinking about baby?" Elle questioned.

"Do fairies eat strawberries Mummy?" She asked in all seriousness with a high-pitched voice.

"I honestly couldn't say. Perhaps we'll do some research online later." Elle couldn't think of a better response. "You know we could ask Nana Ness too, she used to tell me all about a place called Frin. She said that's where the real world is, the magic world. And I think she said fairies live there..." she chose to add, drifting off into her thoughts again.

Suddenly she was back in her childhood bed, looking up at Nessa, she was tucking her floral blankets up around her throat.

"I don't know how you can sleep like that Hun, I'd feel strangled." Nessa said grinning at her small Elle.

"It's safer." The little girl said as if it were fact.

She was about six years old. Her dark hair thick around her head, spilled over a ruffled pillow. Her big, wide eyes beaming from her face, making it look small. She had large pixie like features. She'll grow into them Nessa thought stroking her forehead.

"Tell me a story Mama." Elle took hold of Nessa's hand and pulled her encouraging her to sit.

"Hey Ness, you coming Baby?" A man's voice bellowed from across the hall. Nessa rolled her eyes and sat down.

"He can wait." She winked and Elle giggled. "I'm telling my baby a story. Move over Hun." She said as she playfully shoved Elle across the bed to lie down.

Nessa's head rested against Elle's on the pillow and the girl smiled as she caught her mother's spicy scent in her button nose. She couldn't name the smell but knew it came from the bottle Mama kept in the top of the pantry. She'd left it out once and Elle being curious, took the bottle down and opened it up wanting to take just one sneaky sip. Nessa had caught her and yelled. Elle didn't understand but knew she'd never touch that bottle again.

But at least now she knew where that strong scent came from. She liked it. It was so familiar to her now.

Nessa began to speak. To tell Elle of a beautiful place with peach skies, three suns and sweeping fields that went on and on. Flowers and creatures like none on Earth, places so ancient they'd absorbed the emotions of thousands of beings. So thick with their auras you'd feel it yourself. She'd tell her of a happiness so blissful and sweet.

Elle didn't ever want to fall asleep. She wanted to listen to the magic, and hear of the fairies that flew in blue flames, of men so magnificent, handsome and charming. And of feelings so free and happy.

She loved to hear her mums hushed husky voice and finally would give in and allow her eye lids to grow heavy and finally close. Promising herself she'd only rest them, keeping her ears open. Then gradually her mother's voice would fade and she'd slip into her own world with peach skies and flaming fairies.

She'd wake to find Nessa smoking a cigarette in the kitchen while she cooked bacon, wearing some man's shirt she'd never seen before.

"How was your night in Frin?" She'd ask and dish out some breakfast for her baby and her good friend.

Elle frowned. Why haven't I remembered the stories before now? I wonder why Mum stopped talking about Frin?

As Elle pondered over the stories her mum once told her, she printed pictures from the computer of fairies and magical beings for Mai to colour in. Then together they sat for hours, colouring and talking. Elle thought that perhaps she loved it even more than Mai did. It gave her something to do, a peaceful distraction. She adored all those pretty images so carefree and delicate. Mai was becoming her only friend and Elle enjoyed spending time doing things she liked, even though perhaps it wasn't entirely healthy.

Once Mai had gone to bed, tucked up safe and sound. Elle decided to find more fairies and wonderful creatures for her. As the evening wore on, she'd found links to websites containing articles that supported the existence of such magical things.

The more she looked the more she found. She was utterly absorbed.

She leant back, unfolding her legs and stretched. They'd lost circulation. She always sat crossed legged on chairs, her feet tucked up under her. Nessa told her not to numerous times as a girl, but she'd never grown out of it. She rubbed her tired eyes and turned back to the screen to continue reading. Elle was completely engrossed.

Perhaps mermaids, fairies and pixies really did exist. Mai would love that she thought, a hunt for magic. Actually, I would too. She hoped they did exist. Somehow, the world would seem less drab and cruel and more mystical and wonderful if they were indeed real, even though her rational mind told her it was impossible.

Finally, Elle turned off the computer and sat staring at the blank screen for what seemed a long time in the silence. She began to feel guilty and stupid. Researching mythical and make-believe creatures?

You're a grown woman for goodness sakes Elle! Reality smacked back into her hard. I'm just a mindless single mother, no job, no direction, no ambition, no money. Living with an older man who swept me off my feet, he's practically over me, I'm over it! Does he even care about me? And now I'm obsessing over fairies? Finding pointless things to day dream about, purely to avoid facing the truth.

The world was no longer magical, or romantic, or special. And even when Elle thought of the times when she'd thought it had been, she declared herself plain wrong. She'd quit love, didn't believe in romance. All those times she'd felt carefree and alive now just seemed silly.

Once she would run wild through shopping malls; her glee was further inspired by the people who looked on thinking she was strange. She didn't care. She was having fun. She'd find brick walls to balance along when she'd go for a walk, just to add interest, barefooted and cold. Sleeping in the middle of football fields, just so she could watch the stars creep across the universe. She would dive into the icy ocean for no reason at all, totally clothed, just to feel awake and excited. Now the dip of a toe was enough to turn her away.

And why? Because Toby had finally convinced her that her behaviour was inappropriate and immature. Despite these little things being what made him love her in the first place. He was probably right she thought. It was no longer practical or grown-up to desire being unique and free. Becoming another droning statistic, like a proper person. Like everyone else, was what she should aspire to be.

Over time, depressingly she began, without even mindfully doing so, cutting herself off from friends and family. The very few she had left. She and Toby were both passionately opinionated people. Only Toby's ideas and opinions now over-powered hers and they'd always end up arguing over something she'd said that didn't quite fit Toby's perspective.

So, she stopped expressing herself. She stopped communicating with him. Elle knew she was shutting down and shutting off but couldn't seem to curb the rippled effects. She didn't know how to change now. She was down and probably miserable to be around, therefore chose not to be around anyone.

Elle had now lost all motivation to call or contact or visit anyone she once knew, what would they say if she told them life wasn't perfect for her anymore? What would they think if they came to realise that she was no longer the happy person that they'd always known? She knew they'd blame Toby, tell her to leave. But for some reason she felt compelled to stay. Maybe because she knew it was not all his fault. It was her, she'd had a choice and she'd made the wrong one.

She thought back on the dinners they once hosted together, long afternoons in the kitchen following new recipes she'd found. Mai sitting up on the bench with flour on her nose, wet rivulets running through the powder on her cheeks. Left from her sorry tears over an accidental egg breakage. Toby would wander in and out of the kitchen to gleam a blueberry here or to dip his finger in a bowl there. He'd spin Elle around to the mellow, soulful music she played loudly while she baked away.

She'd be tidying up as the doorbell would ring. A buzz of excitement would course through her. She'd do her excited squeal thing she didn't even notice she did, unless Toby pointed it out, dash Mai down from the bench. Realizing she'd missed some food stuff from Mai's face, she'd quickly wipe it away before sashaying toward the door. The night would be filled with laughter and food, music and joy.

It was awesome for her to dress up and throw parties, something to look forward to, a bit of fun. But she tired of it. Toby aimed for this as a lifestyle, endless friends, food and drink. He didn't understand the effort, the cleaning, the preparations. The pretending required on Elle's part.

She began finding it hard to continue to smile and be buoyant after she and Toby had argued before their friends arrived. And that became more often than not. Or he'd chose to pick a fight once everyone had left, usually over something she'd said during the night. Or because of something inappropriate a man had said to her. He was always so jealous and suspicious.

It was too hard for her to fake happiness when all she wanted to do was wallow. The energy, the effort, she couldn't muster it anymore. It easier to hide away, easier to do nothing and easier to be isolated and sad.

Elle pulled out the pictures she'd printed the night before, showing Mai as they ate their fruit salad for breakfast. They always got to share breakfast together as Toby would still be sleeping after his long night shift. It was their special time, without interruption and hovering judgments.

Mai was happy with the pictures, her eyes lit up as she examined them one by one in great detail.

"This one looks like my friend Trey." Mai claimed almost dropping the banana from her fork as she held up the yet to be coloured, black and white image.

"Is that someone from school, one of your friends?" Elle enquired.

"No Mum, Trey lives in Frin." Mai said in such a way, that Elle could imagine the eye roll that would accompany it in the years to come.

Elle shook her head at the innocence of Mai's attempted sarcasm, clearly it ran in the family she decided with a smirk. He lives in Frin? Elle decided to question Nessa about the stories she'd once told her as a little girl, Mai's imagination was obviously growing. Their joint interest in the mythical and mysterious was something she treasured. She'd love to pass down those amazing stories she'd grew up on. Elle was keen to relive those memories too. Perhaps involving Nessa would build a stronger bond between them.

"Hi Hun!" Nessa exclaimed as she hugged Elle. "Didn't expect you, I'll put the kettle on."

"Thanks, a coffee would go down well, I haven't had my morning dose yet." Elle smiled as she watched her mother dash off to the kitchen. She nodded absentmindedly as Nessa chatted away about something inconsequential while she made the coffee.

Nessa always had a classy yet naturally unkept appearance. She always looked like she'd just grabbed clothes from the unfolded basket and chucked them on yet somehow made it look good. Her hair was in a stylish bob. One side was longer and hugged her face tucking under her chin just a little, the other side shorter, bobbing around her earlobe. It had a slight wave in it, no matter what she did or how she slept it forever looked like she'd spent hours styling it.

It was once as dark as Elle's but over time the greys began to streak it. Elle liked it. It didn't make her look older. Elle thought it made her look serious. Her eyes were a startling icy blue, almost glacial and catching. You couldn't look away, they weren't necessarily warm eyes, piercing but hollow. Captivating. It was the small smile lines that took away all that harsh intensity. Elle knew she looked like her mother in many ways but those eyes were all her own.

"I wanted to talk to you about those stories you'd tell me when I was little." Elle said out of the blue, not really knowing what Nessa had been talking about, her smile quickly melted.

"What are you talking about?" Her tone harsh as her face fell. She sat as she placed the coffee mug down in front of Elle.

"You surely remember? All the stories of fairies, peach skies, the three suns? All those magical things? I remembered Frin the other day. I haven't thought of that place since I was a kid. Mai reminded me, she's been interested in all those cute girly things lately. She's even got a fairy friend." Elle explained smiling gingerly, not understanding the strange reaction. "I just thought it would be nice if you'd spend some time with Mai and tell her some stories. The way you used to tell me. She'd love it. I would too."

"You need to stop encouraging her right now Elle." Nessa said sternly, seriously. "That silly stuff is all forgotten now. We don't need to go looking back on childish things. Honestly, I thought you'd be more mature than that."

Elle's heart started pounding and she felt a lump in her throat. Her mother had just made her feel stupid and she couldn't help but recall the day she'd given birth to Mai and the reaction she'd received from Nessa.

"I don't understand what the big deal is at all. I thought you'd want to spend more time with Mai." Elle's feigned calm at her mother's tone dissolved with one massive sob. She blurted the question she assumed she'd never receive an answer to. "What's wrong with Mai? Why don't you like my daughter?"

The storm behind Nessa's eyes calmed as she put an arm around Elle.

"I love little Mai. I always have. But I worry about her. Those stories are nothing but trouble. Get her into ballet or some kind of sport. Don't let her become obsessed with all that stuff okay?"

Elle nodded not understanding why. She searched her mother's eyes for a clue, an answer. Nothing made sense, little girls have forever loved angels and mermaids and it never did them any harm. Why can't mine? Elle considered as she sipped the coffee in an attempt to relax.

"I'm sorry I upset you." Nessa stated as Elle was about to leave. "I'm afraid for you. It's just that I thought I was going to lose my little girl once and I don't want that to happen to you okay?"

"What do you mean Mum? Why would you be afraid for me and how am I going to lose Mai? I don't understand what you're trying to say. All I asked was if you'd tell your grandchild some fairy tales. It's not a big deal. Your reaction was so weird." Elle stated frowning.

"Just listen to me. I know what I am talking about." Nessa's grip became firm on Elle's shoulder. "You don't want Mai turning out like Grandma." She added through gritted teeth as if she'd rather not be saying it out loud.

"Grandma?" Elle hadn't heard a word about Grandma since she was Mai's age. Her confusion and worry intensifying. "Grandma died when I was little. What about her? What the hell does any of this have to do with her?"

"Nothing." Nessa mumbled as she walked away from Elle, leaving her standing there by her car, keys in hand, utterly confused.

Grandma? I don't get it. A simple request and she makes it so strange. Elle shook herself off. Mum probably had booze in her coffee again she thought. Yes, that was probably it. It's becoming a problem and I'm not going to let her upset me. Forget it Elle. Forget it.

Elle took Mai home and in direct violation of what Nessa had told her, she whipped out those colouring pictures and began to colour them with Mai. There is nothing wrong with colouring pretty pictures with my child. Elle told herself. But the thoughts played in the back of her mind, swirling and dancing. Teasing her to engage.

As it was her nature she finally conceded. Grandma? She just couldn't resist now that Nessa had brought her up. It was such a long time ago. She had vague memories of her that seemed surreal. She wasn't entirely sure if her memories of Grandma were even memories. Perhaps they were just a child's dreams of a comforting, jovial woman who made her feel safe.

Golden afternoon light, poured down on the two of them, so warm and dreamy. Elle looked at her Grandma and smiled. She's so pretty Elle thought. Her blue eyes sparkled. Her long hair was grey, sliced up with a little leftover youthful darkness. It was sleek and appeared to shimmer, like she'd sprinkled it with glitter. Besides the grey hair, in the face, Grandma looked young and cheery.

They drank some pink sweet liquid from glass jars as tiny fire flies swirled about leaving trails of light. They giggled together. And there was an animal there. No, it was a person, an animal person, talking to them, giggling with them. The sky seemed different. Elle noticed it only briefly, it wasn't blue as it should be but a pleasant shade of peach, a champagne kind of colour.

The grass she lay upon was a vivid green and soft. She recalled running her fingers through it. Eyes closed listening to the comforting conversation of her loving Grandma and her animal person friend. All she felt was peace, she was content to lay there forever.

"Mum?" Mai pulled Elle from her reminiscing or perhaps day dreaming.

"What is it Mai?" Elle replied.

"I'm done colouring for now. I'm really tired."

And suddenly she did look tired. Elle looked to the clock; they'd been sitting there for hours. I shouldn't let my mind wander so far, Elle chastised herself. She'd pondered too deeply and now felt guilty about her divided attentions.

She tucked Mai up into bed, told her stories of goblin men, rainbow horses, dragons and those fairies which her mother had to told her to avoid. Once Mai had fallen asleep Elle kissed her good night. She switched the light off and stood in the doorway a moment looking over her exhausted daughter's shadowy body. The light streaming in from the hall making Mai seem smaller than she actually was.

What did Mum mean about Grandma and what's she got to do with Mai? What is Mum afraid of? Elle closed the door, leaving it wedged open to allow a pyramid of light to point towards her baby. She headed back to the kitchen more confused than ever.

It was a terrible trait, over thinking every single detail. She just couldn't help it. Maybe I'd make a great detective Elle considered for a tiny moment. Maybe you should become something a little more realistic. Elle scrunched up her nose at her own inner voice. She took a bottle of beer from the fridge and twisted the top off. She liked that excited fizzing sound it made. That makes you an alcoholic, her mind was so judging sometimes. Whatever.

Elle sat pitying herself as she drank her beer. Maybe my mind is right. She tipped that last few mouthfuls into the kitchen sink and wiped over the dishes that sat there from dinner. Should couldn't shake a bad feeling, a shadow had moved in and settled above her thoughts like a threatening storm. Something, some kind of connection between Mai and Grandma. Is that what Nessa had hinted at?

She wanted to know more but was tired, hours of scrambled overthinking had got her nowhere besides exhausted. She was yawning every few moments and decided to shower in case Toby came home from work and wanted to pay her a little physical attention. She doubted that he would but wanted to feel fresh and clean just in case.

She wasn't even sure if she wanted him to touch her the way he used to, but she was human, she craved love and feeling wanted. He appeared to have lost all interest in her physically. And emotionally, her mind added for her. Some kind of affection, even the slightest interest, to make her feel desirable. Just something to hold onto and feel good about. Something to make her feel human.

Elle picked up her fat novel and began to read. Submersing herself into the fictional life of some interesting character who had love and attention, who had passionate sex and adventures. It was the next best thing, she read until her eyelids began to droop and the words began to blur. She folded the corner down. Looked at the glowing digital clock to estimate how long until Toby would arrive home, then turned off her lamp.

Almost immediately she was asleep. She dreamt of a cheery old lady making out passionately with a half animal, half man creature.

Chapter 3

Elle woke to Mai tapping her on the forehead. She groaned and rolled over, it was the weekend and she liked to try and sleep late on weekends. Later than usual in the least. Mai was persistent.

Once Elle became coherent enough, she felt a twang of panic creep up into her chest. Where was Toby? Usually he was in bed with her when she woke. Did he have an accident on the way home?

She jumped out of bed suddenly wide awake. Picking up Mai, she hurried down the hallway. Elle shoved the lacey lounge room curtain aside. Looking out onto their dead-end street, she saw his blue sedan parked in the driveway and her panic ebbed.

"Let me guess..." she mumbled as she put Mai down on her breakfast stool and headed toward to garage.

Sure enough, there was the back of Toby's head, the computer screen creating a glowing back drop for it. And now she felt dumb for caring so much.

"Coffee?" Elle asked, trying to keep her emotions in control

She didn't want to let on that she'd almost had a mini meltdown over the possibility of Toby being in an accident. If he didn't want to show that he cared about her, then Elle sure wasn't going to give him the satisfaction of having something she didn't. A little tit for tat, but she really didn't care.

"Sounds good." Toby said without even turning to look at her.

And so, my day begins again Elle stated to herself as her familiar melancholia set in. When Toby left for work that night Elle decided a distraction was required, to shake off the monotonous boredom of her day. She knew exactly how to keep Mai occupied as she did so. She hit print on as many magical images as she could, Nessa could go to hell.

Once Mai was cozied up with her pencils and crayons and stacks of papers Elle scanned the net for interesting facts and old-fashioned mythical stories. She came across a website dedicated to the existence of fairies. Probably fake but none the less interesting.

Beautiful photographs of flowers and foliage seeming to pose for the camera, weaved together with words about their truthful realness. Elle's fascination was powerful. She was so entranced by these amazingly delicate forms. She made sure to bookmark the page and write down the address and then double check it. So realistic and pretty, elegant yet naughty. Giggling, enticing, begging her to come play.

"Mum, I'm so hungry." Mai cried as she tugged at Elle's arm. "I want a drink too."

"Just a minute Mai, I won't be long." Elle didn't even look away from the screen.

She was hooked. Eventually she completed reading the current article she'd found interesting and sat back. Fairies, what am I thinking? Who has issues now Elle? Her mind teased meanly.

She looked to the clock, it was past 10pm. Turning to the lounge, instantly guilt set in. Elle ran her fingers through her hair as she sighed. Poor Mai, asleep in front of the television surrounded by pencils and a ridiculous amount of papers. Half a biscuit in hand, a bottle of water by her side that she'd claimed from the fridge. In that moment Elle felt stupid. Completely ridiculous. There was no other word for it.

She scooped up her sleeping baby and took her to bed. Tucked her in and kissed her. Elle turned off the computer, picked up all of Mai's incomplete pictures and went to bed. She sobbed for what felt like ages as her mind served up an onslaught of bad mum insults.

Fairies? How stupid of you, ignoring your child, she fell asleep on an empty stomach. Because of fairies? Eventually, her tears stopped coming and her sobs weren't so convulsive. She focused on a big black nothingness until she finally slipped over that fine silky line between dozing and sleeping.

Toby was in the shadows, watching her. She could feel it, and then suddenly, from a high up perspective she could also see him. It felt as though they were inside an echoing cave, it was dark but chopped geometrically with shards of dull light. Half his face was lit. Utter terror inside was all she could feel. Her very core was terrified. He came running at her.

It was Toby yet some what a monster. Identifiable as Toby, but monster like with his face snarling, a monster wearing Toby. Elle screamed and ran as he plunged towards her. She couldn't get away, he was just a step behind her no matter how fast she ran.

He could have grabbed her at any moment and Elle knew it. He was playing games, feeling her panicked fear was what he wanted. Elle gave in, she was exhausted and the horror inside threatened to make her explode.

Her fear was physically painful and she stopped running. Elle turned to face Toby the monster, better to get things over with quickly. He looked slightly amused as he drove a long shard of that dull light he'd plucked from the atmosphere, straight into her heart.

An instant later she began to feel warm and the darkness started to recede. A blue glow began to radiate and she opened her eyes to a peach sky, dusted with golden smeared clouds. She could hear a sweet humming buzz and that old woman's giggles.

They've come for me, finally they've come for me. Once the darkness had lifted enough she rose to sit cross legged, on the grass. She looked to her left and there crumpled and grey lay Toby the monster. He whimpered and sobbed like a lost child as a swarm of blue glowing, surrounded him.

Elle woke in the dark hours of the morning, hazily stirred. Toby was kissing her and stroking her hair. She startled and pulled away from him abruptly. Her frightened emotions towards him in her dream were still there, fresh and terrifying.

"I'm sorry. I was having a dream." She murmured at his offended reaction. The residue of fear still gripped her heart, yet knowing it was only a dream she felt silly.

"I'll let you get back to sleep." Toby said, clearly taking her response to his touch negatively.

He left the room and Elle lay staring at the roof. She wanted to finish her dream, grasp at it, recapture it like a helium balloon string that had slipped through her fingers. To see how it would all play out. Though once she closed her eyes, she realised she'd lost it and all she could do was watch it fade away.

By the time Elle woke in the daylight hours of the morning, all memory of her life like dream had faded. She'd wanted to hold onto it so badly and yet now it was nothing more than a finger print on a pane of glass. It was there but it was faint. Thinking about it only made it more elusive. The dream occupied Elle for most of the morning. Toby had asked her for a coffee to which she shrugged and left the room. He asked her on numerous occasions what was on her mind.

"Nothing." Was Elle's reply as she continued to pick at her bottom lip.

It was one of her lesser habits, but one of her more revealing ones. It told the world a number of things about her, things she didn't really want the world to know. It said she was deeply involved in thought, more so than was usual for her. It spoke of nervousness and also advertised that she was completely and utterly disconnected from the world at that time.

"Look we need to meet up. I need to talk to you." Toby told Elle over the phone as she sat in the kitchen of her mother's house.

"Sure okay." She said wondering why home wouldn't do. "Where do you want to meet?" Elle looked at Nessa with a frown.

"How about that new café you like, say 2pm?"

"Sounds fine, I have to pick up Mai around half past though." Elle said, deciding it would be good to have a reason to not hang around long. She felt curiously confused. Since when does the man I'm in a relationship with want to talk to me? And why not at home? We're breaking up perhaps? "What's this about?" she decided to add.

"I'll talk to you when I see you okay?" And Toby hung up.

Elle frowned, looked at her phone, and pushed the hang up button. She pouted her lips and chose to accept the outcome regardless. She picked up her hand bag and flung the phone into it, flicked her dark hair over her shoulder and grabbed her keys.

"Looks like you're off then?" Nessa noted.

"Yeah looks like it, Toby says he needs to talk." Elle said slightly annoyed, she'd wanted to talk with her mother about Mai and Grandma and clear up some of the odd things that had been said. Maybe gain a little clarity if Nessa were sober. But the phone rang the moment she'd sat down.

"I hope it's nothing too serious." Nessa commented whilst she walked Elle to the front door. "Maybe you should try to act like you're listening to what he's saying though."

"What's that supposed to mean?" Elle turned back with an accusing frown.

"Nothing, you've just been, I don't know. Sort of deep in thought, preoccupied I guess you could say." Nessa stumbled over her words. "Maybe you could stop picking at your lip and focus on the present. You're always staring off into space, it isn't anything necessarily new but you've been worse of late."

"Sorry, I'm just thinking that's all." Annoyed she scrunched her nose. Do I really seem so distant? she questioned herself.

Elle arrived at the café and ordered the coffee, ashamed that she was so shy toward the attractive barista. She sat in her favourite spot over-looking the beach, within glancing distance of her tattooed barista.

I think too much? How could I not think? I need to sort myself out, Mum throwing me cryptic messages and Toby needing to talk to me? And they wonder why I'm so internal? I can't help but over think.

Elle looked up at the wall clock and it was already 2.15. Where is he? I'll need to leave soon. He's consistently late. Why bother giving me a time if you're not even going to be here?

She felt eyes on her and glanced toward the barista. He was watching her. She sighed and rolled her eyes and looked back out to sea. Trying to smooth her furrowed brow. This handsome guy seeing her right now was all she needed.

Elle knew her frantic concern and overpowering stress was visible. She tried hard to extinguish it. She blushed slightly as she looked back to him with a weak smile and a lazy wave. He's so late, she thought again. Typical Toby she declared as his car pulled up out front.

He stepped out all suave and celebrity like. Mum's right. He does think he's better than everyone else. Toby sat down across from her, eyed his coffee and pushed it away. Obviously, there was something wrong with it. Not that Elle would have ever been able to know exactly what.

"Look Toby I don't have long, you're late." Elle said.

"Yeah this won't take long." He stated as he took his mirror like pilot sun glasses off, folded them and placed them on the table. "You gave my computer a virus."

"Is that what this is about?" Elle half laughed. "Really are we here to talk about a computer virus?"

"It's serious Elle. It's going to cost a lot of money to get fixed."

"Sorry I was wrong, this is about money?" Her amusement quickly turning to crankiness, all the while completely aware of the baristas steel eyes observing the situation.

"No, actually it's about neither."

"Then what is it about Toby? Why'd you have me meet you in a café to discuss your computer?" Elle was clearly annoyed. "Surely we could have fought about this at home?"

"I'm not looking for a fight Elle. That's why. I'm worried about you." He reached across the small timber table, uncurled her fingers from the coffee cup and held them. "All those websites you've been obsessed with, mythical stuff. The virus came from one of those stupid fairy sites."

"Obsessed? Stupid." She pulled her hand back. She folded them both in her lap beneath the table. "That's a bit harsh isn't it Toby?"

"You've been researching that stuff for months now. You talk about strange things and something called Frin in your sleep. You know it's Mai's birthday next week, don't you?"

Toby sounded strange. Distant and fading in her ears. Elle zoned out. Began picking at her lip and focused on a dark spot on the concrete café floor. She was staring at it but not really seeing it.

Her mind went mad. Months? It's only been a couple weeks, a few at most. I'm not obsessed, interested perhaps, but obsessed? Okay, I did forget Mai's birthday next week. That's understandable, I'm a little preoccupied. It's not like it's been and gone and I missed it. Just, preoccupied that's all.

With what Elle? Her mean mind questioned. Fairies, stupid fairies, and mermaids and goblins and elves and all those things that aren't real. I think stupid and obsessed are the perfect words. Her mind was getting snarky and Elle told it to "shut up," out loud, without meaning to.

Suddenly snapped back to reality with Toby staring at her. Sitting there calmly watching her, with his perfect hair and his smart clothes. Mum's right she thought, he totally thinks he's better than everyone. Better than me.

She still felt him looking, the barista, intensely studying her. She could even see him at the edge of her vision, though she dared not look. She was so upset and irritated she didn't care what that stranger thought.

"You know that Toby? I'm done here. I have to go get Mai. I don't need to listen to you tell me what I should and shouldn't be doing, as if you even care." Elle could hear herself grow louder with each word. "You don't care. Just leave me alone. Next time your computer gets a virus go have a deep and meaningful with someone else."

Elle stood up bumping the table in her flustered state spilling the coffee. She didn't look back, tried to hold her head high even though she knew everyone, including her barista was looking at her. She hurried to her car. She knew she was going to cry, she just didn't want anyone else to know it.

She dried her tears and walked into the preschool feeling a little self-conscience. She'd seen mums who'd been crying, trying to pretend like everything was fine. Besides the red rimmed eyes and over exaggeration of life being dandy, she would have almost bought the lies. Elle hoped she could pull it off. Or hopefully everyone would feel too awkward to actually ask her what was wrong. She wouldn't have told them anyway.

Elle picked up Mai and went straight back to Nessa's house. She hadn't had the chance to talk with Nessa earlier. Even though Nessa was not the motherly type, her presence still offered comfort. Nessa didn't seem at all surprised that Elle was back. She made Mai some cheese and crackers with chopped fruit and sat her down at the table, while Elle made the coffee.

Nessa and Elle sat together on the back deck. Her mother had gotten all creative out there on that deck one breezy afternoon. She'd painted the floor boards green, strung shells and drift wood to the beams. Tiny shards of sea glass tinkled together as a gust blew up. It was a creative space, whimsical and totally Nessa.

"So?" Nessa asked expectantly waiting to hear the goss.

"So, Toby thinks I'm an idiot." Elle shook her head and rolled her eyes. "Maybe I am. I don't know, time apparently has been slipping away from me."

"You're not an idiot. But you do come from an interesting line of women." Nessa said while looking into her coffee cup.

Nessa knew she should tell Elle more but she didn't want to. She'd made decisions long ago to keep the truth from her. But in this moment, she genuinely wanted to make her child's life easier, wanted to make her life make sense. But after so long and so much withheld information, it was not easy decision to make. What to share and what not to.

Elle didn't quite understand what Nessa meant but then again, she didn't understand most things she said. She seemed to like riddles, only giving half the truth or sometimes only tiny hints.

"I know you told me not to encourage Mai, but I didn't see the harm. I think it's me who's interested. Toby's worried." Elle decided to share.

"Why didn't you tell me this?" Nessa blurted, she honestly hadn't realised how far Elle's condition had progressed.

"You told me it was silly and childish and not to encourage Mai. Why would I tell you I was the one who was interested after hearing you say the things you did?" Elle said sighing. "I just don't know what's wrong with me. It's all so addictive."

"Look, I think I need to tell you about Grandma." Nessa decided, this was far worse than she'd imagined. "She's not dead."

Elle's jaw dropped, her world suddenly spinning. She closed her mouth, trying to regain some composure and sat looking blankly at her mother. Trying to absorb what she'd just heard. Grandma, sweet giggling Grandma. Not dead, alive?

"Where?" It was all Elle could manage to verbalise.

"This isn't easy for me to tell you Elle." Nessa began tearing up.

"Where? Where is she?"

"She's not well okay. I thought it was best you didn't know. I didn't want you to go looking for answers and getting all lost like she did. Like I almost did." Nessa was crying now. "I don't want you to end up like her."

"Where Mother? Where is Grandma?" Elle was still blank. Dull. Nothing. It was the only question she could grasp.

"She was institutionalised." Now she was sobbing uncontrollably and Elle didn't really care.

Wow. Ok. I need to leave. Now. Elle collected Mai and her things and was again heading toward her mother's front door. She just couldn't soak in anymore just now. For years and years, she'd been told and had actually believed that Grandma was gone.

Dead, that's not something that can be undone in one confession. I need some air Elle thought. As she started the car, Nessa put her head through the window.

"Don't do anything dumb Elle. Okay?"

"Like what Mum? Tell my daughter her grandmother is dead? Of course not."

Elle knew it was a low blow, but she had no care for kindness right now. Clearly no one cared for her. Not Mum, not Toby.

She looked into her rear-view mirror back at her little girl sitting there, holding onto her favourite doll. A ratty hand made one that Elle had stitched together when she was pregnant. It was meant to be a boy doll, all blue haired and denim wearing. But Mai loved it all the same.

"It's just you and me baby girl." Elle said to the reflection of her pretty child, as she drove away to a place she didn't know right now. Mai smiled. At least she cares.

Elle pulled up at a cheap motel. Just off the highway only 15 minutes from home. She needed space, needed to think. She didn't want to lie in bed half asleep over thinking and warping her thoughts into a strange dream tonight. She wanted a free space to hide and be calm and perhaps get a good full night sleep.

Elle took Mai from the back seat and helped her shrug on her backpack. It was in the shape of a teddy bear, all pink and fluffy. Mai had filled it with all her toys and dolls, which Elle had to empty besides her absolute favourites, replacing them with clothes for the night. She locked the car, slung her own bag across her shoulder, took Mai by the hand and headed toward reception.

Mai raided the mini fridge in the musty, moss painted room of all its small milk containers. She loved the little complimentary portions with their foil lids, just enough for tea, coffee or a little girl's mouthful.

Elle sat on the bed. It was stiff but she knew she'd have no trouble falling asleep tonight. Life was complicating and confusing and becoming increasingly exhausting. She second guessed almost everything of late, all her relationships seemed to be falling apart. Elle couldn't decide if it was her fault or not.

Toby doesn't love me. Maybe he's cheating? I've done nothing but be there for him. Cook his meals, wash his clothes. I don't deserve to be ignored. He's supposed to love me, care about me, at least make me feel like he does. Her resentment toward him was growing and she knew it.

Mum, lying to me all these years, Grandma alive? I can't wrap my head around it. Institutionalised, but why? She was always so happy and normal. Despite not knowing what was a memory and what was a dream, Elle couldn't shake the thought that something was terribly wrong with it all.

Even through her mind was still racing, the new environment, as unappealing as it was, lifted some of the weight she'd been dragging around. A space that belonged temporarily to just her and Mai was divine.

After a quick cheap meal of tomato pasta in the motel's small restaurant, Mai and Elle went back to their room.

Elle put Mai to bed with the television playing quietly and started to run a bath. An excuse to relax and let go of it all. I'm looking horrible she thought of herself as she stripped by the mirror. Her face was looking older and she knew it shouldn't. Not yet. Her eyes were red rimmed, looking like she'd been crying even though she hadn't. Dark circles threatened to take hold and move in for good.

She'd lost weight she realised. Her hips less round, her breasts less full. She sighed as she sank back into the hot water. It felt good, like slipping into warm silk, hugging and holding her warm and light all over. Elle closed her eyes and lay back, soaking.

Her eyes opened to that champagne sky. Feeling nothing but calmness deep in her bones. Her jaw wasn't clenched, her shoulders weren't tight. Like she'd been holding her breath for too long and it had finally been released. Elle was laying, comfortably naked beneath a weeping willow, the sun glowing down through it. Each leaf encircled in a tiny halo of shimmering gold. She'd woken to what felt like an eternal afternoon.

Suddenly someone stroked her hair, lightly brushing it from her forehead. She didn't jump, not even flinch. It was natural, like she foresaw it coming. Looking up she met the eyes of her sexy barista, they were deep and steely.

Smiling down at her he continued to stroke her hair. A long breath escaped as she closed her eyes to rest and enjoy, feeling dreamy and dozy with her head cradled lovingly in his lap. He leant down to kiss her on the mouth. His full lips covered hers and she couldn't help but whimper. Her body melted.

She could smell him, exactly as she'd imagined. Rich roasted coffee mingled with a masculine earthy aftershave. Elle thought she was relaxed before, but with his kiss left the last residual tension that had been clinging on. Like it had been swept up and carried off with the breeze.

Her entire body was loose, her anxiety gone, her bones had turned to dust. Elle's only sensation was in behind the cage of her ribs. Her heart was swollen and about to burst. His kiss seemed to suck her very life essence out. She trusted completely, unquestionably that he would return it. This stranger, this feeling, she loved him and in one warm breath against her ear, she knew she couldn't live without him now.

After an eternity breathing in and out his kiss, he pulled away and hazily Elle emerged from her peaceful coma. Her eyes opened heavily like she'd almost been asleep but he was still there, unmoving, unchanged, just loving her. She knew he did.

She lay watching him, his jaw so strong and his eyes wide and intelligent, smiling at her. They were the colour of steel, not blue but not grey. His hair a dark blonde and a mess, a perfect mess she mused. As if it were meant to be that way. His hands were big and strong. The way he stroked her hair and cheek, so gentle but firm, those hands.

Something caught her eye, a glittery spark. Moving her head slightly to see what had bounced around in her peripheral. It was small and quick, zipping back and forth and then abruptly it was still.

Hovering inches before her nose, a small figure no bigger than Elle's smallest finger. Its skin was blue and pale. It was female and naked, she could almost see right through it. She could see it's weaving veins and its rapidly beating heart. Surrounding it was a flaming, flickering blue aura. Elle knew what the creature was but couldn't recall in words. She reached out with both hands and gently cupped it between her palms.

"Wait!" He exclaimed.

"Ouch!" Elle cried out and let go. A blazing trail faded off into the distance as it flew away with a faint howl.

Sitting up, she held her hands to her mouth blowing softly on the angry red burns. He took her hands from her with his own and resumed her efforts, blowing gently.

Looking deep into her eyes, Elle could hear his words within. Despite his mouth remaining in that comforting smile. You are beautiful. You are precious. You're also naïve and sweet. His smile smirked a little and he tilted his head to the side just a fraction. I love you.

Elle heard it as if he'd said it and she believed it within, without words, without actions. She felt it about his very being, his energy, his aura was love. For her.

Suddenly she gulped for air. She couldn't breathe. Elle stared into his eyes with pure panic ripping through her. I can't breathe she thought. Groping at her own chest with fear. I need air. He kissed her palms and looked into her big, terrified eyes.

"Open them." He said and instantly Elle knew what he meant.

Opening her eyes, she found herself underwater. She couldn't see. Her hair swirling about her thrashing body. The remainder of her breath escaping in gurgling bubbles, she could hear the thuds of her pounding heart and of her body banging against the tub. Reverberating through the water to deafen her ears.

Elle reach out, grabbing the tubs edge, pulling. Her face pressing up and out of the water, gulping for air. After a few moments, the panic subsided and she regained a steady breathing pattern.

Once the water had been coughed up from her aching lungs, she became bewildered. It was a becoming a stable feeling in her life.

I almost drowned in a motel bath tub? How cliché, she thought. I must be exhausted, falling asleep like that.

Smoothing her hair back out of her face, she winced as her palms stung. Frowning she raised her hands to her face. Burns? Her heart dropped. Confusion was now an understatement. This was a whole new world, something more than confused and she didn't know what it was. She was beginning to question her very sanity.

A violent shiver. The water was cold. So cold, she climbed out quickly. Now flustered. She almost slipped on the grimy tiles as she reached for the bath towel, which she knew would be too small, even before pulling it from the chrome rack. She wrapped it around herself and walked into the room leaving dark, wet foot prints on the carpet. The room flickering in the eerie glow of the television.

Mai was still fast asleep in the small single bed, covered in the faded floral cover, just as she'd left her. A little relief flooded back once she'd sighted her girl. Though it ebbed quickly as she looked to the dull glow of the digital bedside clock. 2am. I was in that tub for 5 hours? Panic. Heart racing Elle inspected her hands, not wrinkled. Not even pruned. Just burnt.

Standing in the middle of the room, in her towel, she scanned. Everything just as it was. Yet Elle couldn't help the feeling of something having changed. Something was intensely different.

Sleep, I just need sleep. I'm too tired, too emotional, my minds playing games with me. It felt like hours before she slipped into a disturbed dormancy. Elle's dreams filled with tender steel eyes and a passion she'd never felt before, swirled with images of Grandma and little burning beings.

She woke feeling lost, tired and emptier than ever. She rushed home to get Mai ready for school, back in the car again she drove that boring drive. They arrived at the school to find not a single soul present. Elle rushed Mai from the car non-the less. Reaching the gate, peculiarly it was locked.

"What day is it Mai?" She inquired of her little girl.

"It's Saturday Mumma." Mai beamed up at the mother.

"Here I was, thinking it was only Thursday. Silly Mum. You are such a clever girl." Elle praised while frowning with concentration. I really am losing it. "Ice cream then? You didn't want to go to school anyway." She gave her girl a wink, in an attempt to act as if she wasn't even slightly tormented.

Chapter 4

"Look I'm genuinely concerned about Elle." Toby said into his mobile phone, as he paced in front of his car prior to entering work.

He'd been searching for Elle and Mai since he'd arrived home from work to find them missing. She's always home, he'd told himself. Troubled by the idea she had somewhere else to be, perhaps that's why he was now so panicked.

He'd taken that fact for granted. He'd never come home to a house full of silence at the end of a long night shift. There had simply always been the warm sleeping body of the woman he thought of as his, lying there in his bed when he arrived. Toby was feeling a loss he couldn't describe and it unnerved him.

"She didn't come home last night. Her phone is off and I have no idea where my girls could be."

"She'll be okay Toby. Elle found out some difficult truths that I probably should have discussed with her sooner. It's time I told her everything." Even as Nessa said it she wasn't sure that was true. "She will come home when she's ready. She will need your support."

"I don't know how to do that anymore. Elle has totally shut me out. It's like I'm living with a robot, life goes on around her and she withdraws more and more into herself. She's always in her own head."

"I know, I know. This isn't new Toby, she'll keep her problems to herself until she processes them as best she can. She'll try to fix things on her own and it takes a toll. I do think she's coming to understand she can't take on the world alone. Don't panic, give her some time. Just let me know if you hear from her."

Nessa pressed end call and began to pick her lip, the crease in her forehead deepening. She slapped her own hand away. I can't let this get to me. I thought we were passed this point.

She took the vodka from the pantry cupboard and her crystal shot glass from the window sill. Nessa liked to keep it there so when the afternoon sun shone through, it would cast rainbows across the room. She would stand in her kitchen watching the magic and remember things she'd attempted to convince herself weren't real.

There was beauty and mystery and magic in this very physical world of hers and she'd found her own way of connecting with it. She threw back the nip of vodka she'd poured. It didn't even burn her throat anymore. She was so used to it. And another, just for luck. I can connect with it and shut it out she convinced herself as she swirled the last drops of liquid in the bottom of the little glass. Oh Elle, this can't go on. I have to end this. Right now.

"Where have you been?" Toby demanded as Elle walked in the door. Very real concern tinted with anger displayed in his face.

"Shhh! Mai's asleep." Elle whispered sternly glancing down at the sleeping child she carried against her chest.

She took the sticky, ice cream covered baby and placed her down on her bed, pulling up her light blanket to cover her. She could feel Toby glaring perplexed into the back of her, from the door. She stroked Mai's head and turned to face him knowing she couldn't avoid the situation any longer.

Elle walked by him trying to come off as if he were bugging her and continued down the hall, knowing full well he'd follow. Outside she decided. I need air for this conversation. Elle sat down on the slatted bench crossing and tucking her legs up beneath her, folding her arms. Finally, she lifted her head and made eye contact with Toby.

Toby looked Elle over, everything about her body language screamed she was not open to him at all. She was all tucked up, limiting her own body space. Small, compacted. Protecting herself. He knew she was not open to what he'd say, or even how he felt. But he loved her.

He'd been such a wreck when he found her missing, he understood he had to try harder. Had to show her that he did love her and didn't want her to ever leave him alone again. He tried to tell himself he was a proud man, he didn't need a woman to complete him or to support him. Deep down he knew it was all lie. He was in fact an arrogant, egotistical man. And deep down, he knew that too.

Toby almost smiled, she looked attractive like that. Sitting there all defensive. Trying so hard to be seem something tougher than the lamb that she was and he thought it was cute. Her big eyes bright in the reflection of the kitchen lights glowing from inside.

He loved those eyes, they poured forth all her truth. If she were happy or sad, it didn't even matter how hard she tried to hide it. Regardless of what noise came out of her mouth, what stories she blabbed at him, her eyes always spilled her guts. Though right now, he couldn't read them and it worried him. They seemed shadowed, a haze of something playing out behind them.

She was wearing a pretty dress, yellow straps crossing over her chest. Elle was partial to dresses she'd told him, they were comfortable and versatile. She'd gotten defensive toward him when he'd questioned her about her clothing choices. Asking him why he wanted to know or why it even mattered. He'd told her it didn't matter at all and that she always looked beautiful. It was just that normal girls liked to wear jeans and t-shirts every now and again. Elle had then responded grumpily, saying that perhaps she wasn't normal.

The one she wore now was knee length. He liked it. I like her. He frowned trying to make sense of his own feelings, trying to figure out what he was going to say because he knew she wouldn't speak unless he spoke first.

"Where were you?" He asked again.

"I needed air, I just wanted some space." She stated.

Elle began staring at a stone imbedded in the concrete below her. She thought it was weird and interesting that she could so clearly see the small grey pebble set into the concrete. And, she could also see a blurry version of her coral painted toenails peeking out beneath her folded legs in her peripheral. She focused on her toes and the pebble faded away into a wavy blur as her toes became clear. She wiggled them and watched them blur, as she once again returned her focus to the pebble. So weird, she thought.

"Elle! Elle?"

"What Toby? What is it?" She was frustrated, he'd broken her concentration. Her attempt to be somewhere else.

"You're not even listening to me. I said, have you organised anything for Mai's party? Her birthday is in 2 days." He was very obviously angered. But he also was baffled by her. He didn't know how to simply say I love you, or to let her know how worried he'd been. He didn't want to appear vulnerable or weak to this strange wonderful creature. Being defensive was his way.

"2 days?" Perplexed. "It's not until next week. You said so yourself, yesterday in the café whilst you were lecturing me on computer viruses." She exclaimed unfolding her arms.

"Elle, you've been gone for days."

"No, it was only one night."

"No Elle. Not one night. Days." Toby sat. stroked his chin and sighed. He was disturbed. What's going on with her? He wasn't sure if he should be mad at her, or perhaps he should hug her? Or maybe he should do nothing.

Elle was quiet, trying to assess this information. It just can't be possible. Mai and I stayed in that motel last night. Came home, got ready for school. Only it wasn't school. I'm just a little confused that's all. Am I losing my mind? Or is Toby losing his?

"Toby I just need time to think." It was all she could manage to say, with time and consideration it would all become clearer she thought.

"No, you don't. You've been gone for days. You've had time. Let's just get back on track okay?" Toby seemed worn out suddenly. "Elle, I love you. You understand right?"

"Well, yeah." She said uncertainly. Do I know that? "I think I know."

Instantly she knew she'd lied. She didn't know that at all. She knew what love was. She'd finally felt it now. In a dream; and it didn't feel like this. It didn't make her angry or make her feel used. It didn't make her feel ugly or hopeless. It didn't have words. It was pure emotion. Emotion so strong that she wouldn't care if she'd never heard a flimsy, worthless word ever again.

Those steel eyes came back, haunting her from the depths of her mind. Flustered and warmed all at once. Elle could feel that kiss, lingering distantly in the cells of her lips. The real thing is far better she thought to herself. The real thing? It was a dream! Her mind snapped back at her.

Toby was sitting there watching her. "So, you love me too, right?" He asked after minutes of silently studying her.

"I do love you Toby, what we have is real." Elle replied feeling panicked at being put on the spot, trying not to hurt him. It is real, not a dream. Nothings perfect.

"I'll sort this out ok?" Whatever this is, she contemplated.

Toby seeming satisfied got ready for work. Elle knew what she had to do but decided it best to wait until he left. She potted around the house like she usually did, made herself one of those uncultured instant coffees that Toby hated. Attempting to appear her normal self.

However, on the inside she was a storm of whirling thoughts. She couldn't let it go. Days slipping by unnoticed, Mai's birthday 2 days away. Really? Grandma and the burns, those steel eyes just watching her the whole time.

Finally, Toby was heading for the door and Elle was feeling a suppressed buoyancy. She felt a guilt at her excitement of him leaving the house, though she knew how to make it up to him. Elle put on her light and happy mask and directed her act toward him. She bounced toward him, giving him a peck on the cheek and said goodbye. She'd never been a patient person and now that Toby was heading off she could finally do a little homework. Perhaps find some tangible answers.

"I could get used to this." Toby said as he grabbed Elle by the waist and pulled her close for a deeper kiss. "See you tonight." He added with a wink.

Elle smiled back and waved as he drove down the street. Once his car was out of sight she dashed to the computer. Logging into her bank accounts she discovered she'd indeed been charged for three nights. Three nights? I don't understand. It was one night! She tried to convince herself still.

I can't have been dreaming in a bath for two days. Could I? Surely not. What about Mai? She'd have come woken me? She can't have fended for herself all that time. It can't be true. There must be an explanation. She sat back perplexed, her mind couldn't comprehend an explanation.

She spun on the swivel chair, around and around and around watching the patterns her eyes were inventing on the roof. Like a whirlpool of light that wasn't really there. After giving herself a headache, still nothing made sense. She jumped up swayed to the fridge and took down the magnetic calendar, checking the dates.

Right there, the 16th was circled in pink. Mai's birthday. I need to organise something, but first...

Elle called her neighbour Jilly. A short and chubby, old lady. White haired and cutesy. She was an interesting thing, communicating with each of her three deceased husbands via tarot cards and mediums. She always had intriguing stories to tell after her weekly appointments with clairvoyants.

She was a good woman and Mai loved her. She may have loved her more than Nessa. Jilly was always happy to keep an eye on Mai if needed, she liked the company. And right now, Elle needed to take care of something.

The following morning she dropped an excited Mai with Jilly, she got in her car and headed to her mother's. Elle felt excited yet anxious, not knowing what she may learn about the woman she'd seen in her dream. But feeling determined to know more.

Nessa rushed out to meet her as she pulled into the driveway. Before Elle could even open the door, Nessa was already giving her an earful.

"Bloody hell Elle, I was worried about you."

"I need answers, I want to go see Grandma." Good girl Elle, straight to the point. She praised herself on being assertive.

Resignation seemed to wash over Nessa as she replied with "Come inside, we'll talk."

They both took an end on Nessa's old lounge. It was ratty but comforting. She'd had it since Elle was a girl. Actually, the more Elle looked around, not much had changed since her childhood. The same paintings hung on the walls only now they were faded into ghostly people and scenes, in a hazed world of dust.

Nessa had interesting little trinkets and statues that she'd collected from flea markets and garage sales and second-hand shops over the years. They too sat sprinkled around the house, suspended in time collecting dust. Her musty curtains still hung in the same windows. Nessa still had Elle's room partially made up, girly and flirty. Stuffed bears and a few remaining dolls that were now far more creepy than cute to Elle.

It was as if Nessa's home was almost frozen in time, perhaps more glacial. Always appearing the same and unchanging however, sometimes a difference was detectable, even if it were unnoticed. Maybe that's why Elle kept coming back, it was like there was a mystery lurking that aroused her curiosity and called her back.

She loved her mother but she was complicated and confusing, draining. Elle would think they were on the same page occasionally, only to realise they weren't even in the same book. Finally, her thoughts settled and she knew what she wanted to ask. Her eyes stopped roaming and settled on Nessa's icy blue ones.

"Why were you so upset when I gave birth to Mai?" She said firmly aiming to seem determined.

"It's complicated okay? It's not that I don't love Mai, it's just I thought the chain was broken." Nessa said awkwardly as she watched herself strangle her own fingers. "I thought you'd lead a different life."

"The chain was broken? Lead a different life from what? I don't get it Mum, you need to just tell me."

"When you had Mai, I knew it would happen all over again, that's why I didn't tell you about Grandma. You know, just like you and Mai; Grandma and I never knew our biological fathers." She looked up and into Elle's eyes as if pleading for mercy, as if begging for no more.

"You'd always told me that Grandpa, your dad had died when you were pregnant with me." Elle couldn't help frowning, she was concentrating so hard waiting for everything to click into place. Forcing the information to just work together but it wouldn't go.

All her puzzle pieces were wrong like two were mixed together, the version of life she'd been told and the one Nessa now hinted at. No matter how hard she tried to jam them, they just refused to form a bigger picture.

"You also told me my father ran off with another woman." Elle reminded her.

"Well apparently Elle, I figured killing people off and making them bad guys made life easier. Turns out it doesn't." Nessa was becoming sarcastic and defensive. "I never knew my father and yours ran off the morning after we'd slept together. I'm sorry I lied, I had to. It helped to keep the truth from you."

"So, you and Grandma never knew your fathers either? Was it like with Mai?" Elle's brain strained to keep up. With every question, a million more seemed to need asking. She tried hard to stay on track.

"Exactly like Mai. We both ran into men who seemed to be angels, gods sent to us. Both of us, like you Elle. We were unable to resist. They were handsome and dreamy, loving and kind. One magical night together and then they disappear to haunt you always. Next thing a baby is on the way. And you're alone."

"Doesn't that seem odd to you Mum? Generations of women have been totally taken off guard to the point of having sex with a stranger and then he literally disappears never to be seen again?"

Elle could hear her anger rise. For so long she'd punished herself over Mai's conception, not because she didn't want Mai, but because she was an intelligent person. She didn't sleep around, she wasn't weak in the knees over every guy who looked at her longingly. It wasn't who she was. She was in control. She'd always wanted children but her image of how that would go was very different. She didn't even know his name.

Elle shook her head trying to rid herself of the shame she'd felt the day she decided to declare her pregnancy to her mother. She couldn't even give her a name. Worse still, she couldn't give her daughter a name.

"So, you thought that if I had a boy, he wouldn't end up like me and sleep with some stranger?" Elle added sarcastically. "Is that all it really comes down to?"

"No; well yes. It's complicated." Nessa struggled. "There is so much more to it than just that."

"Tell me. Just tell me. I want to know."

"I don't want to encourage this Elle. I can't just tell you."

"Encourage what? I'm trying to sort myself out, my brain is just a swirling mess and weird things are happening, I just need some clarity. You obviously know far more than you're telling me. In fact, you're lying to me."

Elle was standing now. She couldn't help but run her fingers through her hair and flick it back over her shoulder, pacing back and forth across the room, picking at her lip in thought. She'd been asking the right questions she'd thought, but she was getting strange strangled answers in return. Nessa wasn't giving her anything mouldable to work with.

If anything, Nessa was feeding her bemusement, heading her off in directions she hadn't even considered. She'd come hoping for some peace, that her mother would lovingly sit down with her and explain some of the mysteries of her life. Possibly clear up some of the misleading information that she herself, had given. But instead Elle felt as if she were becoming shrouded in the heaviness caused by years and years of lies.

"I know you're having these fantasies Elle. I know you are. You can't keep hiding it. And you can't keep going there either." Nessa bossed. She stood now too, her icy eyes roaring.

"Fantasies. Going where? You make it sound like I'm crazy!"

Nessa considered her next words and sighed. "Going to Frin, you can't keep doing it. I know you don't get it. But one day you'll find a reason that will make you want to stay forever and you'll lose everything."

Nessa looked exhausted now, emotionally, mentally. She went to her pantry and took out the vodka, not caring what Elle thought which she usually did. It wasn't often that she didn't have alcohol running through her veins but it wasn't something she wanted her daughter to know. Didn't want her to witness. Elle followed her to the kitchen not wanting to let go of the conversation. She watched Nessa reach for the shot glass. I should have known.

"Frin? You're speaking of the stories you'd tell me when I was little? Now you sound crazy Mother." Elle scoffed, eyeing the vodka. Wondering why she were even listening to her. "Next you'll be telling me Mai's fairy friend Trey is real!"

"Actually, that's exactly what I'm telling you." Nessa gave up with a nasty attitude. "And just so you know he isn't a fairy. Fairies are tiny little lights, small beings that fly in fire."

Instinctively Elle rubbed her palms together.

"Trey my dear, is the who is responsible for placing these seductive men in our way, generation after generation as you pointed out. Trey is real, just as real as Frin, just as real as you and I standing here." Nessa let it out as if purging poison from her system.

She took her shot, forcibly putting the glass down while staring aggressively at Elle. She took another shot as she watched her only daughter furiously leave the house, slamming the door behind her.

Elle stopped her car, parked at the headland and looked out over the ocean. Shaking her hands out, she lay her forehead onto the steering wheel. Gazing down at her bare feet and coral painted toenails. She loved that colour, it wasn't red and yet not orange. It was something entirely different, a shade suspended in the mix. She took a breath and rolled her shoulders. The tension was growing again and her pain was screaming, soon squealing, but for now she could manage screaming.

What the hell is going on? She thought. So now Frin is real and some magical guy named Trey, who isn't a fairy just to be clear, is placing men in my life, to what? Tempt me? Impregnate me? And what's he doing with Mai? My fantasies are real? This is ridiculous.

So obviously I'm not some desperate housewife whom daydreams a little too much, I'm clearly the spawn of an insane line of women and finally my times up. Time to go nuts or become an alcoholic like the rest of them. Can't beat them, join them. Mum lying to me, inventing people, then killing them off so I could appear to have a normal upbringing? Normal; nothing could be considered normal if it's hung around with Nessa too long. My own father, never really existed?

With her mind blown, Elle chose to believe she was going crazy. It was far easier than trying to make sense of it all.

Chapter 5

Elle just wanted to drive. She didn't even know where she was going. Just exploring if anyone asks. Who's going to ask? She turned down one street and turned into another.

They were lined with brick houses seemingly all the same design, only the orientation was different. How creative. However, each had its own occupants tastes on display. One had a plain bare lawn. Next door had lush bushes and shrubs, flower beds and a little mouldy water feature.

The next had wind chimes dangling everywhere and a grotesque amount of garden gnomes. Another had a swing set, basket and soccer balls, hula hoops and bikes strewn across the yard, clearly a family home. Despite all their artificial, decorative differences, essentially, they still all remained the same. People were like that she thought, all the same on the inside, decorated on the outside.

She told herself not to keep putting on the same blinker or she'd end up going around in circles, mix it up a little Elle. Left, then right, right then left again. That was about as deep as she'd allow her thoughts to go in this moment. Her brain felt dead, it had been overloaded with lies, corrupted with confusion. There was nothing she could do except shut it all down.

Not wanting to go home yet. Satisfied Mai would be having fun with Jilly who was probably reading her palm, or her tea leaves, possibly both. She continued on, knowing she couldn't be a good mother in this state. Elle so badly wanted to be a good mother for Mai and often wondered if she was. Nessa would want to be a good mother to me, wouldn't she? Does that mean lying to our children?

Elle pondered if she already had committed the same crime. Perhaps not on purpose, though she knew she'd omitted some truths. Mai didn't know her biological father and she was so young she hadn't specifically thought to sit her down and explain that Toby wasn't her real dad. She was only a little over one year old when they'd met, so in Mai's eyes Toby had always just been there. Does she think Toby is her Daddy? She doesn't call him dad. Am I lying to my child? Eventually she concluded that she wasn't.

What Nessa had done was fabricate entire relationships that had never existed in the first place and proceeded to convince Elle they had been real. Mai would know the truth someday but for now she was still too young. I will never lie to my child she decided. I'll tell her too much if I have to.

Elle was so angry at her mother. She didn't even know where to begin, perhaps she felt betrayed. Or maybe she had an unrealistic view of what a mother should be and when her own turned out to be simply human; someone who made mistakes and lied here and there she took it hard.

Elle knew she'd wind up back with Nessa. There was a strange thing about being someone's daughter, about being someone's mother. There was a bond that no matter how violently one hacked and knarred at it, the connection was just always there.

I'm tired, so tired. I need coffee. Suddenly she knew where she needed to be, or perhaps wanted to be. Those steel eyes, coffee, aftershave. The very thought of him almost made her eyes roll back in her head. She groaned and shocked herself with the very physical reaction she felt even at the idea of him. Him? Him who? She'd didn't know this random man.

Starting the car, she headed toward the café reminding herself it was all just a dream. A loving, realistic dream. She had feelings and emotions toward this stranger now because of it. And she didn't even know his name.

Elle had seen attractive men before, every day. But none caused her to fight her own body, in an attempt to restrain it from contorting with pleasure from a simple thought. Calming herself she stepped out of the car and walked into the café, she was hit with the smell, so warm and arousing the second she entered. She stopped, her eyes like magnets paired with his. A palm frond brushed her leg just below the hem line of her yellow dress and she shivered.

Her mind now swarmed with deliciously naughty ideas. He was smiling at her as if he knew something. Knew her better, knew about her dream. His eyes unwavering from hers, his smile grew as he gently flicked his head back indicating she should come in. Elle gulped, she wasn't prepared for this. Him, actually knowing what was on her mind. Or did he? Standing in the doorway acting quite weird. Now she felt embarrassed as she confirmed with herself, he was simply reacting to her oddness.

She walked closer and stood by the counter. Refusing to look at him even though she could feel his eyes resting easy on her. She took a breath as she fiddled with some business cards placed in a holder on the counter. She could smell his smell and her belly grew tight. Just being near this man, this stranger made her heart pound.

She felt alive. It was like all the depressing and draining thoughts dissipated like a fog withdrawing when the sun showed up. The feeling of her life spiralling out of control seemed to slow and hover giving her reprieve, allowing her to take a breath. A whole refreshing breath rather than the short, panicked ones that simply kept her alive.

Elle tried to sneak an unnoticed peek at him but he was still looking at her with that steady smiling gaze. Those eyes knew her, she was sure of it and they'd never shared more than a few words as she ordered her coffee before. Before her bath tub dream that is. He knew her now, he really did. She told herself. Taking another breath, she picked up a business card, took out her wallet and slotted it in purposely, as if she actually required it and wasn't stalling. Stalling for what? Her mind harassed her. What are you going to do?

With her composure reclaimed she looked up. Be brave Elle. She looked right into his eyes and there it was. Clear as day. I love you Elle. Written into the very pores of his skin.

He turned to tap out the used coffee grind, wiping out the filter basket in preparation of more. She stood still, attempting to absorb his telepathic message, trying to decipher if perhaps it was all in her head. Again, he turned to her, and as if in response to her silent thinking. Elle, I really do.

This time he made a sound. He chuckled a little and shook his head as he returned to his job. An- other worldly sound, strong and beautiful, Elle had never heard something as lovely or frightening.

Something within her was lit. She loved him and didn't even know him. The emptiness, the confusion, the complicated way life had become, melted away around him. Her everyday life just didn't seem real, didn't seem to matter anymore. He placed the take away coffee cup onto the counter as she watched his hands place the plastic lid on top and press it down into place. She was now desperate to put her lips to it. She'd know the smell; She knew it was as close to him as she'd get in this physical waking world.

"Elle Florence." He'd said it with such simple eloquence.

She'd never thought of her name as pretty, or unique or special until he'd verbalised it. He slid the coffee across the counter toward her with a gentlemanly tilt of his head.

"Thank you." She said hoping the pink in her cheeks was a gentle blush and not the flustered redness she could feel.

Smiling she took the cup, not even once caring to consider when, where or how he'd learnt her name just glad that he did. She turned to take her favourite seat. Without thinking, she spun back a little too quickly to face him.

"What is your name?" She blurted.

"Torian Amos." He replied as if prepared, his strong jaw supporting a brilliant smile.

He was leaning on his hands against the counter, they were big and attractive and looked as though he was once a landscapist, builder or something similar. They were earthly and well used. Masculine hands she thought, and he makes great coffee, he's practically perfect. And again, there was that smirky smile of his.

She worried a brief moment thinking he could read her thoughts and brushed it off. His smiled brightened again and she felt what it meant, even without him saying it out loud. You're cute, you're funny. I like you.

"Torian." She giggled like an idiot school girl.

Taking her seat, she quietly scolded herself for her immaturity. Watching the waves roll continuously. Today was calmer than the last time she'd visited but still that coastal breeze.

She absent-mindedly pondered the gulls swooping then swinging away wildly, the view from up there must be spectacular. A big blue below and a big blue above, floating suspended between the two. Decorating the empty space between two huge important things. Like her, between life and death. Decorating the in between.

The café wasn't busy this late in the afternoon, and she was thankful. It was easier for her to hear his movements while he worked. The hissing steam that billowed up to meet him, causing tiny beads of sweat to form across his well-made nose. She watched as he patted his hands against his thighs, making his pants pull tighter around his solid, rounded backside. Every now and again he'd flick his head to one side, displacing the hair from his face.

Occasionally too, he'd glance at her. His grin would pull up as if he found it amusing that they kept making eye contact, even though they were both trying to have a peek on the sly.

Sipping her rich coffee, but not too often. She wanted to stay and smell and drink in the very presence of him. Torian. I like that name she thought, it suits him. Torian, Toby, Trey, that's funny she rotated the idea in her mind like the dregs of her brew in the bottom of the cup. Toby? What am I doing?

Suddenly, as if day dreaming and walking right into a sign post she was completely aware of where she was, who she was and what she was thinking. This is not a dream Elle, this is real life. Practically having an affair with a sexy barista. Or considering it. Torian, you mean. Her mind stated. I'm with Toby! And what about Mai? What the hell am I doing? Immediately, the short trance of a carefree life fell. The guilt and stress and pressure raced back in to replace it.

Putting the coffee down and pushing it away, she picked up her bag and headed straight for the car, purposely fighting the urge to look back at Torian and those eyes of his. Those gorgeous eyes, were watching her she knew, as she moved along looking at the ground frowning with shame.

The second she sat in the car her mind began to chastise her. What are you thinking? You're going to run off with this random coffee guy? You only know his name, that's literally it. He could be a murderer or worse. You're acting like he's the answer to all your problems just because you had a steamy dream about him? Because he makes you feel all flirty and cute? This will only complicate things further. What kind of answers are you going to get from him?

He's just looking for a little action and the way you were acting, he certainly thought he'd found some. You think he loves you because you imagined some telepathic messages? Grow up Elle. You're just a sad, lonely desperate woman with an over active imagination. This is not fairyland. This is the real world, get with it. Focus on Mai, Toby too. You want answers? Perhaps do what you should have long ago, see your Grandmother.

Chapter 6

Elle walked up the leaf littered path. It was a quiet place, eerie maybe, but she liked it. Young, freshly planted flame trees were mingled with big, ancient trees that appeared to be going bald. Their leaves in shades of burnt orange brown floating, fluttering to the ground like a butterfly's genocide.

She stopped. For just a moment. One leaf spiralled rapidly, then swooped and slowed. Rocking back and forth upon the air, like a baby's cradle before delicately caressing the earth. Deceased. I will find the answers she confirmed within.

Allowing the trees to haze out of focus she saw the sky beyond, brilliant white cumulonimbus clouds bound forth on the horizon. Their bases heavy, lined with a dirty grey. Threatening to take over the watery blue. A gust swirled around Elle, taking the dead leaf, giving it a second life. Sweeping it up against the tall cast iron gates she'd just opened and walked through.

Continuing on toward the building, ivy devouring it from its base. A thick ruffled blanket of green. As it grew higher it thinned clinging and clawing at the terracotta coloured brickwork, trying to swallow it all. Only the large bay windows of the bottom floors were safe.

The windows were imposingly tall. The glass looked thin and blurred with age, like looking into the eyes of the elderly. Obscured, yet wise. The lichen covered path lead to a stone arch. Draped with dry lifeless vines, perhaps ivy too that had been sliced at the base by the garden maintenance people.

She passed through the arch and shivered as the combination of creepy death plants and cool electrified wind of the impending storm engulfed her. Reaching the door, she could see it was clearly old, smooth areas where people had run their hands over the years, wore at the intricate carvings. As if curiosity enticed a need to feel.

She pushed the door. It was heavy but slid away easily revealing black and white checked lino. High pastel green walls seemed to curve down around her. Hesitating, she suddenly wasn't sure this was a good idea. Her breathing became shallow and her heart was pounding in her ears. Panicked at the thought of what she may learn. Trying to keep her steps light, despite feeling heavy. They echoed regardless. Sucking in a breath, she continued forward toward the impressive timber desk carved in a similar fashion to the door yet there were no worn areas here. Maybe people felt less inclined to be openly curious when they had an audience she mused, especially when the audience was the small, white haired lady behind the desk.

Elle ran her hand over the carvings to spite all those who'd felt they couldn't express themselves. A throat cleared. It was the old lady. She was just as impressive as the creation she sat behind despite being small physically. She had a strong vibe, a presence. A sassy attitude was obvious from her demeanour.

"Can I help you?" She questioned impatiently from behind slightly tinted, silver rimmed glasses. The large open space made her strong voice echo and boom.

"I'm here to see my grandmother. Eleanor Florence." Her voice shaking in contrast, the acoustics of the space didn't portray her feigned bravery as she'd hoped.

"Eleanor Florence? No one's been to see her for a very long time." She looked up over her glasses at Elle. A soft look passed over her eyes, a fondness perhaps. "I'm sorry; that's none of my business. Follow me, this way Miss."

Standing, the woman reached a pointed hand, indicating they go down the hall. "You said you were Eleanor's granddaughter?"

"Yes, my name's Elle. I was named after her actually. I haven't seen her since I was very little. I remember her as this cheerful chubby woman. Her eyes and hair sparkle in my memories of her." Her mind drifting back to the vague, warped flashes of memories and dreams of her grandmother.

The little lady was no taller than Elle's shoulders. Elle could see straight over the top of her white bun, pinned precariously upon her head. She remained silent as she listened to Elle's reminiscing, it wasn't the first time she'd heard this kind of idle chatter. She knew it was best to allow visitors to talk and remember.

She didn't need to say anything, just listen. It was important, because what was behind those doors in the next corridor where not always as welcoming as loved ones imagined. It wasn't always easy, the chit chat she knew, was often nerves.

They turned a bend and followed that un-ending black and white plastic look floor. Elle watched her feet hit it as she continued to walk. That's not white she mused. It's black and yellow.

The white was old and yellowed with age, the black she decided, isn't even black but faded into a dark grey. Some places she noticed had been rubbed raw and bare, like a gentle acid had corroded it away. It seemed peculiar to her, how her mind tried to trick her into believing the ground was a simple black and white when clearly on closer inspection, it was not at all. Why does that happen she wondered? Make things easier, smoother to comprehend. Is that why Nessa lied to me? Make things easy. Smoother?

"Excuse me?" Elle cracked open their solid silence. "What colour would you say this floor was?"

"Black and white honey, but I don't see why that matters."

With those words she stopped and turned to a door, it was white and just like the rest they passed lining their walk. No different at all, though Elle thought if she had enough time to observe them all, that surely, they were each very individual.

The little woman lifted the hem of her navy coloured coat producing a large ring with dangling keys. She selected one without a moment's hesitation, unlocked the door and pushed it inward away from them.

Elle looked to her as if waiting for directions but the woman merely stood by the frame facing down the hall. Her hands clasped in front of her holding the keys. Perhaps she'd been in the army or something Elle thought. All stern and regimental dressed in her navy suit, poised and well postured.

"Good luck." The woman said plainly.

Elle inclined her head toward her and mumbled thanks before she moved to the open door. She peered in. It was a small sized room, with an antique dresser in one corner, only big enough to hold a beautiful silver hair brush, comb and mirror. There was a wooden chest, a wicker chair. And then there was the bed. White cast iron, in tall swirling patterns, trimmed in a greenish tarnish. Elle wondered if all institutions had this same kind of gothic creepiness, or if it was only the old ones. She liked it, it had character and interest. Holding the manic energy of all those who lived and passed through here. Interesting but still creepy.

She stopped, knowing her mind was again focusing on the details to avoid recognising the frail, lifeless woman lying on that gothic bed. Elle walked into the room, trying not to think of the potent old person's smell that was thick in the air. Is there any kind of ventilation in here?

She went to the window and like the ones at the front of the building, it was tall. It made her feel minute in comparison, all that smoky glass bearing down on her. Just like life. She unlatched it and slid the window up a few inches, until she realised it would go no further. Possibly for the safety of the patients she thought, even though it was covered with heavy close-set bars and old metal gauze.

She returned to the door and found the yellowing flick switch for the ceiling fan. It was so high up she doubted if its effects would be felt down here on earth. She liked the metallic whirring sound it made however, it sliced through the silence making it a little more comfortable to bare.

The small, hawk eyed woman was gone, retreated to her post. Elle closed the door and pulled up the single wicker chair to her grandmother's bedside. At first, she didn't dare look at her, what if I can't deal with this? She questioned herself. You're tougher than that, don't be stupid. It was one of those rare times her mind agreed with her.

So, she looked. Really looked at her grandmother. Her skin was the first thing she noticed. It was so fine and almost a grey blue shade, she didn't want to touch it in case it broke beneath her fingers. Her hair was still that grey she'd remembered so long too, but no longer did it shimmer and reflect the light as she thought it would. It was dry, dull. Limp.

Her cheek bones protruded, not in a harsh frightening way but in a way that wasn't natural for the living. Her eyes were closed and she did seem peaceful, a hint of a smile. That secret smile made Elle's heart slow a little, a relief brushed against her like a purring cat.

Elle placed her head down onto her grandmother's lacey crochet bed spread. She decided to risk her grandmother's fragility and took her hand. Her fingers held the memory of warmth and Elle felt a calm, an okay-ness came over her as she concentrated on breathing in and out.

"I'm here Grandma, Elle. Remember me? I'm here with you. I have a beautiful little girl now. Her names Mai and she'll be five tomorrow. I've missed you so much. It would have been nice to have you in my life." She rambled. Elle had no idea what to say to someone who obviously would not respond. "It's been so hard."

The darkness began to seep in. She'd lost track of time, or perhaps she'd fallen asleep, she wasn't sure. But it was late and she needed to get home to plan for Mai's birthday. Elle closed the window she'd opened, it was getting chilly and she could smell the rain coming. She made sure to switch off the ceiling fan too but still it felt cold.

She carefully opened her grandmother's wooden chest in search of something warm to shrug over her shoulders, to fend off the icy evening air outside. She found a shawl. It had a funny, musty smell that made Elle wrinkle up her nose. It'd been in there a long time, she swung it around her shoulders and hugged it to her body. Instantly she felt a warm snugness that made her shiver.

Before closing the chest, she dug a little deeper and found a small fancy bottle labelled Lily of the valley. Spraying a little into the air she observed the tiny droplets hover, before descending toward the floor, Elle swooped her face into the mist and inhaled. It made her smile. I remember that smell. She took the bottle to her grandmother and pressed the golden pump.

"Now you're a little more like you used to be." She whispered as she tucked a loose silver strand of hair behind her grandma's ear, deciding that next time she'd brush her hair for her. There will be a next time? Her mind piped up. I guess so, Elle responded.

Returning the perfume to the chest she saw the corner of a small leather-bound book, peeking up from some ivory shaded garment. She took it and stroked the cover. Eleanor Florence. Grandma's diary.

Opening the first page, words like miserable, distraught, lost and hopeless jumped off the page at her, grabbing her by the throat. Elle felt a hard lump, a choking sensation rising. Threatening.

Dear Diary,

I really need someone to talk to. Looks like you're it. I'm tired of asking myself questions I can't answer. Is this all life is? Why am I so different and feel so alone? Why does nothing satisfy me? I am done with this constant gnawing boredom. I feel like I am slipping. I have lost all motivation, I can't act anymore on this stage of life where everyone is expected to perform and be perfect for their audience. Surely, I can't be the only one whom feels like nothing is real. Nothing is genuine.

I feel so lost, like I am searching for something unknown. Something that will make everything feel better. I want this pain and loneliness to end. Right here and now, I can't take it anymore and I can't even explain exactly what it is. With each passing day I feel more and more miserable. I sometimes wish life would just end for me, the sooner the better.

Dear Diary, I feel so horribly hopeless. Can you help me?

Eleanor.

Elle slammed the book shut and put it in her bag. Like the shawl, she didn't think Grandma would mind all that much if she borrowed them until she returned. She looked her grandmother over one last time.

"I'm so thankful you're here." She said. "Even if you don't know I'm with you. You make me feel not so alone. Thank you."

Chapter 7

Miserable? Lost? Grandma felt the way I do. Elle sadly, felt relieved that she wasn't the only one and was anxious to continue reading grandma's diary. She tried to put it from her mind, she had something far more important than herself to think of in this moment.

Mai's birthday, it had come around so quickly and desperately she wanted to make it special. Magical, she thought as she flicked the blinker on and turned into the driveway. Elle called in on Jilly and Mai to let them know she'd arrived home, after some home baked treats and tea Elle asked Jilly to keep Mai just one more night. She had an idea.

Hurrying home, she went straight to the closet and dug out streamers and balloons from birthdays and parties past. Gathering all of Mai's pretty fairy pages and pictures she took them all to Mai's bedroom, closed the door and began to work.

It was late when Toby arrived home. The house was dark and quiet. Entering the kitchen he flicked the light on, put his brief case down on the bench and leaned over it. It had been a long shift at work. Toby managed a chain of nightclubs. The classy kind he told himself. He'd soon realised the night shift was when he was needed most, it was when most of the stuff ups occurred. Perhaps it was the young inexperienced staff combined with intoxicated patrons, regardless the reason, Toby had decided to change his day shifts to night ones. It made a world of difference at work almost halving the incident rate.

He knew within himself that he was overly absorbed in all things related to his job. He thought it made him important, like his job made him a worthy man and he believed that people envied him.

Not Elle though and sometimes that frustrated him. She never put any kind of ranking system on people. To Elle, Toby was an equal with the man who collected their garbage every Thursday and he knew he was better than that. He tried to make her realise how important his job was, how important and powerful he was but she always, innocently seemed to be able to emasculate him.

Toby kicked off his shoes and pulled off his socks. He always felt naked without footwear. Not like Elle he thought to himself. She appeared over dressed, unnatural even, with something on her feet. He walked down the dark hallway feeling the lush cream carpet between his toes.

He was in a good mood despite work, especially after his talk with Elle, she seemed distant, but she's coming around he thought. Quietly he opened the bedroom door and pushed it open. The bed was still made and Elle wasn't there. Her car was parked out front, where is she? He frowned, worried that his promising thoughts of sorting things out were premature.

Returning to the hall he quietly opened Mai's door. There she was. Elle with her back turned to him, up on her tip toes trying to attach a pink balloon to fishing line she'd hung from the ceiling. Her head tilted back looking up, made her hair fall forever, half past her rounded backside. Her waist tucked in at just the right spot he mused. Her short, shorts she reserved for home made her legs look long. Her calves looked neat and smooth when on her toes like that, cocking his head to one side for a different perspective. Finally, having absorbed her with his eyes he cleared his throat. She dropped the balloon and spun around. Elle beamed.

"Like it?" She asked waving her arms around the room.

Obviously, she was proud of her efforts and she should be, he thought. The room looked great. She'd tacked different shades of green streamers from the floor up, at varying lengths. Among the streaming grass she'd cut out and stuck Mai's drawings and fairies all over the place. From the roof more streamers, masses of them, in shades of peach, champagne and gold. Balloons in Mai's favourite colour of pink, bobbed seeming to be suspended in the air all on their own.

It did look magical, something any little girl would love. Elle looked back at Toby, who was still admiring the room, leaning on the door frame with folded arms.

"She will love it." He smiled answering the clear, what do you think? Look she was giving.

He held out his arms toward her. In happiness at her achievement; she bound to Toby and hugged him. Dying to see the look on Mai's face. With her head against his chest, she wondered if things really could go back to normal one day. And then, those eyes.

Invading her thoughts, she almost felt mad at Torian for stealing her brief moment of sanity. She'd been distracted and she liked it. And now, he was smiling at her, telling her she was loved. Her chest suddenly constricted and she pushed Toby away.

"What's wrong Elle?" He was still gripping her upper arms.

"Nothing." She said as she pulled out of his reach. "I haven't baked Mai's cake yet. That's all." And she hurried off down the hall.

She listened as she cooked, to Toby showering and brushing his teeth. Heard him click off the bathroom light and enter their room and close the door behind him. He's waiting for me, her brain said. We haven't had sex in ages, I can't even remember the last time. I don't know if I want to. She had wanted it for so long, so why did it now feel weird? I didn't want the sex, I wanted the love, the comfort, she answered herself.

Elle couldn't hault her nervousness from increasing as she took her time packing away the eggs, flour and milk. She spent a few moments rearranging the sprinkles and opened the fridge to double check Mai's cake. She'll like it.

Switching off the light and leaving the room, now feeling like this was all a strange dream. Her whole life a warped dream state. Maybe Toby's asleep? I did take a long time in the kitchen and it was well past midnight. He's been at work and surely tired. Elle snuck in quietly stripped off her clothes leaving her underwear in place she carefully lifted the heavy blankets and snuggled in. Her head had barely touched the pillow before Toby rolled toward her.

"You took forever baby." He murmured as he reached an arm around her bare waist, nuzzling at her neck.

"I just wanted Mai's cake to be perfect." Elle could feel her body tense as she lay unmoving.

"It will be. You're perfect." He said sleepily between nibbles to her neck.

Elle could feel his chest press against her side as he wormed his arm underneath to encircle her with both arms. She closed her eyes and tried to enjoy the kisses he placed against her. But she couldn't. She felt trapped, like he'd never let her go. It's in your head, relax. She listened to herself and took a breath and tried again. She began to caress his arm, gently stroking back and forth wondering if he could tell it was forced or not. Elle could feel him harden against her thigh and instantly knew he had no clue. Would he even care?

Elle knew exactly how this would go. They'd rarely have sex but if they did, it was quite predictable. She'd been here in this spot so many times before and suddenly she was curious as to why she'd missed it so much.

After he's done nibbling my neck and ear, he'll kiss my mouth and move his left hand to my right breast. He'll start slow but get rougher. When I begin to think he's too rough he will slide his hand down my belly. Stroke each of my thighs once, then move his hand up the inside of the one on my right. He'll pull my underwear aside and cup my crotch while making that wild animal sound. He'll scoop my legs up and over him as if he's cradling me. Before I know it, he'll have pushed his way into my body.

Invading me, yet before I've even had time to contemplate if I want him there, he'll be done. Pulling out of me spreading his goo all over my belly.

Elle couldn't help but give herself a run through of the events unfolding. She knew it off by heart and it made her cringe. Made her anxious. Made her angry. The emotions afterwards were hardest to deal with, once it was all said and done. He'll peck my forehead and weasel himself out from under my limp legs. Make his way to the bathroom leaving me here, empty, messy.

He won't care that I wasn't satisfied or even know that he hadn't made me feel good or special. I'll feel used and depressed. Like a messy piece of meat. Like some dirty rag thrown in a corner. That's what I've been waiting for? Why would I want that? That's not love. It's something else entirely.

Torian's face entered her mind and she smiled, such a sweet distraction. She wriggled and tried to imagine it was him touching her, him pressing his lips against her skin. But she couldn't make it work. He'd never make me feel this way.

Somehow, she just knew he'd make her feel sexy and erotic, beautiful and loved. Torian would make love to her soul, not destroy it. He'd make love to her body, not use it. No, she couldn't fantasise it was him touching her in this moment, what an insult.

Opening her eyes, she was again snapped back to the physical happenings in the present. She'd been wrong. Toby had totally skipped the mouth kissing; he was already up to the left handed, right boob grope. Elle wasn't into this at all. Her stomach was churning and her teeth were clenched. She didn't like it and she felt dirty. She pushed his hand away. He returned it. She pushed him away forcibly this time and started getting out of bed.

"Elle, what's going on? Where are you going?" Toby called to the shadowy figure of Elle leaving the room.

Perhaps once, she'd have returned to talk to him about how she felt. Explain to him what she wanted and needed from him. But she'd done that. Numerous times. She'd found it so pointless talking to a man who obviously didn't listen nor care. She'd waste no more time talking to brick walls. Simply didn't have the energy for it.

Elle showered. She needed it. She sat in the bottom and cried. She traced the patterns on the floor tiles with her long slender fingers. The hot water streamed over her head, her hair creating a wall around her face. A little dark cave that blocked out all worldly sounds. All she could hear was the eerie sounds of water pounding down around her ears and the echoes of her own weeping.

It was surreal, her chest heaving and feeling sad but not really knowing if tears were falling. They mingled with the water cascading around her. Maybe it's all my tears. Her heart ached, she wanted to be held and not in the way Toby offered. Just hugged, embraced, allowing her feelings to fall, pour and flow naturally. I am so alone; this life is too hard. I can't do it anymore. So, she cried.

Once the water began to run cold, she pulled herself up from the tiles using the slippery soap dish. She just felt so lethargic and old. Drying herself and wrapping a towel around her body she crept from the bathroom and into Mai's. Elle dimmed the lights as low as they'd go without being completely off and climbed into her daughter's bed.

Lying there looking around at the slice of a magical world she'd created for Mai. Five tomorrow, I can't believe it. That little girl was the only light in her life, the one thing she could trust to be true and she treasured her. Be happy for her. She forced a smile and fresh tears burst forth and this time she knew they existed, knew they belonged to her. She felt like a terrible mother, trying to hide all this pain and confusion and fight on, playing make believe so Mai had peace in her little life.

Still in her damp towel she watched the dim glowing light bounce off the gold glittery streamers and the shiny stretched balloons. If I could simply silence my mind, with an empty head I'd have some peace. Why do I have to be so different? So complicated?

Her final thought before falling asleep was; What's wrong with me?

Chapter 8

Flickering light intruded as her eyes stuttered open. Peach skies, it must be sunrise. She simply knew it was. She could see a glimmer peeking up from the sweeping hills in the distance, the sun again keeping its eternal promise to always rise.

However, there was a second sun, very distant, higher and flickering duller. The sky was dome like, peeling up and back away from her, scattered with those shimmering, dreamy clouds that held the golden warmth of the suns. The air was fresher than she was used to but it was warm, like she had been dipped in a tepid liquid wax. The atmosphere coated her comfortably.

She was beneath that old weeping willow, just as before. She liked that tree. Standing up, feeling the soft grasses on her bare soles and moved toward it. Gnarled and rough. Touching the bark, she considered how it was rough but a rough different to the one she knew. This was somehow pleasant to feel against her palms.

There was a curious beetle scurrying up the wood, blue iridescent wings folded back over it's body like a lady beetle she thought. Her eyes tracing its path as its tiny legs carried it higher and higher. Looking up into the branches, seeing them reach and paw at the sky, or perhaps praising it and then turning away and weeping back to the earth in worship.

The shades of green among the leaves were many and unusual. The light shining through made them glitter, like monochrome Christmas lights. Yes, she liked this tree. Moving around the trunk, stepping over the roots that grounded it she allowed her fingers to trail over the bark.

She was feeling good. Simply good. As though she'd been slipped some kind of relaxing drug that made her chilled and docile. This was her happy place. All was forgotten. All safe and calm. This was all she knew, this moment, this place. She felt not one ounce of fear or sadness, of loneliness or stress. She never wanted to leave this place where all her worldly worries disintegrated.

Rounding the trunk, her eyes met another pair. Torian was standing there, his feet slightly apart, his hands in the pockets of his jeans. They sat low and she could see those delicious muscles reaching up from his groin. His broad shoulders where slightly drawn forward, his head tilted to one side. His messy dark blonde hair flicked and tousled to one side. She wanted to touch it.

His smile was slight but she knew it was there, she could see it in his eyes. He had an honest air about him like he had the inability to speak a lie. There was also a childlike playfulness, sparkling at the edges of his aura. An innocence that made her want to take him and hold him and care for him. He was just so big and masculine and she knew he'd never physically need anyone to protect him. But she wanted to protect his heart. Love it and keep it safe forever.

"Torian." She said it like naming a god.

He came closer and she allowed him. He stood before her and was at least a head taller. He took his large warm hands and placed a palm on each cheek, his fingers tucked into her soft dark hair beyond her ears, he tilted her face up to his. Torian looked into her pure blue eyes, as if searching for permission. Slowly he leaned in and kissed her. Full on the mouth and deep. She melted into him.

Swiftly moving his hands to her waist to support her as she relaxed and languished into his kiss. Again, he was absorbing her life, taking it from her and she gave it willingly. Elle could feel the exchange of her life between them like a pulse. It was essential to her very being that he kiss her like that. Her heart pounding in her own ears, her chest caged a blissful agony. She feared she'd explode and yet she kind of hoped she would.

Torian moved his arm further around Elle's waist holding her close, moved his other behind her head, entangling his fingers into her hair. Elle was utterly loose and free. Like she'd wash away, all light and liquid. Torian took his moist lips from hers between beats and again looked into Elle's wide eyes with his playful grey ones.

"I love you Elle." She knew it. No need for words.

Taking a step back from him, she took the corner of the towel tucked between her breasts and pulled it free. She allowed it to fall to the ground, leaving her standing in the warm morning light, nude. She felt free like a creature, a powerful natural beast with no rules only instinct. She went to him and embraced his large firm body.

Suddenly he pressed against her a little firmer and she felt something unlike ever before. As if her body really was melting into his. It felt like he was softly splitting, his ribcage opening. Being pulled apart to let her in. Her eyes closed and she allowed this exquisite sensation to take over. His body was melding over hers, forming one being.

He enveloped her. Elle could feel Torian all over, his touch everywhere, every inch of her skin burned with tingling pleasure. Her skin flush with heat, her pulse hurrying her along. Every intimate and naked cell of her body was feeling him. This was different and new, he was like water sweeping gently all over her. And then pleasantly, he was inside her too. She was full, every part of her.

Skin burning beautifully, insides about to explode, it happened. Wave after wave, she came. Drugged on an erotic high her eyes flew open and she could see that sky, that tree. She wanted to scream out with pleasure, scream out at this whole-body release. But she was exhausted.

Slowly, carefully she felt him melt and withdraw from him. Pouring off to leave her feeling light and satisfied, lazy and loved. She looked at him looking at her, happily but with slight concern.

"I'm fine." She said into his worried gaze.

She smiled completely satisfied then collapsed totally into his arms. She had no fear, no doubt. He'd never let her fall. Elle slept breathing in his coffee aftershave scent until afternoon crept in.

She woke, how nice it felt to wake naturally. And to feel fully restored. Torian was still there holding her, she knew he would. Hunger finally convinced her to move. Standing, Torian reached down to help her rise. He handed her a dress of a light organic fabric, embroidered with flowers.

He studied her as she dressed, put his warm inked arm around her and they began to walk. There didn't seem to be any need to exchange words, he felt her needs and wants and she simply knew he did.

They walked together for a long time but it didn't make her tired or bored, she felt no physical strains. Elle kept on going and so did Torian. She was interested in the landscape.

Everything looked different with this peach like sky. Though most things she saw were in fact different and she didn't think the lighting of the atmosphere would change that. In the distance she saw a herd of large animals. At first, she considered them to be elephants only they had no trunks, and their legs were far too slender. Their ears too, were smaller and perked up, flicking about trying to catch unknown sounds. Birds flew overhead but Elle couldn't recall their species, or if she'd ever seen them before at all. They flew slow, more relaxed. The tall grasses looked like an ocean, the breeze made the seed heads ripple with such a precise rhythmic motion.

Finally, they reached a hilltop and as they began to descend Elle saw what looked like a gathering. Lots of people and lots of beings. Everyone engulfed in a translucent sphere of happiness and joy. There were long communal tables drenched in candlelight, laden with juicy meats, piles of strange fruits, sloshing water bags and large wooden pitchers of something potently aromatic.

Happy people and beings, indulging in drink and foods. Dancing, some were naked and sleuthing all over others, children giggling and running in and out from between grown people. She wasn't sure who or what was down there, but somehow it didn't worry her. It all felt so natural; like home.

This was a whole new world, a world where her emotions and feelings couldn't be hidden, a place where words felt so useless. A place she'd never been but somehow it was home. She was meant to be there.

As they approached Elle could see more of those little fire flies. Fairies, she corrected herself, zipping about. She saw beings tall and small as she gazed around, everyone appeared to be smiling at her. Something caught her eye, a silvery glimmer and she turned quickly to catch it. Nothing was there. She heard a familiar giggle and spun again to find the source. Again nothing.

She felt she knew who was teasing her, playing games with her but she couldn't settle her eyes upon her. It was Grandma, she's here, Elle exclaimed inside. She peered through the people, stood on tip toes to peer over. No matter how hard she tried, her sight would not connect with Grandma.

Torian took her hand and led her further still into the cheerful crowd. It didn't faze her one bit to see a bare breasted woman with a goat's bottom half. She had two children by her side, both also with goatly features. It didn't occur to her that anything was strange about a statuesque man with spectacular, muscular white wings draped stately down his bare back. A couple, fox like yet humanoid, making out passionately felt commonplace.

Her rational mind told her it was all so unreal, that this wasn't really happening, it was just a dream. But she allowed the thoughts fade away, turning to ash. This was her dream. Her most wonderful dream and she would relish in it while she could.

Torain led Elle to a tall man. She could sense his power and see his magnificence. His aura which shone radiantly towered above her. His hair was long and dark. It fell smoothly down his chest and strapped neatly to his head with a leather band around his forehead, a golden bejewelled emblem in the very centre.

He was a beautiful man to look at, his brow strong, his jaw firm. Good looking, but not in a sexy, rough around the edges way like Torian. She realised she couldn't help but compare them. His eyes were emerald green and looked far too deep into hers. Like he was reading her deeply. She could sense a stern and solid personality but he also held a humility. Perhaps a big soft spot inside.

She'd never seen anything like the garments he was wearing before. All draping and manly, light but durable like a gentle amour. It was very clear he was in charge. He stepped forward to meet her, eyes always watching. He held out his hand and Elle took it without question. He seemed so familiar but she couldn't recall how.

"It's nice to finally have you here in Frin Elle." His voice echoed in her ears.

Frin? Her mind registered. Don't go there anymore. Nessa's voice sounded hollowly from her mind.

"We've been waiting for you, we weren't sure you'd come to us, we have Torian to thank for that." Putting his hand on her shoulder, he bent down for a closer look into her eyes. "You are so much like Laura, aren't you? The resemblance is uncanny. She has been dearly missed, your presence will be such a delight."

"Who is Laura?" Elle was almost hypnotised by his eyes.

"She is the very beginning, the one who helped me guide Frin for so long." A shadow passed over his startling eyes and he broke his gaze with Elle. "Laura was, is a very important part of Frin's beginnings and yours too Elle. I'm sure you will hear about it all soon enough."

"Who are you?" Elle asked, the feeling of knowing him from somewhere had grown. He was familiar to her.

"I am Trey."

Trey. Trey? I know that name. Mai spoke of him. Mai, my baby, where is she? Slowly a lump began to creep up into her throat from some distant place. Her ribs seemed to constrict crushing the air from her lungs. Her heart beating, bashing at her insides.

Elle's eyes darting like a kitten full of terror. She spun, searching, eyes wide and welling. Torian took her in his arms, he could see her sudden fear, her confusion, her utter panic.

"She can't stay here! It's too soon, she doesn't understand. She will feed the darkness!" Trey's voice boomed inside her head as she struggled to grasp reality.

"Open your eyes." Torian told her desperately.

Elle could see his pain, but she had to go. Now.

Chapter 9

Elle opened her already open eyes. The scene had changed. She was now looking up at a white ceiling. Florescent lights, far too bright, blinded her. The synapses of her brain firing with confusion like a little frog eating dinner in a mosquito storm. She didn't know where she was and her eyes weren't adjusting quick enough to combat her rising panic.

She tried to sit up but couldn't. Reaching for her arm, she felt the needle in her vein tug. She'd been hooked up to a drip. Her clothes gone, replaced with a stiff white hospital gown. Hospital? Where is Mai?

"What's going on? Where am I?" Elle began calling out, her panic audible. A nurse rushed in looking at her as if she had risen from the dead.

"What's going on?" Elle demanded again.

"I'll get the doctor for you, and call your mother in. She just stepped out." The pretty blonde nurse retreated, all the while watching Elle like she was an experiment.

There was nothing for Elle to do, other than lay back onto the fabric covered plastic bed and try to recall how she'd come to be in hospital. Only her last memory was of Toby. In bed. With her. She'd showered and slept in Mai's room. Having that dream. It had been so vivid.

She could still feel the way Torian's arms wrapped around her as they'd made their way to the gathering for food. Oh, I am still so hungry! Who is Laura? And why would I look like her? Where's my baby and where's Toby? Her mind snapped questions at her from two realities. What's happening to me?

Like lightening striking a tree, the sparks of guilt burned her soul. Soon a raging fire, her dreamy love affair was eating her up. So clear in her mind and she couldn't release it. It was far too real, making love to another man, sex with a stranger. She didn't even know if it was sex, it certainly felt like an intimacy on the same level. Her body responded, tingling in places she knew she shouldn't. She blushed as Nessa walked in, as if some how she'd hear her thoughts and know what she'd done.

"Darling! I'm so glad you decided to join us!" Nessa beamed as she leant down to hug Elle.

Nessa scanned Elle's eyes, curious to know if she could take away any information without Elle knowing. She couldn't. It's still too soon, Nessa thought. Elle can't work it out. She doesn't understand yet.

"Decided to join you? What do you mean Mother? It's Mai's birthday and I wake up here, strapped down and plugged into all this stuff?" Elle blurted a little too loudly as she gave a sarcastic tug on the cords tapped into her body. Anger slowly seeping in, adding to the cocktail of mismatched emotions already there.

"Oh Honey, Mai's birthday was nine days ago now. She loved her room though and the cake. Both beautiful, you did a great job." Nessa knew the time to tell all was imminent, Elle was on the verge of losing everything. Her family, everything she'd worked for. Just a little longer, perhaps I can still stop all of this.

Nessa was torn, watching her daughters uncontrollable spiral, knowing she couldn't tell her everything. Knowing what was happening but not wanting to fully reveal all she knew. She'd worked so hard for so long to keep the truth from her only child, she wasn't completely prepared to quit just yet. She still had a chance.

Every word Nessa spoke after the mention of 'nine days,' was deleted from Elle's mind. It did not even enter it. Nine days have passed? And Mother's so calm about it. Elle swimming in an ocean of perplexity. Every time she tried to grasp at even the smallest handful of sense, it rolled on to evaded her. And the pressure of it was making her buckle.

Staring at the ceiling, she noticed a smudge. I wonder how it got so far up there? Shouldn't it have been cleaned it? This is a hospital after all. The longer she peered at it, the less it actually seemed to be there, perhaps it was just dust on her eyeball. Or one of those sun spots you got from looking into a light for too long.

Either way she wasn't impressed with that smudge, be it real or not. Mai's birthday. Elle didn't want to focus on that. She kept looking back to where the fantasy smudge was, but once the idea arose in her brain it kept persistently coming back.

Five, Mai's five? And I missed it. Somehow. Resignation settled in, I'm going mad. Tears began to pool, lining the rim of her eyes and finally, one popped forth moistening her dark lashes.

And then heaving, harsh sobs consumed her body. What would happen to Mai if her mother went mad? Who would look after her? Toby? No, he wouldn't take on that responsibility. He liked her and was nice to her but he wasn't the fatherly type, had no patience and wouldn't put in the effort to actually raise a child. Not like Elle wanted to. Nessa? She'd barely raised Elle, hell, she still had trouble acting like an adult sometimes let alone have the nurturing attributes a caring mother should have.

The truth was that Elle wanted the best for Mai and in her opinion, she was it. She knew someone else could probably feed her, send her to school, tuck her in at night. But no one would ever love her child like she would. A mother's love can't be replicated. She wanted Mai to have that. A mother's love. The very thought of not being the one stable person in Mai's life killed her.

"Elle?" Nessa questioned tentatively after allowing her sobs to subdue. Nessa remembered what it was like. The utter confusion, the lost time. At first, she'd loved all those beautiful, fanciful interludes until she came to hate them. "Tell me about Frin."

And just like that. A piece fell into place, sucked together like magnets. Checkmate. Finally, a move was made that she could be sure of. Nessa Knew. Elle took a breath, a deep clear one. She didn't feel mad, sad or anything at all. Her insides as still as death.

Lazily rolling her head toward Nessa, hearing the scrunch of the pillow case beneath her messy hair she looked into her eyes. Who is this woman? Numbly curious about this stranger, she decided to speak.

"I met Trey." Nessa began to cry and Elle didn't really care why.

"How is he?" An angry yet wistful tone was there.

"I don't know. I didn't ask. I remembered Mai's birthday and panicked. Torian told me to open my eyes." Elle could hear herself talk, as if she were listening to someone else. A hollow echo in her head. It was almost as if she was becoming external of herself. She didn't want to talk aloud, she didn't want to talk internally. She wanted to be hushed, surrounded in silence. In the dark alone.

"Who is Torian?" With the mention of his name Nessa could see a slight light return to Elle's eyes, they were directed at her but glazed and glassy. Like Elle were looking not at her but through her, into some where else.

He's important, this Torian Nessa knew. The blank look in Elle's eyes told her she'd say no more. She's closed. Shut down.

"I'll call Toby and let him know you're awake. I sent him home to sleep, he's been worried. He's been here with you for so long. Mai's with Jilly so don't worry about her."

Elle rolled her head back to gaze at the other wall. Don't worry about Mai? I've missed her birthday and clearly nine days of her life. Spent months so self-involved while she occupies herself. My poor Mai probably would be better off with someone else.

Tears again started to flow. Welling, then over flowing the bridge of her nose, escaping her face and dousing her pillow. I'm a terrible mother. Her eyes wouldn't stop leaking and she didn't mind. Elle wanted the poisonous thoughts and feelings to be gone, flushed away.

Chapter 10

Toby heard Elle get into the shower. He was still laying propped up on one elbow. He wasn't sure what he'd done wrong. He thought she was into it. We haven't had sex in so long I thought she'd want it as much as I did. He knew she'd be in the shower until it ran cold. She always did it when she was in a mood he didn't understand. Frustrated he lay back in the darkness listening to a fly buzz around the retro lamp shade.

This relationship was so much harder than it was promised to be. Sure, Elle was beautiful and interesting and he knew he wasn't the only man to think it. He often felt he had to fight to keep her but was it worth it? He was told she'd make him happy, told she'd be all his dreams come true. But then again what mother wouldn't say that about their own daughter?

Finally, the sound of the shower petered away and stopped. He waited but Elle didn't come back to bed with him. Toby slammed his fists down onto the bed beside him with clenched teeth. This is not what I signed up for he thought angrily. I'll be talking to Nessa about this.

Toby stirred from sleep, feeling someone watching him. Mai was standing there supervising his slumber.

"Good morning Mai! Happy birthday." Toby scooped her up and threw her into the bed with him.

Mai giggled her funny little giggle, it was contagious and he couldn't help but smile. Someone cleared their throat from the door way. Toby sat up a little embarrassed. It was Jilly, she was totally unaware of the privacy she'd breached or the boundaries neighbours usually kept. She'd let herself and Mai into the house

"Toby, I can't wake Elle." She stated. "Mai raced straight in, excited about her birthday, jumping about amazed with her room. I thought Elle would wake but she didn't."

"Okay, thank you Jilly. She's been exhausted lately. I'll go wake her soon. Thanks for having Mai, we really appreciate it. We'll see you this afternoon for Mai's tea party?" Toby asked hoping she'd take the hint and leave his bedroom so he could dress.

"You sure will. I wouldn't miss it for the world!" Jilly beamed at her as Mai leapt from the bed for a hug. "Have a great day little one."

Toby waited to hear the front door close before he got up and reached for some pants. Mai jumped about screeching repetitively that it was her birthday. It was a little more than he could handle in that moment, he'd slept badly thinking about Elle and her mood swings of late. One minute all loving the next ice cold. Forever pondering something he thought.

"Let's go wake Mummy, she's so happy it's your big day today." He suggested.

Toby nabbed Mai from the bed and spun her around, her giggles becoming uncontrollable. He swung her over his shoulder and left the room. Opening Mai's door and walking in.

"Let's tickle her." He laughed, Mai raced to her in agreement. He grinned as he watched on, it faded as he began to sense something was wrong. Elle was ticklish, and a light sleeper. She wasn't moving. Unresponsive. Looking over her body, stunned he froze, she was just so still. Too still for even sleep. She was pale, unnatural.

"Mai honey? Go check out the cake your mum made. It's in the fridge, it's so awesome."

Toby tried to keep the waver from his voice but he felt tears threatening his feigned strength. Mai climbed down and rushed off to the kitchen, he stood a moment longer his eyes glued to the limp woman on a small girl's bed. He fell to his knees beside where his complicated woman lay.

"Elle! Wake up, Elle?"

Toby was afraid. Elle's breathing was so slight that he wasn't sure if he were imagining it or not. He placed his head down on her soft chest and strained his ears to hear Elle's heartbeat. It was present but quiet, like it didn't want to waste energy on a thick lively pumping. He shook her. Nothing. He couldn't even get an eye flicker from her. She won't wake.

In his panic her picked her up like a baby, tucking her towel around her when it slid exposing her naked skin. She was so heavy, a complete dead weight but somehow lighter. He could feel now that she'd lost weight, her ribs hard and bumpy beneath his palm. He carried his lifeless creature and lay her down on his bed. Took his mobile from the bedside and called Jilly.

"I need you to come back immediately. Something is wrong with Elle, I'm calling an ambulance. I don't want to worry Mai on her birthday. Elle would be distraught." He hung up and called an ambulance.

Days passed unnoticed as he sat in that hospital room watching over his comatose partner. So still, so pale. The doctors said it was her body's way of getting some rest. She'd switched off. They couldn't tell him why or how or even when she'd wake. He couldn't understand why she couldn't just sleep like a normal person. He was angry at her but also sad and worried. He hadn't been to work since that day.

The day he'd found her practically dead in Mai's bed, in nothing but a towel. He briefly considered if he were to blame for her coma, the sex? The conversation? Something I did without knowing?

He was so thankful for Jilly, she'd continued on with Mai's birthday. She'd welcomed her preschool friends and their parents into their home and hosted the entire party alone. Mai had asked a couple times where Mummy was but Jilly expertly changed the subject and distracted her with fun and games. She had then continued to do the same every day since.

Day nine Nessa turned up. About time Toby thought. Probably drunk under the table to whole time. He didn't particularly like Nessa but she was an unavoidable situation. She was Elle's mother first and foremost but she was more, Toby felt like he owed her something and she played it against him. It was probably what he disliked most about her. She was manipulative and he hated himself for not realising it sooner.

He'd called her from the ambulance to let her know Elle was on her way to hospital. She seemed relatively calm, not at all what he expected from her. Nessa had been quiet and distant and not at all the distraught mother he'd planned for. The reassuring comments and it'll be okays, weren't needed.

Nessa paused by the door to Elle's suite. Toby stood to meet her, the look upon his face was fearsome, his heavyset brow and strong features only made it worse. He held up a hand to stop her from entering the room.

Best let him think he has the upper hand for the moment Nessa thought and obliged his request to speak in the hall. She could feel his anger, like warbling petrol fumes as he followed her out.

"What is going on Nessa?" He asked in a fiercely hushed voice, before she'd even turned to face him.

"What do you mean Toby? I don't know what's wrong with Elle?" Nessa's body language was defensive but fake and she was clearly playing dumb. He was taken aback, it wasn't what he'd anticipated. He frowned in concentration, she's not telling me something. He shook it off, Elle's in a coma. What could she possibly know. But then again, this woman.

"It seems obvious to me you're hiding something. I don't even care what. I don't want to talk about it. I want to know about our relationship. Me and Elle. You said it would be something it very clearly is not." His volume rising.

"Please keep your voice down Toby, you're making this seem like some kind of business deal gone bad." She felt relieved that he wasn't going to question her about Elle's state, he wouldn't believe her even if she told the truth. This topic she could deal with. She waved her hands about in feigned exasperation as if he were dramatizing the circumstances as she continued. "I played match maker, nothing more. I thought we agreed not to talk about it."

"I want to talk about it. You were more than match maker and you know it. What I want to know is why?" He was still fierce but not as loud. "Why did you set us up like that?"

"I thought you'd be good for Elle and for Mai." Nessa tried to be as sincere as possible. "She needed stability, a real relationship. She has that with you."

"No, she doesn't." Toby couldn't help but shake his head and turn away from her, putting his hands into his pockets. Peering out onto the grassy patient's garden through the tinted windows as he kept speaking. "What we have is difficult, confusing and bad for both of us. God knows she's smart and beautiful, but she won't let me in. I love her but there's so much going on in her head and she won't share it. Who knows, maybe we could've worked once, but she's become so depressed and withdrawn. I just don't think I can do it anymore Nessa."

Nessa looked him over, she could see he was truthful. The pain in his eyes shone with the relaxing of his features. He didn't want to leave her and he didn't want to stay with her. He was torn. Nessa approached him with an amped up earnest.

"Toby please just give her some time." Nessa took him by the wrists and looked into his eyes. "You can both recover from this. Just some time. Please Toby? Think about it." She was totally begging and she didn't care one bit. As long as she got what she wanted.

"When you asked me to go meet Elle that night my life changed. In so many ways. Amazing ways and terrifying ways." He was drained and Nessa could see it, his soul screamed exhaustion. "I just wanted you to know that."

"Go home Toby. Get some sleep. Things will seem better after some rest. I'll call if there's any change."

Toby drove the long way home. Thinking about the night he met Elle. He'd been home, watching some reality tv show, not because he liked it but because there was nothing else on. His mobile rang and he answered. It was Nessa. She gave him the details of when and where Elle would be. She told him to hurry and ended the call.

He remembered feeling excited and getting ready as quickly as he could. Nessa had shown him pictures of Elle and he was attracted visually right away. He knew who'd he'd be looking for, the curvaceous woman with long dark hair. Her eyes were round and innocent and a brilliant shade of blue. Her mouth was full but not too full. It had a curve, like a hidden smile reminiscent of some happy memory she kept reliving forever.

Despite feeling a little anxious and intimidated, he couldn't wait to finally meet her in person. Nessa had prepped him for this moment for months now. Toby had met Nessa through a work mate, Lawrence. He was higher up within his company and Toby always liked to get on the good side of someone who could help advance his career. Lawrence had been sleeping with her on and off and she'd said she was trying to set her daughter up with someone decent.

Lawrence passed Toby's number on to Nessa. Toby thought he was doing his work mate a favour when he met up with Nessa for coffee one bright morning so long ago now. He never expected this complicated life to be spawn from that one meeting.

Nessa explained to him Elle's likes and dislikes, what interested her and what did not. She claimed she wanted him to have a good chance at capturing her attention. Nessa told him she wanted a good man for her perfect daughter but Elle was stubborn and wouldn't accept blind dates she offered her.

Nessa told him that he could never let Elle know it had all been set up. Elle would never forgive her for going behind her back and Toby would be the one to lose out in the situation. Elle had to believe she'd chosen Toby, that it had been destiny.

He recalled walking down those long stairs and out onto the beachy timber deck. She was already there, waiting for a man that wouldn't show. Nessa had made sure of it. Standing there, leaning over the wooden railing. He watched as she lifted her hand to run her fingers through her shiny dark hair and flick her head to whip it around over her shoulder. He could see a bottle of beer in her hand, interesting for a woman in this place Toby considered.

Glancing around he saw blondes with perfect tans, made up faces with their manicured fingers holding colourful cocktails. But then there was Elle taking a swig from a bottle, looking out at the ocean as if no one else existed. She adjusted her feet, black heels. He wondered if she wore them often as she shifted them again, crossing her ankles. Maybe not.

Though it was her dress that struck him. He'd never forget that shade of red against her ever so slightly sun kissed skin. It hugged her shapely body. It traced the smooth sweeping curve of her tucked waist, expanding to coat her swelled hips and round backside like she'd been dipped in rich red paint. He could see her lovely calves beneath the hem. He could imagine himself touching them yet afraid he may never get the chance.

He remembered drawing in a breath before approaching her and casually commenting on the sea. He couldn't remember exactly what he'd said, only that she'd turned to him. Her eyes had a distinct green in them, like the ocean, perhaps reflecting it. They certainly were not the complete blue as shown in the photos. And then she smiled. That smile. Toby sighed, he'd never forget it. His heart stuttered a moment as he resketched it into his mind for safe keeping.

He pulled into their driveway and sat behind the wheel a little longer, considering. "I'll be patient Nessa. I won't go."

Toby lay down on his bed, calmer with his decision at home. He could smell Elle's scent lingering in their bed sheets as he dozed. Feeling like he'd only just closed his eyes his phone buzzed jerking him wide awake.

"She's awake." Nessa's voice told him as soon as he picked up.

He didn't even respond. Deciding to skip the shower, he changed into fresh clothes as quickly as he could. He wanted to get back there. Back to her. He didn't think she'd ever wake. Sitting with her, day after day, talking to her, pleading with her to just wake up. He'd begun to accept that maybe she never would. Relief flooding him, life may return to normal. No more telling Mai Mummy's on holiday, no more excuses to the boss. Just me, her and Mai.

Arriving at the hospital he made his way to Elle's room, he knew the halls by heart. The lefts the rights. He knew which machines made coffee in a way that was bearable for even his fussy palate and which ones just ate his coins. He knew which nurses began their shifts, he knew which to talk to and which to avoid. He rounded the last corner and opened Elle's door.

She wasn't the smiling, sexy angel he'd filled his mind with, the one he'd met that night years ago. She was haunted and shadowy. Her face ashen and gaunt. Her curvy soft body seemed to be deflating before his eyes. Elle turned to look at him and gave a weak smile. Her eyes held no hint of that mysterious oceanic green this day. They didn't even seem to sparkle, cold glassed orbs. But she was awake.

"When can we go home?" She asked him in a voice that just sounded sad.

"I'll talk to the doctor and we'll leave as soon as we can." He said approaching her.

He was paranoid that if he went too close she may slip away again, especially if it'd been him that made her do so. He wasn't sure if he was meant to kiss her or hug her. It wasn't like she'd been on a holiday as Mai had been led to think. A self-induced coma for nine days. He didn't know how to be.

Elle sensed his lack of confidence and smiled weakly. A new sensation for the poor man. She turned away and was about to close her eyes before she suddenly sat up, startling Toby and bursting into tears.

"What is it?" Concern gushing from his pores.

"I'm afraid to sleep." She cried, her eyes pleading, begging for help. "What if I leave again? What if I can't come back? I can't lose Mai because of those fairies."

"Come back from where?" His shoulders tensed. Fairies? She really is in trouble. She can't keep rambling like this.

"Just don't let me sleep okay?" She gripped his arm, hugging it to her. "Promise me."

"I promise Elle, I won't let you sleep." Her grip loosened and he felt her relax a little.

Toby moved another pillow to help prop her up, stroking her hair he felt his heart swell. My poor strong woman, so broken and sad. He felt incredibly weak himself. Knowing he really couldn't do anything for her. So, he talked.

He told her about Mai's birthday, about how she had tripped and cake had landed on the shoes of another parent. But it didn't matter because that parent hadn't brought a gift so obviously it had been karma. A faint smile passed over her eyes.

He told her about Jilly and how she'd walk into the house as if she owned the place. She'd almost caught him naked when he'd made a quick dash from the bathroom to the laundry for some underwear in the dryer. She had totally seen his white butt as he raced back down the hall. However, she was polite enough not to mention it.

Toby thought that if he told her something funny enough to crack into her shell, that perhaps she'd warm up and come back to him. She didn't. So, he told her about work, about the dramas and issues he had to deal with. Patrons who weren't satisfied, ignorant staff and his bosses who thought they were the big shots making decisions when they weren't at all hands on within the business. He just kept talking until his voice grew hoarse. He was tired now too. And had nothing left to say, even though he was sure Elle had been busy inside her own head the entire time. Busy with stuff he'd never understand, stuff she'd never tell him anyway.

He called the doctor and he gave Elle an injection. Something to help her sleep the doctor had told him. Elle didn't want to sleep but she needed to. She'd been staring at her own warped reflection, trapped in the chrome curve of the meal table for at least an hour now. Engrossed within herself, she didn't even register awareness of the shot being given.

Slowly but surely her eyelids became heavy. Finally, she crossed over that velvety edge. Toby waited until her breathing steadied and knew she was fast asleep. Slightly worried she was gone again he hoped for the best as he kissed her forehead and tucked her hair behind her ear.

"This is hard Elle. Watching you do this to yourself. Having you shut me out. But I am here for you. I love you."

Knowing she'd be out for the night he left. Deciding to pick up Mai and take her out for a nice dinner. I'll take Jilly too, to thank her for all her help. Yes, we'll have a nice normal dinner. Who knew what life would be like when Elle returned home. Just one more nice, normal night, for Mai.

Chapter 11

Toby was wrong. It had been months since Elle's episode and things were relatively normal. He'd anticipated so many various scenarios, the top of his list was that it'd happen again. In which case he'd decided he'd be out the door immediately.

He loved her and what she offered him. As much as he couldn't stand the thought of what people may say about his relationship break down. He'd decided it would be better to leave, than to be known as the man keeping a broken woman.

Toby was pleased that wasn't the case, pleased she was back into her normal routine. Pleased she was cooking his meals again, pleased she was washing his clothes. And pleased she didn't complain about it. Again, she was laying out his work clothes on the bed and washing the grot from his dinner plates. He didn't like doing it and was glad he no longer had to.

In the time that'd passed he came to resent her a little, it frustrated him to look back on how weak and hopeless she'd made him feel. How undignified it all was. He was better than that and didn't deserve it. Especially now that she was back to her old self. It wasn't fair she'd put him through it all for nothing.

At first, she'd been quiet after her time in hospital. So much quieter than she'd been prior. But she seemed connected, not so out of it. And Toby was grateful. No one would know what had happened, no one would suspect a thing. He felt the need to keep up appearances and now he didn't have to lie anymore. He wanted people to envy him, envy his life, his job, his woman. He did not want anyone to know his life was anything but perfect. Elle had put all of that at risk and it annoyed him.

Elle was spending time with Mai and meeting Toby's friends with him in cafes. He was happy she could hold a good conversation with them. In his eyes it only made them envy him more. He had a lovely clever woman and it was these moments he appreciated her. Out in public making him look better.

Things he thought, were good. She spoke, she cleaned, she slept, she did what she was meant to do. She'd even had sex with him a few times. Yes, things were good. Elle had been referred to a therapist and he figured it must be helping. He made sure to seem interested after every session.

"How did it go?" He'd ask as soon as she walked in the door.

"Yeah, great." She'd say, smile and head to the kitchen to make his dinner.

The therapist had put her on medication after their very first meeting and once she adjusted to it, she was almost her old self. Toby's internal torment ebbed. He was feeling strong and in control again.

Elle wasn't going anywhere and he didn't feel like letting her now either, not with her better. He could get over the trouble she'd caused him as long as it didn't happen again. The medication, being taken under his watchful eye was the best thing that'd happened to them. To him. Things are okay he mused with a contented smile.

Chapter 12

"Just pretend." Nessa said firmly. Leaning forward on the edge of her chair, holding Elle's hand. Trying to convince her. "It's the only way you can get through this and keep your whole life together."

Nessa knew this was the ideal time, to get back on side with Elle. She still had a chance to stop history from repeating and Nessa wouldn't let this chance slip by without a grand effort.

Elle had been dismissed by the doctors under the strict conditions she regularly meet with someone to talk out her issues. Elle agreed reluctantly, she hated spilling her guts to strangers who frankly she didn't think sincerely cared. But she hated hospital more. Anything to just leave and get home to her baby.

Though, she was afraid. Afraid she'd slide back into some fairy tale land that existed in her head. Afraid of real life too. Elle didn't want things to go back to how they'd been, normal. However, she didn't want to appear abnormal either. All she wanted more than anything was peace. She wanted the constant internal monologue to quit. A nice quiet, calmed content inside yet no idea how to achieve it.

"Elle, I drink for a reason." Nessa spoke without eye contact. "It's the only way I've been able to control this problem." Yes, problem, the perfect word.

"I still don't understand it all Mum." Desperation poured from her lips.

"Alcohol keeps me numb enough to get through the day without slipping away."

"You're telling me you're an alcoholic, so you can be normal? So you can live life? You're telling me you've been to Frin. That this has happened to you? This is real? Or are we both just insane?" Elle's eye again poured tears, she didn't know she had so much liquid left on the inside. It was all so overwhelming. "Why haven't you told me about Frin? About this....problem?"

"But I have told you Elle. You remember the stories?" Falling silent for a moment while Elle absorbed, she looked to the outside through freshly washed windows. Clean enough to seem invisible. Another storm growing. There'd been so many of late. The hairs on the back of her neck rose just thinking about the electricity it harnessed.

When Elle didn't respond she continued. "Look, I've been where you are. Only worse. I was alone and depressed, men, partying, nothing made me feel better.

One day I'd had enough. I hate to admit it, but not even having you made me care much about anything but myself. So, I slipped. Into Frin. It felt right. I'd convinced myself you'd be better off without me. Convinced it was the only way. It felt like a beautiful dream, a week passed and I'd all but forgotten you, my life. But something pulled me back. A spark of memory, of a small girl with tears in her eyes. It was you. I woke and it was devastating." Nessa gulped. Holding back tears she didn't want to free.

"I looked into the mirror, I was old. My hair greying, my body destroyed. Thin and old. That's all I was anymore. But you Elle, you'd grown. You weren't my little girl anymore. It was heart breaking, to think I'd been so selfish. I'd missed years of your life. You'd been alone, placed with strangers while I lay in an eternal sleep no one could explain. And you know what? You didn't need me anymore. I hated Frin that day. Hated who I was, hated Laura. Hated Trey for ever sucking me into his world." Nessa stopped talking again and looked away. Her lips pursed and appeared to be done.

"Mum, please. Go on. I want to know." Elle reached for her mother's hand begging for more.

"I promised myself that day that I'd create a different path for you. A better one. I was going to be stronger than my own mother. I was better than that, better than your grandmother. I thought this insanity had spared you, spared Mai. I was far younger when I first slipped. I honestly thought I'd succeeded and broken the chain. But now it's happening again and I fear there's nothing I can do to stop it." Nessa broke, composure fallen. Placing her head down on Elle's lap she bawled.

"Mum, don't cry. It's not your fault." Elle didn't know who's fault it was. She felt compassion for Nessa's raw emotions in this moment. This would be a hard thing to express to a daughter. To anyone. No one would believe it. They'd be locked away. Like Grandma.

As she hushed and stroked her mother's hair she tried to slay the irrational, difficult thoughts that kept on coming. Elle figured her mother was trying to tell her, that Frin was a real place. But only a real place for them? Like a secret world only accessible by a special map that only they had? An insanity reserved for the Florence women? She tried to let the idea settle. A very special mental illness restricted to her bloodline.

"So, I pretend? Fit in and act functional like everyone else? I can't drink Mum. I can't do that to myself or Mai. How do I do this? Pretend?"

Nessa lifted her head with renewed spirit. *Perhaps I've done it. Convinced her. I can keep her now.*

"It's not impossible. See your therapist. Do not tell them about Frin. Nothing at all. Talk about your real life, your depression. Forget Torian, never think of him. Let them know you're tired. Stressed. Medication will keep you numb enough. You won't slip,

I promise you." Even as the words wisped from her lips, she knew they sounded disgusting.

She basically had asked her daughter to die on the inside. But she so desperately wanted to keep her from Trey. She didn't want him to win. She hated him and she knew Elle would be favoured, appearing so much like his beloved Laura. Elle would hold a special place in him, a place she could never forge for herself. Brand new tears sprung, Elle didn't know why and Nessa would never have explained.

"Elle you can do this. Do it for you, for Mai." She pleaded. "She needs you and you can't be there for her in Frin."

Torian's eyes bore into her from the darkness of her mind, he seemed to always be there, watching safely from the shadows. Elle could feel him inside her, something had happened when they connected in that strange wonderful way. He was and always would be a part of her now. How could she ever possibly forget?

"Can I ask? If you and I can slip into Frin, then perhaps Mai can too. I feel so happy, so right there, I wouldn't need medication or need to pretend." Elle's heart raced with excitement, despite questioning sheepishly. Nessa had been pushing for the opposite, the hard road. Perhaps this was the simplest solution, why fight? If it is in her genes, maybe it's just how it's supposed to go. She could be happy with Torian and Mai. Why fight? "It could work couldn't it?"

"No, you can't Elle! That is the stupidest thing I've ever heard." Nessa immediately was outraged. "Who do you think you are questioning me? This is exactly what I'm telling you not to do." Nessa grabbed at Elle's face, gripping her firmly. "Mai is too young. She can't cross yet. You want to leave her here motherless and alone? Forget Frin. Forget it all. Don't be so selfish."

"This is all so stupid!" Elle yelled with frustration as she reefed her face from Nessa's hands.

Elle lay back onto the uncomfortable bed again, trying to ignore Nessa's presence. That mark on the ceiling, it's back? Her thoughts drifted in and out of real and not real.

Suddenly her heart fluttered as she recalled a conversation with Mai. Mai had told Elle of Trey long before she'd first slipped into Frin. Before I recalled Mother's childhood stories. Mai was the reason we began researching fairies, the reason I began to dream of Frin. Mai. Oh god, Mai. Elle's fluttering heart became a pounding in her ears. Nessa can not know, Nessa can not find out Mai has slipped into Frin. Never.

"Look, Toby will be here soon. Is there anything else you'd like to share before I go about my mundane life?" Elle's sarcasm was heavy and she didn't care, anything to hide her shocking epiphany from Nessa. She hadn't had enough time to process her own opinions on the whole situation and didn't appreciate being ordered around by someone who'd made a hell of a lot of mistakes themselves. Perhaps she's wrong? Wrong about it all.

"I know you don't quite understand but I am doing this for you and Mai. For your family. You don't want Mai growing up the way I did, Grandma in and out of my life. And as much as I hate to admit it, you don't want her growing up like you did. I know I wasn't there enough. But I made tough decisions, tried my hardest. I love Mai, I want the best for you both."

Elle thought perhaps Nessa held a grudge against her. Had she made too many sacrifices in her own life because of Elle and couldn't shake the resentment? She seemed far too angry for some reason, holding onto hurt?

Nessa was beginning to sound desperate pulling out huge guilt cards and whipping words like love around. Elle wanted more from her. She decided she wouldn't accept the opinions being spoon fed to her, the ones Nessa was trying her hardest to convince her were the only ones available. She had her own mind and in it, Nessa was coming off as far too adamant, far too persistent. Something was up.

Toby arrived announcing they were getting out of this sterile place before she had a chance to fish for anything further. Resigning, she picked up her things and started for the door. Nessa passed on some silently stern looks and Elle heard them loud and clear. Pretend. She could do that, fake it all. Her shoulders slackened at the very thought of it. But she had time. Meanwhile, pretending it was.

Chapter 13

Elle was home. The days blurred like heat waves on concrete. She didn't actually care. She was content knowing one day had passed into the next without feeling anything. The best part of her day was bedtime, like reaching the height of a gentle wave knowing she'd sleep and wash up on the low of a new one.

One ended and another begun, it meant she was moving forward. Toward something. Wasting time, heading toward the end of life and for Elle in this pretend world, it couldn't arrive soon enough.

Moving forward, wasn't that what she'd wanted? She woke. She rose, helped Mai get ready for school. She'd begun kindergarten now and liked it. Elle smiled and appeared present when Mai talked on and on about her friends and the things she'd done at school. Elle would nod and comment at appropriate times while driving the same road again for the millionth time, without thinking about how much she hated it.

She'd begun to notice pointless things about their monotonous route like how many guide posts lined the few straights. Like the trees that stood abnormally tall among the general consistent height of the others to her right. She started observing the faces of passing drivers, headed to where ever it is that normal people go daily. She felt they all looked depressing and selfishly it made her feel better. Maybe I'm not the only one here existing soullessly.

She'd kiss her baby good bye, pretend she couldn't hear the gossipy mums by the gate call her name. She'd flick her hair back, pull down her sunglasses and look in the opposite direction as if something had caught her eye. Reach blindly into her hand bag, pull out her mobile to see the time. Pleased she completed this imaginary check list in time to reach the car and avoid conversation.

She'd drive to the headland and just watch the ocean a while. She knew she had time before Toby woke and got up so she'd been sneaking this stop into her mornings. It helped so she thought. To have a quiet moment without his supervision to just sit and be depressed. To over think things.

It seemed amusing to her that the sun was out. Fluffy cotton candy clouds floating out amongst the faultless blue sky. The light connecting visibly with the brilliant green waters, sparkling away all glittery like. It looks happy. It's the weather for happiness. She imagined colourful kites, giggling toddlers chased by loving parents, climbing obscenely shaped playgrounds.

It made her feel all the more helpless. She didn't feel that joy, couldn't feel that joy. She felt like storms, like rain, like gloom. But here was this sun, blinding her, taunting her. The sun made her feel fake. She couldn't admit out loud that she hated this pretty day, one she envisioned everyone was enjoying. It wasn't normal.

Alone in her car was such a relief, to just feel how she felt. Allow it to wash her and soak into her bones. She was herself in these moments and she missed herself. She let tears fall salty and slow. Grieving for Torian and a love she never really understood, grieving a life she could never have. Grieving a home, she wasn't sure was real. Crying for the loss of all those blissful emotions, the loss of her very self.

Being sad, being empty, this wasn't so hard. She could do this. But what she couldn't do was pretend. Elle had never been good at it and it was becoming harder and harder like pushing boulders up a hill. To pretend things were good, one had to actually care. And Elle no longer really cared. All her actions were simply steps repeated from the manual of a life lead with normalcy. Her smiles were empty. Her eyes were soulless. She couldn't even bear to make eye contact with herself in a mirror anymore. It only made her sadder.

This isn't who I am. I never wanted Mai to look at me without a smile upon my face. She knew her emptiness would be visible to others so, she avoided others. Elle was sure Toby could see it too but he was okay with it as long as she kept on pretending. As long as she assisted in keeping up the appearance of a happy relationship. Elle was beginning to hate him. The resentment she felt toward him was well past dislike. She knew he didn't really care if she was actually okay or not. And she didn't even care about that.

Toby. You'd better head home before he wakes her mind ordered. And she knew she should. Gritting her teeth and angrily wiping the very honesty from her cheeks she started the car and begun the mindless drive home.

"Where were you?" Toby bombarded the moment she stepped in.

"Just chatting with the mums at school, the kids have a dance next week. It's a beautiful day out."

Ah lying. She'd become good at it. All she had to do was make sure the pointless words spilled from her mouth were in an upbeat tone. Elle had never considered herself a liar and had sworn once to never lie to Toby. Though now, she did just about every day. Possibly multiple times. Toby seemed satisfied with her answer and headed to his office.

"Making coffee Elle? I'll have one if you are."

Of course, I'm making coffee. That's what a normal person does for the one they love. Elle made his espresso and made hers instant. She wouldn't drink it, just cup it as Toby drank his and rambled at her about all the important things he'd been up to at work. She tried to remember to make eye contact regularly and nod when required.

Occasionally she'd be pulled a little too inward and he'd call her back. She'd stare too long at the grain in the wood of the table she leant upon, trying to block his sound from her ears. Her mind forming faces, both kind and monstrous. Fading too deeply they'd become animated. She'd chastise herself, lift her gaze and open her ears to Toby again.

Elle made sure she washed his clothes, washed the dishes, vacuumed the carpet and wiped over the benches. She made sure to cook meals he liked and allowed him to initiate sex, when ever he wanted. Day or night. This is what couples do she reminded herself, despite this she still blocked it out.

She lay, with her jaw clenched, breathing deeply staring at the lamp shade in the centre of the ceiling. It was an odd shade of orange brown, like a beer bottle only paler. Like it had been blown and stretched a little too far. The glass had small knobs around the edges and a draping, sweeping pattern around the sides. Like a glossy solid cake attached to her roof. When it was switched on and when she dimmed it just right, it cast golden light in shards and spheres, a shadowy light. She liked it. It was retro, modern houses didn't hold character like that she pondered.

Toby groaned and she felt warm liquid spew onto her belly. Pulling her back into her body, slapping her with what she was trying to forget was happening. He got up and walked toward the bathroom. Her breathing grew laboured and she squeezed her eyes shut. Her heart was swollen and it ached. Simply ached.

Elle opened her eyes again, wide, trying to let the air dry them. Took a deep shuddering breath, the painful woo sound that was released was unavoidable as she slowly blew it out. I can't cry now, I can't, she yelled at herself inside as she tried to regain composure. Toby returned, lay down beside her and kissed her forehead.

"I love you Elle."

"I love you too."

Her pain was too much. It was easy to lie to him, much harder to lie to herself. Rolling over she pulled the blanket up around her throat as tight as she could, wishing somehow, she'd find the strength to silently strangle herself.

She wasn't sure if Toby knew she was crying or not, either way he made no acknowledgement. Elle waited to hear his snores before quietly getting up out of the bed. She sensed her way through the house not wanting to turn lights on. She wanted to be alone.

She slid the glass door open only wide enough to squeeze her naked body through. It was noisy. And the silence made it worse. She sat bare on the concrete in the icy midnight chill. She didn't cry now. She couldn't. She just sat with her knees tucked up under her chin hugging herself. She didn't know what to do or where to go. Her brain running around playing games, taunting her, teasing her. She wanted someone to hold her hand, tuck her into bed. Hold her lovingly.

She shivered and looked to the sky. It was dark though hinted of a deep blueness. The stars sprinkled sporadically. There was no pattern to it, no meaning. It was just there. Just like her she thought. It looked lovely and mysterious, but really it was an eternal nothing. An empty space no one could comprehend. Just like her.

Elle's weeks passed and flowed into months. She'd done as her mother suggested and went to therapy. She was put on medication and it wasn't long before she was diagnosed chronically depressed.

She stopped therapy after that. But Toby didn't know. As far as he were aware, she was going regularly and it was helping her work through her personal issues. Nessa was right, the medication had numbed her. No more Frin.

The pills became something she hated, she didn't feel anything, no big ups, no big downs. Life was just a monochrome shade of misery now. Like Nessa attempting to hide her alcoholism from Elle as a child, she was trying to hide her daily pill popping from Mai.

"What's that Muma?" Mai questioned one morning as she stepped into the bathroom as Elle was about to swish the dehumanising pill down her throat.

"It's just to help me be a good mum." Elle smiled down at her weakly yet genuinely. Mai was the only one who could trigger any kind of emotion in her anymore, even if it was only a vague memory of what it once was.

"Are you happy Mum?" Mai scrunched her little nose a tad, tilting her head to the side looking into Elle's eyes. Reading them.

"Mai, I am happy that I have you. I just love you." At least that was true, she never wanted to lie to Mai the way Nessa had to her. "But I am a bit sad. I miss someone very much."

"The man with the tattoos? He loves you so much." She said it with such straight forward simplicity. The way only a child could state something so purely.

"Mai, Honey. What do you mean?" Elle was now crouched down, holding Mai's shoulders while scanning her child's eyes.

"Well, Torian misses you and wants you back." Mai peered back just as intensely as Elle, far too intense for a child. As if she were seeing into the soul of the woman she'd one day become. Or trying to communicate on a level that was far beyond her years.

Elle sat down on the tiles of the bathroom floor, running her fingers through her hair, her heart beating a lush pump for the first time in so long. Concentrating on the bath tub taps, trying to grip what Mai had so calmly said. She turned to her, held out her hand offering a cold hard seat on the tiles by her side.

"Mai, now tell me quietly. Have you been to Frin?" There was something inside Elle that was coming alive. This tense creature unfurling from the depths, creeping up to take a peek.

"I have. I was there when he kissed you." Mai giggled like it was embarrassing to her. "You really love him too, don't you? He is handsome." Giggling again, Elle surprised to find herself joining in. She hugged Mai close to her chest.

Mai could feel Elle's heart rhythm, it soothed her and she closed her eyes to just listen to it. While Elle remained silent, thinking.

Mai was with me when Torian and I kissed? Those three days, she wasn't alone, she was in Frin. Right there with us. Her thoughts had been confirmed. She'd been too afraid to talk to Mai, not wanting to scare her, or worry her, or perhaps even provoke the crazy problem Nessa claimed they had. Plus, she'd been too busy pretending and forgetting. But Nessa said Mai couldn't? It isn't the first time she's been wrong her mind snorted.

"Mai, have you been to Frin again?" Elle's revelations quickly turning to concern. What if she can't get back?

"When I go to sleep I go to Frin and see my friends. Trey looks after me, tells me when to open my eyes so I don't get in trouble and worry anyone. Sometimes I want to stay because it is so much fun. But I would miss you. Torian is so sad Muma."

Elle tried to take the information for what it was. Not allowing her mind to over think this time, adding weight where it was not needed. Take the facts. Mai can slip into Frin. Clearly has been for a long time. Torian misses me. Torian is real. She was becoming physically excited, as if her body were preparing for him to literally step through the door whisk her away, saving her from herself, saving Elle from life itself.

"Mai, you can't tell anyone about this. Do you understand baby girl? You can't tell Nana or Toby. No one." Elle's panic being welcomed back by an accustomed host. "Do you understand?"

Mai nodded. Smiling, as if she knew something Elle didn't and ran off into her bedroom. Elle could hear the tinkering of her toy piano as she played.

She rose from the floor and stood, looking into the mirror at the reflection before her and made eye contact. For the first time in a long time. She knew what she'd see and wanted to remember what it looked like. It was there, wisp like and faded but still she looked. A spark threatening fire. She saw hope.

Chapter 14

Elle continued on with her morning routine as she usually would have prior to this new information Mai had provided. Packing sandwiches and fruit into Mai's lunch box. Chasing her around the house attempting to put socks over her squirming toes once captured. Driving her to school, counting the guide posts, watching the faces of passers-by.

Returning home, she made Toby's coffee without being asked. She'd placed it, steaming away, on the bench. He walked by, snatched the small cup and paused looking at her liked she'd done something wrong.

"The coffee okay?" Elle questioned.

"Yeah. But what's this for?" He asked indicating the espresso.

"Oh, I just thought I'd do something nice for you."

"Why?" His suspicion was thick.

"I just feel good. Never mind, I'll wait until you make your request in the future." Elle said dully. Trying to act as if she hadn't just realised that he was completely unaware of her recent dislike toward him.

Toby shrugged, passed on through to his office, coffee in hand. Elle glared after him with his slick hair do, his far too dressy clothes for home. She wanted to tear them off. Slap the arrogance out of him right there and then. The excessive anger he provoked in her was frustrating. How dare he ruin this mood. This is a good thing, her mind calmed her. You're coming home Elle.

Only yesterday she'd have done what was asked, answered his questions compliantly. But today her sass was back. She was feeling things and thinking things, a little of her essence returning.

She put on a load of washing, stood out in the stinging sun and hung it all out once the cycle had gone through. She took up her fat novel and sat on the edge of her bed with it pressed against her lap while watching dust motes glide down on a knife of sunshine. The swirls looked like fuel on salty water. Only gold instead of that toxic rainbow. She blew a gentle stream of breath into them and sent them whirling out of control. She knew how that felt, outside influences sending you mad. They slowly calmed and settled back into their dreamy decent. Elle was beginning to remember how that felt too.

Taking a deep consuming breath, she was feeling an energy build, an anticipation that things were going to happen. Something. Elle shut the curtains and suddenly the microscopic motes disappeared to another realm. Staring into the space she knew logically, that they still occupied yet now invisible in her world. She'd always felt, known that there were more than meets the eye. If only you had the patience to look.

Even as a little girl she could find fascinating worlds within her own. She loved to watch ants, with colonies so large. The tiny creatures out numbered humans, millions to one. She pondered if perhaps someday they'd realise this fact and attempt world domination. Or maybe their aspirations weren't as deadly as humans. They were like people she mused, leaders and workers, building cities and chambers. Caring for their eggs and young. They each had their place, their role, working together for the greater good. In the end she'd decide they were better than humans. They did not burn or squash others far tinnier than they and they certainly didn't do it to one another, the way people did.

Far smaller still, the miniscule beings living on her very skin. She'd watched a show about it as a kid. Only visible under powerful microscopes, but they were there. Living and breathing, devouring dead cells. An invisible world within her own. But it was real. It was there. Frin, maybe, was like that too.

Elle climbed into the bed, lying on her tummy pulling the sheets over her head and started to read in the dim light filtered through the sheets. Time passed slowly and she couldn't concentrate on the book. The words wouldn't form a story. The individual letters bouncing around without focused meaning.

Toby walked in and sat down beside her, stroking her backside through the fabric covering it. Elle cringed she couldn't stand his touch like this anymore. Violent, irrational thoughts swarmed her brain and she ground her teeth waiting for it to stop.

Maybe she could poison him slowly. She'd read many an article about women doing the same. She cooked his meals and he'd never pause to question let alone give thanks. But, these women had had it far worse. Physically abusive husbands and what not. She was being dramatic her mind mentioned and she agreed. He stopped when he could not entice a response, got up and said he was heading to work. A giddiness pulsed through her though she remained still. He wished her luck with therapy that night and left.

Remaining frozen, her ears straining, requesting patience of herself, she waited until the sound of his car was done. She raced out of bed and straight to the bathroom. Taking her pills, she dumped the whole bottle into the bin, happy to be rid of the nasty things. She made a quick call to Jilly and left to pick Mai up from school.

The two chatted easily on their way back to Jilly's. Elle left Mai in Jilly's clairvoyant hands, exchanging knowing smiles with her baby girl before leaving. Climbing back into her car, she headed toward Nessa's place.

Arriving she found Nessa standing on her front deck with arms outstretched toward Elle pulling into the driveway. A joyous look on her face. All her smile lines gathered at the corners of her wide, cold ice eyes. The sun streaming down from behind her made her glow like some harsh angel. She'd changed her hair Elle noticed, a short sleek style and it'd been dyed to it's original black. It suits her Elle thought, made her look far younger, beautiful and dangerous.

"How have you been?" Nessa asked before she'd even reached her. "You look better."

Elle took a seat on her mother's far too soft day bed out back. It was covered in a complete mix of mis-matched cushions. It was totally random but somehow suited the glossy green floorboards.

She waited, looking around, absorbing her mum's place. She was nervous yet determined. Nessa stepped out of the house carrying two coffee mugs, the moist steam swirling from the hot liquid seeming magical. She was seeing her world again, all of it. The minute details that wove together to make it richer, realer. Something worth living for.

"I was wondering when you'd finally settle into your new life." Nessa was saying as she sat down beside her handing her a mug, beaming the whole time. "It looks good on you."

"Mum, you have no idea. I know what I need to do now. I'm going into Frin." Elle said it simply. Eloquently. No need to beat around the bush.

"What do you mean?" Nessa glared, all trace of her previous buoyancy extinguished. She was flustered, the liquid in her mug quivering. "You can't mean that!"

"But I do. I don't know what Frin was like for you, but for me? I was alive, I was loved. I knew what happiness was. I was content and free. There was no pretending." The conviction she felt was almost visible in her words. She knew now it was her only option.

"You can't do this to Mai. You're all she has Elle. I don't even know why you're considering this idiocy."

"This life, isn't a life for me Mum. I'm doing no good for anyone, least of all Mai. I'm faking my way through. I'm suicidal. I don't want to be dead on the inside any more. I'd never do anything to hurt Mai but I can't live like this. She'll understand one day. I just want you to understand too."

Elle knew she was pleading, feeling it was important to have a blessing of some sorts from her Mother. The one person who actually knew what was happening to her and what Frin was. Despite her own personal conflicting thoughts about Frin surely, she'd see the appeal. Something had connected their very souls to this place. There had to be a reason. Elle didn't know why or what for but she wanted to find out. She was a grown woman and it was her choice. Not Nessa's.

"Are you taking the medication Elle? Have you tried all I've asked you to?" Nessa was now standing, pacing. Her dark bob bounced with each thought out step, her eyes darting back and forth as she picked at her lip. Trying to find some way to convince Elle she was wrong.

"Yes, I did everything you told me to but I refuse to take those drugs any longer. I want to feel something, I'm tired of the utter nothingness. I'm numb sure but I can't continue to function like an emotionless robot. I want Frin. I want Torian." Elle blushed a little, her guilt returning. The idea of being a liar and a cheater hounded her still.

"Torian? What about Toby? I can't believe this. He's provided for you, loved you. He's not perfect, but he's the best I could do." Nessa's eyes opened wider as her startled sight connected with Elle's. Her brow wrinkled, frowning. "I didn't mean that the way it sounded." She back tracked.

"I should have known. Just another fabricated relationship. Are you kidding me?" Elle stood as another piece settled into place. Fuming. "I thought maybe you'd give me a chance to state my case, maybe you'd take a minute to consider what I'm telling you but you're so adamant I'm wrong. What if it's you who's wrong? You want this miserable life when clearly, we've been given this ability to choose. That's fine. You made your choice. But I am choosing differently Mother. I am not you. And you know what? I pray I never will be."

Elle slammed her mug down and it erupted spectacularly. For a second, time slowed. Elle smiled. The colour of that milky coffee as it slowly rained down through the sunlight brought Torian to mind. His skin, milky coffee aglow with sun.

"Elle please don't go!" Nessa cried pointlessly clawing at Elle's back as she left the house. Nothing would stop her.

Elle's car roared off and Nessa dumbly went to her kitchen. It was that perfect time in the afternoon when the sun beamed in through her crystal shot glass. Her chest heaved as she sobbed angry, hot tears. Watching the rainbows play all over her walls she insanely began to dance.

Hypnotic, psychotic, her tears raining down as she felt the warmth of the colours melt and reform over her body. She completed one final spin, stopping at the pantry. Reaching up she took down her precious vodka bottle. Took the glass from the sill, dispelling all the colours, destroying the magic so everything returned to its dull normalcy.

Elle was right. Nessa did miss the magic of Frin. The happiness, the certainty, the realness of a home they were destined to have. Nessa missed Trey, she'd loved him so deeply but he'd never wanted her. Stuck in his eternal wait for Laura. That bitch. She wasn't good enough for him, I offered him everything and still I wasn't good enough.

He'd asked her to leave, her negativity even too strong for the calming atmosphere of Frin to overcome. Nessa couldn't stand the thought of facing him again anyway. To have his penetrating eyes hover over her like she was some worthless creature he pitied. She knew she'd made some terrible choices and this was her punishment. A lifetime of nothingness after having it all. She didn't deserve Frin but she had wanted it.

If she'd been honest with herself, she'd know she was envious of Elle. Jealous of her decision, quietly angry that Elle looked like Laura. The woman she violently hated. The woman Trey wanted instead of her. She blinked rapidly as she took shot after shot, her darkness growing to consume her entirely.

She won't get away with this. I'll make sure of it she declared within. She viciously threw her glass against the bland kitchen wall sending tiny shards of chaos showering down. Watching the broken crystals lie dead upon the floor she took up her vodka and began taking mouthfuls direct from the bottle.

Chapter 15

Elle lay her head down by her too still grandmother. She had no where else to go, no one else to talk to. Grandma was there, in Frin. She too had made a choice and perhaps she'd be the only one to ever understand Elle's.

She was feeling a certainty over the decision she'd made and wanted to share it with someone who'd understand. Elle read more of the diary as she sat by the bed, looking for answers, wasting time.

There were no answers, just more slightly slanted words that Elle felt could have been her own if she'd kept a diary. Grandma spoke of her feelings, emotions, her dark and empty soul. Her complete bemusement as to if she should leave her darling Nessa. She'd felt guilt and fear for her child but had ultimately concluded that this was the path that had been lain down for them and that she should honour it. She mused if it were destiny. Some part of a bigger plan, that her insignificant self was required in some predetermined senario.

Elle wasn't completely convinced but it was a pretty excuse. Helping her sleep better at night knowing she'd left her daughter behind to grow up without a mother. For a worthy reason.

Entry after entry Elle read on and soon the words became lighter, happier. More fantastical. Eleanor's pages were soon consumed with words of Frin and Elle couldn't get enough.

She'd written about amazing creatures and one more so than others. A fawn named Corrigan. A being who was half man, half goat. She'd started by expressing she liked him a lot, even detailing sexual encounters. Elle continued on feeling a little like she was invading her grandma's privacy, glancing at her now and again, ashamed yet stunned by the events she wrote of. While they seemed to share an erotic connection they also seemed to be good friends. He'd read her poetry and give her gifts of exotic fruits.

Grandma admitted further in, that Corrigan had been quite a persuading reason for her to remain in Frin. On Earth she'd been so lonely. Like Elle she couldn't handle the falsity of relationships, she couldn't find anyone to suit her, to fit her. Anyone that could accept her for who she was. She felt at peace with Corrigan, found her place and no longer felt the need to adjust herself to accommodate society and it's wishes of her.

The kinds of taboos placed on Eleanor on Earth were strict and she felt herself always fighting, always rebelling to keep her ideas and opinions. From Grandma's diary, Elle deciphered that many unconventional things were perfectly acceptable in Frin.

Perhaps the one that shocked Elle the most given her earthly, humanly upbringing in a closed-minded world, was the sexual freedoms. It was completely okay for Grandma to be in a loving relationship with Corrigan yet be intimate with any other she chose. She wasn't labelled a cheater, she was expressing herself.

Being able to express one's self in Frin was essential to who they were. It made them happy to be free of restrictions and judgments, they embraced all of who they were. They were creative and artistic people, earthy and natural. They didn't fight their instincts and desires. They were free to explore their very basic nature.

Elle found it all so appealing. However, it only made the ache she felt inside stretch, filling her up. She stopped reading. She wasn't sure she wanted to be tempted away into another world just because she thought it would be nice. She wanted, maybe needed a clear cut, unbreakable reason to cut ties to this life she led. Even if it was the most miserable thing she ever had to endure.

Looking over Grandma's withered mannequin of a body she pondered if that's what she'd become, a shell for Mai or even future grandchildren to sit with and watch.

She began to talk to her. Tell her about a life she'd never been apart of. About how when she was little Mummy would go on holidays and Elle would be left with kindly strangers, about how she'd be so happy when she'd come back. The reunions were always the best even though Nessa's leaving was always so unexpected and her return seemed to never come. She spoke of how after an awfully long holiday, her mother returned and they moved house to a small country town.

Nessa was different after they'd moved, leaving little Elle with the teenager down the road. Angie would drop her home late at night and Nessa would be laughing and swaying with a new man, drink in hand.

"He's just a friend." She'd always say.

Despite the changes in Nessa, Elle loved the new home. It was big and airy. Often, she'd be in trouble for opening every single window in the place. The house would be filled with a summer breeze that made her imagine being outside even when she wasn't. Elle would stand, small and insignificant in that spacious lounge room. Close her eyes and focus on her breathing, in and out. Focus on the light air, tickling over her skin. Focus on the scent of jasmine and gardenia sneaking in from the over grown garden gate. Swallowing her.

She told Eleanor about her first pet, a small black puppy. It had been hit by a truck. And she'd witnessed it all. The truck coming down the hill, red dust billowing up around it. Her puppy gearing up to bark and chase it down as if he were some beast on the hunt. She'd called him, screaming yet he wouldn't listen. He was clipped by the very back wheels of the trailer. His small body was flicked out into the long dry grass lining the road as if he were nothing more than a heavy black sack. She told Grandma she felt bad because despite loving him so much, she couldn't even recall his name.

Elle told Grandma about the very first time she'd been drunk. A silly teenage girl at some party, in some house she didn't know the owner of. She'd fallen down a flight of stairs and been whisked away all shameful like, in front of her friends with a broken wrist.

Then there was the first boy she kissed. She didn't even like him that much in the beginning. But he liked her and it made her feel good about herself. They'd sneak from school to kiss in the park nearby. Eventually he'd asked if it was okay if he told his friends they'd slept together. By that time, in her youthful wishing, she assumed they'd be married someday, so said it was fine. He ended up dumping her for some girl who would actually sleep with him, leaving her sad with a fabricated reputation.

Eleanor lay still and unresponsive as Elle let the words of her greatest shame float around her. She'd been 23 when she met a man with broad shoulders and brown eyes. She'd never had a thing for men with brown eyes but this one she couldn't resist. His look, his scent, his touch captivated her so deeply. She'd been spellbound. And let it all happen so easily, so passionately.

Then it was over as abruptly as it had begun. Not long after, she'd felt sick and so tired. One boring day she stood nibbling the crust of some old bread. Wondering why it tasted so good and why she'd not noticed before. And then, like a bag of wet sand it hit her. She was pregnant. To a nameless, disappeared man.

She told her about Nessa's involvement in her pregnancy, how she'd been so relieved she was having a boy. They became so close as mother and daughter, and Elle had been so appreciative of the support. She'd relished this newfound relationship.

Until one chilly morning when the cramps came. Half the morning had passed by the time Elle realised they were not going to stop. Nessa was with her all the way. Allowing Elle to excessively squeeze her hand, crushing her rings around her fingers like tiny cuffs as the pain amped up. Soothing her, comforting her.

The sky that evening was on fire. Like mother nature were expressing her sympathy because Elle too, felt her body ablaze. The setting sun was something outside of herself that she could focus on as the nurse urged her one finally push.

Her baby began to scream as the sun was finally sucked down beyond the horizon into the black place. Blues and purples spilled like blood along the line between heaven and earth as her baby was flopped against her bare chest. She was then congratulated on her daughter.

Tears of joy, she didn't care her baby wasn't the foretold boy. The pain of creating life was over and here in her arms was her child. Her body had allowed another human to exist and she was in awe. Sweat and tears mingled as she stroked the little purple face, it was just them, like the world had been vaporised.

Finally, she looked up to see her world rematerialize. Nessa still stood by the bed. Her hands held up to her face. The look that was upon it was forever etched into Elle's mind. Disgust. As potent as acid. Before Elle's mind had even questioned why, Nessa had rushed from the room.

Alone, six months. Nessa never even called. She did have to raise her baby alone after all.

Then she spoke of Mai, the joy she'd brought her. The harshness of parenting on her own, the things she wished she'd been able to provide her. Never feeling like she was good enough for such a lovely little creature. Being a mother was the most beautiful yet soul crushing thing she'd even done.

She told Eleanor about Toby too. How it was all so complicated, how she felt trapped and confused. About how she never knew if she were coming or going with him. About how he was impatient, demanding and possessive.

And then there was the guilt. Torian had invaded their relationship and she'd allowed it. She wanted him too. Her mind began to think about his kiss, his touch. She stopped speaking. Tears fell as thoughts of him slashed at her.

"Grandma. I miss you." All she desperately wanted, was a reply.

Elle again studying her grandmother's coma bound form, wondered if she really could commit herself to a life like this. Even if I did, I wouldn't be aware of it she told herself.

But Mai would be. Painfully aware of her mother's lifelessness. She didn't want her to hover over her shell, waiting for a response that would never come in her greatest times of need. But I don't want to be a tiny crying prisoner inside this shell either.

"What do I do?" Elle felt a slight squeeze around her fingers and her brow furrowed. "Grandma?"

Nothing. Elle sighed after being thrown off balance again. She was tired of it, her mind playing tricks on her. Like her own brain wanted to sabotage her sanity. She stood looking down on Grandma wishing so hard for her eyelids to flutter open, she'd sit up and smile. Becoming animated and full of colour, asking Elle to bring a couple of the embroidered cushions over to help make her comfortable. Settling in before opening her mouth to say "tell me all your troubles dear."

But she didn't. So, Elle placed her hand gently back down by her side, wiped the tear that fell without consent and turned to the door. Walking into the hall without looking back, she closed the door. Walking away she told herself not to stop otherwise she knew she'd go back. Grandma was the only one who knew what it was like to need to be in Frin. The only one just like me. The only one I can trust. The only one I can't talk to.

Chapter 16

Toby was sitting in his regular café with a couple of his work colleges. Al and Quin. Al was tall, dark eyed and possibly had a hint of Indian in him Toby thought. He always wore a suit and made sure he looked suave and business like. Toby didn't like the way he'd hold Elle's hand just a little too long in greeting or watch her from across the room at events. He didn't like him but he did like to keep his friends close and enemies even closer.

Quinn was more of a beach bum type, he was tanned and good looking. In Toby's opinion he was about a week over due for a haircut but he was well dressed. Well enough to be seen in public with at least. Quinn too, he liked to keep at a distance from Elle, not because Quinn liked her but because the ladies liked him.

Both men were not so much his friends, but they had their benefits. They were well connected and Toby knew he'd never be out of a job should the situation ever arise. They could hook him up with cheap wine suppliers and get him into fancy upper-class events where he could rub shoulders with even more people who'd potentially benefit him too. These were the qualities that kept him putting energy into the relationship. Plus, they usually paid for breakfast.

Networking he called it. Keeping up with the in crowd, making sure he did favours so he was owed some. Making sure he went out of his way for VIP guests and keeping in contact with those who knew people, who were worth knowing. He relished the doors that had been opened to him when all he had to do was fake some niceties.

It was a good day he thought. The sun is out, everything as it should be. He blew out a large cloud of cigarette smoke just as the young waitress placed a big square plate down in front of him. Eggs benedict. It was his favourite.

He crushed the butt into the ash tray as he looked over his friend's breakfast choices. Bacon and eggs, with a side of buttery mushrooms was typical of Quinn. Al always had the avo, ham and cheese open melt on focaccia.

Toby took up his fork and sliced into his food. A large creamy forkful was placed in his mouth and he began to chew. Halfway through he shook his head angrily and slid the plate away from himself as if it were laced with poison. Al and Quinn looked to one another knowingly and laughed. It wasn't the first time he'd done this. Toby was all about standards. High ones, you just had to accept that if you wanted to be anywhere near him. And accept his temper tantrums too.

"Not good enough Toby mate?" Quinn rhetorically questioned mid mouthful.

"It's fucking disgusting." He spat venomously, flicking the edge of the plate making it clatter against the table. "A new cook or something? I won't eat that. Or pay for it."

Over hearing the commotion, the waitress gingerly approached them. She was a red-head, short and a little tubby. Her skin pale and her eyes a bland blue. Toby thought he may actually find her cute if he wasn't so damn frustrated. He valued good customer service and disliked people who didn't have the upmost respect for their customer. The customer is always right and today the customer happened to be him.

"Is there a problem Gentlemen?" She appeared shy, smoothing her apron whilst glancing about at them.

"Yes, there is a problem. This food is horrible. Please tell your cook he requires cooking lessons."

"Sir, I am sorry it's not to your taste. I had this same meal this morning and I liked it."

"We'll you're just a waitress. You'd think a cheeseburger and a fifty-cent ice cream was a four-hat meal." He spitefully spat, feeling attacked. Like she was trying to argue with him.

"Hey Toby mate. That's enough." Quinn pipped up to defend the young waitress who was clearly uncomfortable and possibly regretting her previous comment.

Quinn had witnessed this kind of aimless nastiness in Toby before. He'd asked him what was going on, if he were okay, if everything at home was alright. People didn't just fly off the handle over something so pointless, so he pushed a little harder and asked if he and Elle were okay.

Toby got worse, went mad accusing him of hoping they were having troubles so he could sneak in a steal his woman. Quinn had denied this strongly and stated he only wanted to help a mate. In the end he'd shook his head threw his hands in the air and promised never to again.

"Look sir, I'll take the meal back and have a fresh plate prepared." She was apologetic as she reached for the plate but couldn't make eye contact. This terrible stranger had made her feel so worthless, like she was the scum of the Earth. All she wanted was a pay check, not a mental breakdown to go with it. Tears welling, she turned away.

"I don't want another shit meal." Toby called after her.

"Watch your language would you." Al decided to say indicating a couple with a child only a few tables away, obviously attempting to pretend they hadn't heard the lot.

Toby shrugged as he took a sip of his espresso. Thank god that's decent he thought. Otherwise I'd never come back to this dump again. Picking up his cigarette packet, he tapped one out and lit it up, taking a long drag he lifted his chin and let the smoke flow out slowly, watching it billow down over him.

"Toby, we're eating here." Quinn said, trying to wave the thick smelly smoke out of his face.

Toby had had enough and was on the verge of telling them both where to go when his phone rang. He picked it up, not bothering to excuse himself and walked off to lean against the railing, watching traffic buzz by as he answered.

"What is it Nessa?" Rolling his eyes not knowing if he couldn't handle her right now. He was growing tired of his relationship with his woman's mother. She was one of the biggest reasons he hadn't committed to buying the ring he'd promised her so long ago. She was just always there, telling him what to do and what not to do.

He wished he'd never met her, convinced he'd have been able to hook Elle all on his own. He so desperately wished he could change the past. Meet Elle and work things out of his own accord.

"Elle knows okay? About me setting you both up."

Toby wondered why she was the one who sounded annoyed. And she sounded drunk. Her words slurring.

"What did you tell her Nessa? I really don't need this right now."

"I didn't tell her anything specific. I made a mistake okay? She knows I was involved that's all." The endings of her words merging with the beginnings of the next. "It just slipped out Toby."

"Look don't say anything else to her. I don't care how persistent she is. Just keep your big mouth shut." Toby was pacing now, smoothing his perfectly styled hair down into place. "I'll work something out. I have to go."

He hung up and shoved his phone angrily into his pocket. Feeling a rage germinating under the pressure of the dirt he'd been shoved into unwillingly.

Nessa looked at her blank phone. He hung up on me? How dare he! After everything I've done for him. He wouldn't even have a family if it weren't for me. She took another swig from the bottle. He doesn't even understand the half of it. And he'll lose it all. Very soon and he won't like it. As much as she'd have loved to laugh in his arrogant face when he was all alone. She still needed him. Needed him on her side to help stop Elle.

She cannot slip into Frin. I'll never get her back and I will not be left here to deal with this place, these people alone. I refuse to have Trey falling all over himself like some dirty old man with my daughter. Her irrationally drunken thoughts came and went and she was in tears now. Why didn't he just love me? She had loved him so strongly and now that she hated him, it was with deadly passion.

Nessa knew in the cores of her bone, what the sober truth was. Trey was a good man. Which is why she'd loved him so. She couldn't emotionally handle reliving the conversation they'd had when he'd explained his unbreakable love for Laura but her mind replayed it painfully.

Telling her he'd never compromise the love he had for her and that he wanted to stay true to her memory until they could be together again. Nessa's heart was breaking with every beautiful, honourable word he spilled. But hate brewed stronger, she wanted his words to be of her. Not of some flake who'd up and left him. She'd never do that to him she declared. It wasn't enough. It didn't matter what she said. And she felt foolish and weak for ever begging like she had.

Nessa lay low, stayed out of his way but the anger and sadness only grew until finally Trey had no choice. Her bad energy feeding the darkness, a negativity that had been starved for thousands of years. Was now ravenous and Nessa was a fine meal. She had to leave and Trey told her so. For the safety of them all.

Nessa did. And never returned. Back on Earth after a long stay in a blissful utopia, her feelings and emotions returned. Weighty, full and about to combust. Hatred had spawned and now without the atmosphere of Frin to tame it, she had the ability to feel it's full potential.

She found it so confusing, yet right in her mind, to hold so much animosity toward a woman she'd never met. A woman she was related to. Despite never being there Trey had still chosen her.

And now Elle had grown to look just like her. Is that why Trey wants her so bad? My girl? Never. The thought disgusted her and made Nessa's feelings even more incoherent. It didn't make sense and Nessa didn't care. She'd been wronged and she'd fight to the death over it.

Nessa was losing grip, and she was aware. Her anger taking charge occasionally. She wasn't her usual calm, collected and slightly intoxicated self anymore and could feel her control slipping. Threatening her seemingly sane existence. Her alcoholism too, was becoming harder to handle. Day by day she knew she depended on it more and more. It no longer soothed her seething madness and Elle was making it worse.

I need her back. She needs to stay. Needs a reason to do so. Not even Toby could make her stay she'd finally come to terms with, possibly even drove her further away. But Mai, she'd stay for her.

A moment of clarity swept through her mind. You can't use Mai! She isn't a toy. The moment passed and her mind spoke to her from a depth of swarming nothingness. Yes, you can. It's the only way.

Chapter 17

Elle collected Mai from school and headed home. The very thought of what she was going to do hurt. Elle pulled the car over on a quiet stretch of road and took a breath. Looking into her rear-view mirror she saw Mai watching her. My baby, she smiled unbuckling her seat belt and twisting around to face the true version.

"Mai, I don't want to go home. Is there anywhere you'd like to go?"

"Can we go to the beach?" It only took her a second to decide.

"Sure, that sounds great. We can collect some shells." Glad she didn't have to use energy she didn't have, to come up with something herself.

"I don't have my swimmers though." A small frown melted Mai's smile.

"Hey that's okay Honey, it'll be almost sun set by the time we get there and probably too cold. But we could go again on the weekend? Swimmers and all." Elle knew she was okay with that. Her smile returning.

"Shell collecting then." Mai stated, more so as an affirmation to herself.

They drove. They sang along to the songs they knew as they came on the radio. This was nice. Elle liked it. She hadn't spent quality time with Mai in so long. She was so wrapped up in her own selfish, desolate emotions that she'd barely made an effort. Not a genuine one at least.

Food, school, bath, bed. Elle's wallowing had left Mai to her own devices. And Elle was concerned Mai wouldn't have any happy memories of them together when she left for good. If she did.

In this moment, it was hard. She wasn't so committed to the idea of leaving for good. Committed to Frin and living in her head forever. Listening to Mai trying to sing a song and then giggling at herself for getting the words wrong. This is the good, this is the magic. It can be found here, in my life, in my world. Tears started welling, she couldn't help it. She was so torn.

Here right now with her little girl in the car was the lightest she'd felt in so long. The constriction that had gripped her ribs, crushing her lungs was slackening just a small bit. Could I really leave Mai to face it all alone? This question was ever reoccurring. Don't think Elle. Just enjoy.

Pulling up at the beach, Mai energetically jumped out of the car and raced to meet the sand. Kicking her foot into the air her school shoe flew off, landing with a puff of dry sand.

"Go grab that Mai." Elle laughed as she kicked the other off too.

Mai ran, snatched them up and sat them at the base of a small sand dune. She looked to Elle then eyed Elle's feet. Elle smirked and kicked her foot into the air as Mai had. Her sandal slipped off a little too late and flew straight up into the sky. She grabbed Mai and they huddled together as they closed their eyes laughing, waiting for it to hit the beach.

"That was a close one." Elle stated as it hit only a foot from them.

Mai was laughing, a full happy sound. A beautiful sound Elle thought. She hadn't heard Mai laugh like that in a while. Her smiling eyes reminded her of sunshine, she glowed. With every tiny happy moment Elle's heart felt worse. Leave my baby? How could I?

"Race you to the water!" Elle yelled after one extra squeeze before releasing her and running off.

Mai was happy. She loved her Mummy. She looks so pretty Mai thought. Her hair all flicking around in the salty wind. Chasing her mum, she also thought she needed longer legs. I wish she was smiling all the time. This is fun!

It was becoming late. Elle had used up all her energy and she was tired. She didn't have much after her months of quiet isolation. This outburst of joyous emotion had left her drained, she wasn't used to it anymore. Being alive, active and involved.

Elle waved Mai over from where she followed and retreated with the lapping waves. They sat on the shore line, just out of reach of the lazy waters roll. The sun was hurrying to sink into them and they huddled together and watched.

They talked about the way the water spewed toward them washing over the stones and pebbles giving them a new glossy coat each time. And how when the waters sucked back, they began to dry becoming all boring and dull again. Over and over, shiny gems, then plain old rocks.

"Mummy?"

Elle faced her. For just the briefest of moments like the waves, her heart swelled and then sank. Mai sat in the same way Elle did, mimicking her. Her little legs tucked up to her chest, her elbows resting on her knees. Her rounded baby face cupped in her chubby hands. Her dark hair falling about her shoulders was a mess Elle mused contentedly. Mai's big wide eyes, intelligent and curious. Elle loved her so much in this moment and she prayed Mai knew it. Could feel it all around her.

"This is for you." Mai handed her a small paper-thin shell. Shaped like a little fan, coral coloured. The colour Elle loved. The shell was delicate and partly translucent, whimsical and beautiful. Like it had come from some ethereal place.

"Mai this is gorgeous. I'll keep it forever." Still looking at the precious gift she hesitated. "Mai, can you tell me about Frin?"

"Of course, I can." Elle liked but also feared how easily Mai spoke of Frin. Like it was no big deal, especially after the way Nessa had made it feel like it was. "There are magical creatures. I think maybe the fairies and mermaids are my favourites."

"Mermaids? I didn't know there were mermaids." Elle realised she didn't know much at all. Not really.

"Maybe we can go together again one day? I can show you lots of things." Mai was quite pleased with her idea.

"I'd really love that. Can you tell me more about Trey? Who is he?"

"Trey is good, but he can be sad. He said he has to wait for a woman who he loved a long time ago. He says she is my family like you, he has to wait for her to come back. She has to help him look after Frin because there is a darkness."

"Do you know who he is waiting for? And what is the darkness?" Elle tried to hold off on too many questions, but hadn't understood how much Mai actually knew of Frin. It worried yet excited her.

"Laura Florence, she has Florence in her name like we do Mum. Just like us." Mai smiled at her, feeling grown up that she could give her mother some insight and glad her mum now knew, her stories were true. "He said the darkness is bad and he needs her to come back and help keep it away. He says she's powerful like Mother Nature. Trey would tell you too if you went back to Frin."

Elle tucked Mai in closer and watched the last struggles between light and dark. The sun so low it glowed vibrantly as it lost it battle. The glow drawn away, like one's last breath. Clouds began to shuffle into position stealing the skies once more, no purples nor oranges hovering along the horizon this night, the blue black conquered.

"Mai, would you miss me if I slipped into Frin forever?" Elle wanted to know, and frowned with concentration as she studied the girl for a reaction. Would Mai even understand the reality of such a thing? The concept of forever.

"I would miss you, but I would still see you. In Frin, in my dreams Muma." So simple, so direct. So innocent. "You should talk to Torian. He's been waiting you know."

"I would love to. But I don't know. I wouldn't want to leave you. I love you so much." Hugging her tighter Elle wanted her to feel it and hear it. She meant it so deeply and wished there were far better words to describe it.

"I know." She beamed. "Don't be silly. I would see you all the time."

Elle picked her up, wishing she were still just a baby. She knew too much, had to deal with too much. Carrying her to the car they felt a drop of rain. It was getting colder and darker minute by minute. Half way there the wind blew up, blasting sand whistling along the beach. It slid fast and rough around Elle's ankles. This dry river hissing by sucking the moisture from her skin.

Mai was fast asleep a few moments down the road, she was still all sandy and her hair was a windblown mess. A bath in the morning Elle decided, she wanted to just scoop her up and whisk her straight to bed. Let her have a full peaceful sleep after wearing her out.

Stopped at red lights not far from home, Elle glanced back noticing the hidden smile at the edges of Mai's mouth as she slept. She'd inherited it from Elle. Hinting at some happy memory, perhaps a happy place. I will, I will see my baby in my dreams. Elle thought finally she'd made a solid, unbreakable decision this time.

Pulling into the drive at home, curious as to why Nessa's car was parked in Elle's usual spot. And there was another car behind it. A friend of Toby's perhaps?

Something was off. They never had visitors anymore. Elle felt strange and annoyed. All she'd wanted to do was come home, put her baby to bed, shower and perhaps read until she fell asleep. Night was when she could be by herself. Toby worked most nights and Mai had a regular bedtime. She wanted to be alone.

Elle parked on the lawn and got out of the car, leaving Mai to sleep while she found out what was going on. Nessa walked out of the house to meet her followed by two strangers.

Both women wore smart outfits, their hair tied up neatly. Besides their apparent uniform requirements their features were completely different. One was tall and slender and clearly the older of the two. The other was short and very round, despite being the younger one she was clearly in charge.

Confused and looking to her mother for insight she gained none. Nessa's face frowning. Her intense eyes lacked the usual smiling wrinkles to soften them, her dark bob sharper. She bore a sinister vibe.

"What's going on?" Elle asked baffled by the situation.

"Where's Mai?" Nessa didn't answer. "I hate to do this Elle, but it is for the best."

"What are you talking about Mother?" Elle's annoyance grew as Nessa barged past her and headed toward Elle's car.

"I've been appointed Mai's legal guardian until you undergo a psychiatric evaluation."

"What?" Elle's heart vaporised. "How could you do this? Why are you doing this?"

"It's the best for you and Mai. You need to stop with all this make-believe stuff, sort your head out and get some sanity back in place. You'll end up hurting yourself or your child. We're here to help you." Nessa said it like she thought she was being truthful. She directed the two strangers toward Elle's car.

"Don't touch my daughter!" Elle screamed at the women approaching her sleeping child.

"Elle this is their job, let them do it quietly and sensibly for Mai's sake okay? Mai will be fine with me, you know that. Once you've been checked over she can come home to you."

"Why are you saying this? Make-believe? What's wrong with you?" Elle was in an utter panic. Taking my child? Make-believe stuff, she knows damn well it's not make believe! She told me so!

The taller woman opened the backdoor of Elle's car and reached in to pull Mai out. Elle snapped. She ran toward her and grabbed her clothes yanking her out of the car. Spinning her around the woman lost her footing and fell to the ground. Elle crying out as she tripped over the woman landing hard on top of her. Nessa and the chubby one, were clawing at Elle, pulling her off the tall woman now grass stained and flustered.

"Just take the child!" Nessa yelled as she struggled with her arms wrapped around Elle trying to pull her into the house.

"Mummy? Mummy!" Mai's big panicked eyes peering over the tall woman's shoulders. She was startled awake and afraid, in the arms of a stranger. Her small fragile arms reaching out toward her mother.

That look. On Mai's face, was the last Elle saw before the women shoved the thrashing, crying child into the unknown car. The women climbed in quickly, started the engine, back out of the driveway and drove off.

Elle slumped into Nessa's arms. She quit fighting her mother's forceful grip as she watched the park lights fade off down the street and into the night. Tears of hopelessness ran down her desolate face.

"Not once did I ever think I had to protect my daughter from you." Elle tore wildly out of her Nessa's arms and pointed to the door. Rage painted her face and all she wanted to do was lash out, rip that woman's hair, hit her with the force she felt surging inside herself.

Nessa having never seen this look before obliged. Stopping before closing the door she turned back.

"Just do what I say and things will go back to normal okay?"

"Things will never go back to normal. You've lied to me, played games with me. And now you've taken my child?" Elle's anger was blinding her. Her tears wouldn't stop and they blurred her vision. Nessa was transforming, obscure, smeared. Like some ugly abstract painting. She looked like a monster, a horrid, evil monster.

"You better look after Mai and love my daughter better than you ever loved me. Or I will find you and you'll regret the day you ever gave birth to me." She picked up the lamp that sat pert beside her and with a heart wrenching scream, threw it as hard as she could. So much energy was released and it showed. The lamp smashed into unrecognisable bits, showering down in a musical clattering against the door. The place where Nessa once stood.

Chapter 18

She collapsed. To the floor, sobbing and weeping uncontrollably. In this moment she did feel insane. An insane anger, an insane bewilderment. Nothing was what it appeared to be. It didn't matter if it were this world or not, she knew she'd feel insane anywhere.

Hours passed and still she lay on the floor, aware that the pain in her broken, betrayed heart was not enough to kill her. This sad ache was not enough to end her misery.

Her tears dried. And still she lay. Calm. Elle focused on breathing in and then slowly out. She felt the back of her skull begin to ache against the floor, but she didn't care, she wouldn't move.

Her body felt heavy and limp but that didn't matter, she had no use for it ever again anyway. She wanted to lay there until she starved, until she finally died and decomposed. Until her body withered and turned to dust. How long would that take? she wondered.

She used her eyes to roam the ceiling. Two lights and a fan, decorative skirting board, no that's at the base of the wall she remembered. For a moment she tried to recall its name but couldn't remember. It doesn't matter, she said inside. Nothing matters now.

Still she lay. Watching, unblinking and suddenly time sped up. Her eyes started to dry and sting and still she watched time. Abruptly the sun was up, creeping across the yucky yellow roof as the sun rose higher and higher. Stretching its creepy fingers of light through the windows invading the room. They climbed the wall, reached the roof and bent unnaturally to touch it too. Caressing it quickly then sliding down the opposite wall. Finally, the lights perversive intrusion was over and the peaceful blackness drowned everything again. Still she was unmoved.

She could feel the dry crustiness of where her tears had overflowed, spilling and falling in the opposite direction of each other. Out her eyes, down into the hair by her ears. One to the left, one to the right. She could feel their salty, cracking paths.

She pondered if this was like death. Just a semi active mind, trapped in an inactive body for eternity. Or perhaps she should close her eyes and submerge herself into blackness, like one would inside a coffin. She hoped if it were true, she'd be spared of feelings. She could handle an eternal monologue but not the feelings. She didn't want to feel her mother's betrayal, she didn't want to feel the pain of looking into her petrified daughter's eyes. She didn't want to feel anything. Nothing at all. She decided if she had to spend forever feeling too, then perhaps it meant she'd made it to hell.

Elle became aware of the clock ticking. It became torturous. That unending ticking and that ever countering tock. Why hadn't I noticed it before? Then she heard something else. A car pulling into the driveway, a key in the lock, the door opening then footsteps.

Toby's face came into vision, hovering upside down over her. He was coming in and out of a blur like her eyes had forgotten how to focus. His eyes were worried and his mouth was moving but Elle couldn't hear him. What a strange sensation she thought. She just lay staring at him wondering if this was some weird boring dream or if he really was there.

Abruptly her view of the room changed and she was moving but not of her own accord. Gradually, feeling returned to her fingertips and then her palms. Her nerves rebooting, switching on. Her arms were sore. Toby was holding her tightly, cradling her like a baby against her will. Her ears began to hone in again on a sound. His voice. He was in a panic, perhaps afraid.

"Elle, come on. Can you hear me? Talk to me." His voice was high pitched and broken.

She felt him lay her down on their bed and he placed a blanket over her. He lay down beside her, started to stroke her cheek and her hair. He seemed to be hurrying as if it were the last chance he'd get to touch her like this. He huddled closer. Tucked his arms around her and told her to come back, told her not to go.

It wasn't that she didn't want to respond to him, it was more that she'd been drowned. The hollowness filling her lungs. She had no energy. There was just no point trying. Elle blinked. Her eyes were itchy. She opened her mouth and then shut it, her stomach grumbled. She wanted food.

"Toby." She mumbled.

"Elle, oh my god. Thank god!" He hugged her too tight.

"She took Mai." Elle whispered. Fresh tears rewet the old paths. She was surprised, she didn't think she had any left.

"Where is Mai? Who took her?"

"My Mother."

Toby made Elle some food. It surprised him that he felt good doing it for her. He wanted to look after her. She liked tomato, cheese and a little mayo on white bread. He sliced a green apple too.

"I just have to make a phone call and I'll fix you up a coffee." He told her as he placed the food on the bedside table within her reach.

He found his phone, laying by the front door in the place he'd dropped it when he'd walked in and saw her just lying there. Her eyes open, staring. They were blood shot and she'd been so still. Too still, she wouldn't answer him or look at him. He thought she really was gone this time. Encased in a frozen form. He tried to stop himself reliving that moment. He couldn't lose her now, wouldn't. He'd invested far too much time and energy and in his own way, he did love her. Moments like those made him afraid. He wanted her and needed her.

Walking into his small office he dialled Nessa's number. On the third ring she answered.

"What the hell have you done?" His voice husky with anger toward her.

"I'm doing what's best. I'm trying to help you Toby."

"It actually sounds like you've convinced yourself that's true. You're only doing what's best for you. You always do."

"She was going to leave you Toby. And Mai. Do you really want that? To be all alone again? She was going to slip into a coma again and probably never come back. I'm doing you a favour."

"How the hell would you know that?" Toby's madness was now mingled with bewilderment. How could she of all people predict such a thing?

"She told me Toby. Look you'll never understand it all and to be honest I couldn't be bothered trying to explain it to you. What I will say is this, you haven't helped the situation. You've made it worse. Happiness is what will keep Elle here and you've made her miserable. I thought if she had a good man who made her happy and looked after her she wouldn't be tempted to leave. So, you can go on your merry way now. You've served your purpose. Screwed it up perfectly I might add. She'll stay now that I have Mai. I had to do this. Can't you see that?" He was annoying her with his questions and with his complete ignorance. This was above him and she was tired of explaining her actions to an idiot.

"The one thing I do know, is that you are the one who needs help Nessa. Yeah maybe I haven't been the best for Elle but what you've done will destroy her. You're meant to be her mother. How could you take Mai like that?" He was becoming increasingly frustrated. He couldn't make her see that what she'd done was wrong. She seemed to truly think this was the best thing for them all. Or in the least, make him think it.

"You're a selfish woman Nessa. Don't for one minute, think I'd ever believe you've done this to help Elle or Mai or Me! This is all about you. You are evil."

He slammed his phone down. There was nothing he could say, nothing he could do to change the situation. He just had to look after Elle now. Toby sat thinking his options over. If he took Elle to the hospital, it would be obvious she was suffering mentally regardless of what her mother had done to induce it. If she had any chance of getting Mai back, being seen as mentally unwell on top of the chronic depression wouldn't help.

Toby knew how much Mai meant to Elle, she was her own tiny little world. If he ever wanted the chance to recapture the relationship he'd once had with the sexy woman in the red dress, he knew Mai must be apart of that. Little funny Mai was essential to her wellbeing. All he could do for now was keep her healthy, rested and pray to a god he wasn't sure existed, that she'd recover soon.

He went to the bathroom to find Elle's medication. Searching, he couldn't find the pills anywhere. He went to Elle's car where she'd left her handbag the night Nessa and her goons came to whisk away Elle's very life. He missed Mai too, ransacking her bag he felt guilt. Not only a bad partner but he knew he hadn't lived up to the promise of helping her raise Mai. And he liked her. No, he loved Mai and Elle. He wanted to be better for them both.

Stumped, he couldn't find the pills anywhere and returned to the house. Finally deciding to check the waste bin in the bathroom he found them. She needs these he thought to himself shaking his head. Taking the bottle and a glass of water, he sat by Elle stroking her hair to gently wake her. It was all she wanted to do, sleep or stare at the ceiling until sleep came again.

Elle stirred and Toby placed the pill in her hand, urging her to sit up a little so she could take a mouthful of water with it.

Placing the medicine on her tongue she sighed. She'd hoped the effects had worn off by now and she'd have slipped away. Too late now, she didn't even care anymore. Didn't care about Frin. Didn't even bother to think of Torian. Her mother was right. It was the easy way out. It was too good to be true and she didn't think she deserved it now.

She was a terrible mother, perhaps Mai was better off without her. She wondered why she'd ever considered having more children, she had nothing now, was nothing. The best thing she'd ever done in her life was have Mai and still she'd gone about that all wrong.

Why she'd ever thought she was special enough to deserve a place like Frin, deserve a man like Torian. The idea now baffled her. What would he want with a useless, hopeless woman like me anyway? Grandma was wrong too. She was not essential to some plan, there is no path or direction. No fate or destiny. This life, this world she'd been born into was where she belonged. If she had a smile on her face or not, was of no consequence. It simply didn't matter. She just needed to shut up, take it in and accept it. This is it. This is my life.

Days passed, not that Elle cared much to notice. She'd wake at times and it would be either light or dark. She didn't know the day, date or even the month anymore but it didn't seem to have any meaning or importance. Whether the sun was up or not was her only way of knowing that time was actually moving on without her.

She watched the ceiling for hours unknown in silence until she drifted back into sleep again. She was so drugged up she didn't even dream. Her mind was blank. Behind her closed eyes was like gritty white noise. Her only awareness, was of lying there, waiting until the day came when her breathing would slow and finally stop. She didn't deserve that either she thought. It would be too easy, too simple. It would be relief and she knew punishment didn't work like that.

Toby had taken time off work and he was there most of the time. Elle felt his presence in the room like a hovering spirit. He'd stopped talking to her a while ago, and she was grateful. She didn't want to hear his voice or feel obliged to attempt talking back. She wasn't even sure she could talk anymore. She wanted silence and darkness. Each day she woke to find herself alive only deepened her depression. Sinking further and further into a sludgy abyss. Elle wanted to be left alone to starve. But Toby wouldn't let her.

Every few hours he'd sit her up and force a pill down her throat, make her take a couple mouthfuls of milk. He'd mash banana and spoon feed it to her. Toby had learned quick enough that she was refusing to chew. She wanted to choke to death.

He was lost. And tried his best, he'd held off taking her to hospital so long, that he now felt he couldn't. She won't get Mai back he thought, should she be hospitalized. It won't look good. His only goal was to keep her alive. Keep her next breath coming and pray she'd just wake miraculously one day with a hint of a smile. A spark of life in her eyes.

He'd told her so many times that she just needed to try. Put some effort in, get up and change. Have a god damned coffee. To get Mai home she needed to be present, be okay. She needed to appear normal. Even if she had to pretend.

Pretend. She'd heard that before and it no longer appealed to her. It only enforced her determination to die.

As much as Toby was surprised by his perverse enjoyment of looking after her, he knew he couldn't much longer. He felt proud to be the one, the man she needed the most right now. He knew that without him, she would have let herself pass away unnoticed. He was keeping her here and it was inflating his sense of self-worth. He was needed. But the bills also had to be paid. And they were coming relentlessly. Elle in this state was a burden no matter how much he strangely enjoyed being her life support.

    He'd been considering something drastic for days and now with finances being stretched so far, he decided it was time. It could work. It had to work. Because he needed it to.

Chapter 19

"I want to see my Mum." Mai stated for the millionth time on her way to her new school.

She was sitting, strapped into the backseat of Nessa's car in a crisp new uniform. It was green and Nessa thought it looked far smarter than the simplistic one her old school offered. Nessa had bought her a new school bag too, it was oversized and made Mai look so tiny carrying it.

"Mummy's not feeling well Honey. When she's better we will go see her okay?"

"I just miss her so much. I really want to go home." She began to cry. It was her sixth birthday today and Mummy hadn't even called. She wondered if she'd been naughty, maybe she doesn't like me anymore. She wondered if she'd done something wrong, said something wrong. Maybe about Frin.

"Mai, don't cry. You're having a good time with Nana, aren't you? We made up Mum's old room especially for you. I thought you'd like that?" Mai crying, flustered her and she tried to change the subject.

Nessa was trying. But she had to admit, she'd forgotten what it was like to have a child around, all the time. Mai wasn't like the child Elle had been. Nessa now understood just how much Elle had been beyond her years from a young age.

Elle's school had been so close to home that while Nessa slept off her previous nights drink. Elle made her own rough sandwiches, sometimes just butter and bread if Nessa had forgotten to shop. She'd pack her food and dress, unlock the front door and head off on her walk to school. Her friend lived along the path, she walked alone daily and she'd often stop by. He was old and had a miniature orchard in his front yard.

Tom had lived in the street for years, the nosy type, he knew everyone and what they did. While not knowing Nessa personally he knew of her. Knew she had visitors of night. Her place was usually the noisiest and that Mai was often playing on her own. He'd begun to water his garden at certain times so he could talk to the sweet pixie featured girl as she passed by. On one occasion he'd asked what she'd packed for lunch, finding it was nothing substantial he then started to question each day.

He'd invite her in to look through his pantry to find something yummy to smear over her bread. Often, she'd pick his home-made lemon butter which made him smile. However, on occasions, he was also concerned that this lovely child had entered his home so willingly and that her mother had no clue.

He'd mention that he'd be having home grown apples and maybe some strawberries too for his lunch and asked if she'd like some. She'd always greedily accept. Then telling Elle she had better be on her way he'd give her one last gift. A small bouquet of honey suckle that grew, covering his front fence.

Elle would always thank him, such manners for a small child. She'd wave as she walked the remaining distance to school while pulling the stamen from the small white flowers. On the end of each was a small dewy droplet. She'd place it on her tongue to taste the faint sweetness. It was the best part of her morning, visiting old Tom. Until Nessa found out.

It was a Sunday, Nessa woke around midday after a hectic night. Elle was gone and it didn't take long before Nessa was frantic. She'd finally found her late afternoon sitting on the front porch laughing with old Tom. Being angry, panicked and hungover Nessa over reacted. Screaming at Elle to come home with her. Tom had spoken up in her defence, claiming they'd been gardening and having a good time and that she was welcome to come by anytime. It wasn't a big deal. Nessa had called him a dirty old man and told him to stay away from Elle.

"He's my best friend!" Elle had cried broken heartedly as Nessa dragged her home.

From that day on, Tom watered his plants later in the day. And Elle walked to school, by his house each morning sadly.

She'd also bring herself home. Often it was late before she'd arrive all grubby. Grass stains on her clothes with dirty grazed knees. She would spend the afternoon roaming the street, exploring dark drains, climbing trees and playing with kids she'd met along the way. Nessa would tell her to run herself a bath prior to laying on the lounge in front of the tv. She'd eat the dinner Nessa had cooked alone at the dining table, feeling like a wild beast as she held a tough piece of meat in her hands. Taking it between her teeth, biting hard, pulling, hoping a chunk would break free.

Finally, Nessa would declare bed time and she always got ready quickly. She knew it was mum's time and knew not to encroach. She'd begged and whined once to stay up just a tad later and ended up with a backside so sore she couldn't sit the next morning.

Nessa knew she hadn't been the greatest mother. She'd been young and angry. Drank too much and distracted herself from Trey with other men, hoping one would stick. Hoping one would take his place. But she was older now, wiser. Her alcohol consumption less party, more controlled. She should have been more involved but credited herself with how well Elle turned out anyway despite her recent issues with Frin. She could have been more, done more. But it was in the past now and all she could do was try with Mai.

Elle was an easy kid. Mai was difficult. Clearly Elle hovered over her, did things for her she was capable of doing for herself, if only she'd been given the chance. With the right influence Nessa thought, she might turn out alright too. A bit of tough love was all she needed.

"Look wipe those tears away. Have a good day at school, we'll have such a fun birthday dinner tonight. See you later my big six-year old!" Nessa feigned delight as they arrived at school.

Nessa wasn't a big fan of school pick up and drop off she decided, leaving Mai by the school watching her shrink in the rear-view mirror. It was an annoying task that broke up her day. She'd moved Mai to another school further out of the way just in case Elle decided to stop by. Nessa was intrigued by Elle's lack of fight. She assumed Elle would try to take her back, call her relentlessly in the very least but she hadn't. Nothing. Not even today, Mai's birthday.

She found it strange and worrying, the lack of communication. She knew Elle wouldn't give up, not on Mai and she knew she hadn't slipped. Nessa could feel her presence like a shadowy figure in the corners of her dreams. She had no idea what Elle was up to and was taking precautions. Her house was on the market and she was searching for a rental closer to the new school.

It was a big adjustment. She'd lived in her house for so long, raised Elle in it for a time. There were so many memories, good and bad. Once or twice she'd asked herself if she were going to extremes to keep Elle under control but this was a new chapter in all their lives. It neeed to be done correctly. Freshly. She'd spent most of her life keeping Elle from Frin, from Trey. She wasn't going to give up now. No matter what she had to do.

Mai's new school was great, far more opportunities than the last and the staff was accommodating to their awkward circumstances. Even praising Nessa on stepping up to raise the child of an unfit parent. Only Mai hadn't made all those friends Nessa had promised her yet. Her birthday dinner would just be the two of them.

Nessa had ordered a birthday cake from the local bakery, after picking it up on the way home she made room in the fridge and let it sit. She took her vodka and had a shot, it was harder now with Mai and all the driving. She was careful to make sure she timed her drinking so it wouldn't interfere. The last thing she needed were to be pulled over, found intoxicated and have Mai taken. Yes, it was all such a huge adjustment, difficult but worth it she assured herself whole-heartedly.

"I don't like this cake Nana." Mai sat at the head of the table, the glow of her birthday candles the only thing to keep the darkness from devouring her. Tears glittered like small sad jewels.

"What's wrong with it? I made sure it had flowers and butterflies. I thought you'd like that."

"Mummy always makes my cakes with chocolate on the inside and vanilla on the outside. She uses sprinkles not lollies."

"Well Mummy didn't make your cake this time. How about you blow out your candles?" Nessa was tired of hearing about Mummy. Tired of feeling like she was doing nothing right by this child when she was trying so hard. Resenting her for not recognising the efforts she'd been making.

"I won't blow them out!" Mai slammed her little fists down on the table, a crystal tear falling.

"This is the cake you have. If it's not good enough then get to bed." She said through gritted teeth, holding back the urge to say more, raise her voice further.

Mai got up and stood by her chair. Looking at Nessa she frowned as hard as she angrily could. Bawled up her fists and punched them toward the ground locking her elbows in place. Tears broke free again as she stomped her foot hard against the carpet. Mai glared. Her heart was pounding and her breathing was hard. Mai didn't know she could feel so mad and sad all at the same time. She wanted to hit her Nana, bite her and scratch her.

"I just hate you." She growled like a wild animal.

Nessa laughed. A bellowing hearty, laugh. Mai had transformed into a small beast in the darkness, half her face obscured by dark. Those tears dripped from her shining orb like eyes onto her night gown, her chubby cheeks all flushed with anger.

Stomping her feet and squeezing her fuzzy peach sized fists as she scrunched up her nose. Grinding her teeth and leaning forward. Like she was forcing all her energy to do something, perhaps pull the room and its contents into a whirling tornado and smash it into Nessa. She was trying so hard to physically hurt Nessa without doing anything and all Nessa did was laugh.

Mai ran from the room leaving the birthday candles burning away, creating solid waxy pools on its perfectly iced top. She threw herself down onto her mother's childhood bed and hugged Elle's old rag doll to her chest. She sobbed, listening to her grandmother's chuckles grow louder, meaner as she made her way toward her. All she wanted was her Mum. And she wanted her now.

Chapter 20

Toby made sure Elle was asleep and crept from the room. He dressed in his darkest navy-blue dress pants and a black button up shirt. He chided himself on not having anything less sophisticated in his wardrobe. He now wondered why such trivial things had ever been so important to him. Elle was all that mattered now.

He took his keys from the fruit bowl in the kitchen and headed out the door. In darkness he drove along familiar roads. Usually, he'd have his iPod shuffled with loud specifically chosen songs but not tonight. He needed silence, needed to think clearly to ensure his plan worked. He took deep breaths to calm the growing anxiety tightening his insides. This can't go wrong. It won't go wrong.

His worries grew no matter how hard he tried to calm them so he turned his minds eye to Elle. The way she'd been when they first met, the casually alluring woman. She'd seemed so free, so unaware or perhaps plainly uncaring about what others thought of her. She was not like him. He cared, wanted to be liked and admired. But Elle seemed above all that. All the pressure and drama, to him originally, he'd thought her silly for it. Eventually he envied her for it. She seemed untouchable, a goddess of some kind. She had a confidence and a purpose she didn't have to prove to anyone, she had no need to worry. She was Elle.

For so long she'd intimidated him and he didn't like it. He liked to think himself better, smarter, more attractive than others and

Elle just kept putting him in the same category as the bum on the streets. Tried to make him believe he was equal with the man who cleaned septic tanks for a living. It offended him.

He'd wanted Elle to think he was the best, smartest and most attractive too, he hadn't realised she wasn't degrading him. She really did have such a compassion for all people and she honestly thought people were equals, no matter their circumstances. He'd finally come to learn this. Even in some ways appreciate it. He had to admit that slowly, bit by bit she was indeed making him a better person. A little more like her.

Elle was so different from other women he'd known. He worried often that she was too good for him, that she was out of his league and some day she'd realise it too. So, despite knowing it wrong, he had tried to put her down. Gradually lower her self-worth. The way she saw herself.

All he wanted was to keep her, to have the upper hand in their relationship. Control her. He'd been so busy breaking her down while she'd been happily building him up. His guilt at having a key role in her sadness was now burning his intestines like acid. Even though she'd believed them equals, Elle was better than him and he knew it now.

"I'll reverse all I've done." He told himself swallowing the hard lump in his throat. "I can do this. I can fix this for her."

Toby pulled up. Got out and locked his car. His palms sweaty as he walked the block and around the corner. It took him five minutes to reach the dark house. Not a single light on as he'd hoped. He crept down the side alley, trying to keep himself silent and stealthy. Reaching over the tall wooden gate he unlatched it, it creaked just a little, rust grinding against rust. Gritting his teeth as the sound gnawed at the silence.

Leaving the gate open he made his way to the back of the house, up onto the green deck. Knowing the back door would be locked but that the laundry one would not. Turning the handle, he pushed the door inward as painfully slowly as possible.

Closing the door behind him, he moved into the house, into the hall. The quiet in this moment was deadly, his heart pounding like a herd of elephants, his foot falls like a sledge hammer on concrete.

Reaching the door he'd been looking for, he pushed it open far more carefully than the previous. He knew there were ears in the opposite room. He could see them. The street light shone unnaturally through lace curtains coating Nessa's slightly snoring body in a camouflage of shadows. Toby moved inside the room and closed the door after him. He now felt light headed and panicked. He made his way to the white wooden bed in the far corner.

Mai's eyes flew open but she couldn't see anything, it was black, night time still. She tried to scream but only a muffled sound broke free of the large, clammy hand that was pressed against her mouth. She began to struggle, her tiny heart banging against her chest, rattling her ribcage. She felt warm breath against her ear and she relaxed her struggling as her fear flew away.

"Mai, baby, it's Toby." He picked her up as she calmed. "Don't worry okay? You need to be very, very quiet."

"Toby, I miss Mummy and you. Will you take me home?" Her eyes void of sleep after being startled peered at him, begging.

"Yes Honey, but just for a visit. We can't talk now, we need to be quick and quiet." Toby hugged her and put her down, holding a finger to his lips to hush her he opened the window and carefully pushed out the mesh. "Come on Mai. We're going this way."

Suddenly, from the darkness, the black nothingness she heard a faint voice. Something inside her had been disturbed. Sending ripples down her spine like a fat snake, feeling the cold. Curled up inside her lazily sleeping, its eyelids now fluttered, its tongue flicked. Becoming cautiously aware. Elle's eyes behind their lids moved about searching the black of her skull, wondering what had caused disturbance.

"Mummy?"

Elle's eye flew open. She tried to move but was far too weak. Someone helped her up, it was Toby. A rush of gratitude for him swamped her. The first emotion she'd felt since her devastation.

"Honey." She mumbled, reaching her thin, shaking arms out to her, hoping that her croaky, unused voice wouldn't scare her.

She held Mai, for so long. She never wanted to let go. Elle stoked her hair, breathed in her child's familiar smell. Finally, she held Mai at arms-length to soak in the sight. She remembered the face but she looked older now. Like a wisdom had formed, something inside had changed. Elle forced tears back, she's not my baby anymore. And she knew it in more ways than one.

"Look Elle we don't have long. I have to get Mai back to Nessa's before day break." He didn't want to say it, he knew she wouldn't want to hear it.

She paused a moment, considering running away with Mai. Then looked to Toby and nodded. It was a futile idea. She was too weak, Nessa would hunt them down, involve the police. Cheap motels, on the run. It was no way for Mai to live. Not a life. But in this moment, she had her baby. She chose not to be greedy.

"Can you leave us Toby?" Her vocal cords warming up.

"Sure." Obliging, he walked out closing the door behind him. He was just glad he'd pulled it off without being caught. Glad Elle was awake and verbalised words.

Elle snuggled Mai up in her arms and lay back with her against the puffy pillows, tucked the blankets up around them and stroked Mai's brow. Taking a deep breath to relish.

"Mai, I need to talk to you like a grown up." Finally resigning herself to their situation. "I don't think I will be here much longer. I need to go and your Nana has to look after you now."

"I don't want her. I hate her. I want you." Her voice quivering, about to snap.

"Baby girl, don't cry. Of course, I want you with me always. Never forget that. But I am not allowed anymore. This is how it has to be for now." Telling her not to cry when all she wanted to do herself, was breakdown, was hypocritical but she continued regardless. "I'm going to get better and find out more about Frin. We can see each-other there right? Maybe we can find a way for you to stay too?"

"You can't Muma. Trey told me. He said I am not old enough yet. I need to grow up and have a baby girl, like you did first." She frowned. "But I could visit you like I am now?"

Elle chose not to waste this precious time questioning Mai further on the statements she'd made. She'd find out for herself soon enough.

"Of course, you can visit me. All the time. And when you are a woman with a girl maybe you can stay a while longer. But I need you to remember, never talk to anyone about Frin or having babies or Trey. Especially not to Nanna."

"I won't."

"I mean it. Nana hates Frin and she will try to stop you if she ever knew you could slip. I couldn't bare not seeing you. Promise me Mai." She didn't want to scare Mai with her intensity but she wanted her safe until the time came when they could be together again.

"I know Muma, I won't tell. I promise." Mai sighed and cuddled closer. "I'm sleepy now, can we go to sleep?"

"Okay. Let's go to sleep. I love you Mai."

"I love you too." She said through a yawn.

Elle couldn't sleep now. She felt like she'd slept a lifetime but Mai had no concept of that while at peace in her mother's loving arms. So, Elle lay awake awfully aware of the girl in her arms. She can not join me in Frin but she can see me. I can see her when she dreams. It consoled her a little.

Toby didn't know it yet but he'd given Elle an escape route. Having Mai in the flesh made her want more and now she knew the only way was to be in Frin. Time was considerably slower there but she'd have far more contact with Mai than the current arrangement. Freedom, happiness and no more stealing sleeping babes from their beds. I can have my girl.

As her mind raced, working out details her eyes bounced about the ceiling without seeing it. How, how, how? Torian.

His name swirled around her brain like wine being tasted, pondered for the very first time. She'd been nothing for so long now, staring at the blank canvas of her mind. Monotonous and uninspiring. She feared the overwhelming contrast of colours spewing forth. Thoughts and feelings boiling over.

"Elle, Elle...." Toby hastily spoke as he shook her shoulder. "You fell asleep. I need to take Mai home."

"Don't ever call it home." She looked down at Mai not knowing if she could physically let go. "Sorry. Just, let me come with you."

"I don't know." Distrust all over his face.

"I won't do anything stupid. I understand she has to go. I am okay with that. Please Toby?"

"Fine. I'll carry her to the car, you grab the blanket. Are you alright to stand? You haven't moved for weeks now."

"I'm fine. Don't worry about me. I need to be there to say good bye."

Mai woke on the trip back to Nessa's so they spoke about everyday things like her new school and new houses they'd been looking at. For Mai's sake, Elle and Toby remained upbeat yet both were disturbed by the lengths Nessa was going to in order to keep Mai away. Nessa had never meant to help me, she's punishing me. My own mother wants to damage me. Elle couldn't think what she'd ever done to her to deserve this.

Parking in the same place he had earlier in the night Toby took Mai from the back seat and carried her. In silence they made their way to Nessa's house, around the back and to the window. Mai's window screen still leant against the house where Toby had left it. They stood beneath Mai's window not sure how to let go or say good bye.

Mai's grip around Elle's neck was tight and Elle didn't want to push her away, force her to release. So, she allowed this long last hug.

"Now you be brave, be good for Nana okay. It might be hard but you're strong. You make sure you grow up into that wonderful woman I know you'll be." She gulped the pain back down to the ugly place it came from.

"I'll miss you Muma. I promise to be a good girl for Nana. I'll keep our secret too."

"I love you so much Mai. I'll make it to Frin and I will be there for you always. I promise." Elle risked Toby overhearing but she needed Mai to know that she wasn't abandoning her, she'd be there for her in the only way she knew how.

"Okay Muma. Bye." Finally, her grip relaxed. It was time she knew.

Toby lifted Mai into her bedroom, through the window. She just stood there. Quiet tears melting away from her eyes. She was so small, dark hair framing her sad face while she stood, raw and alone peering from the dark at the one she loved.

After a pause Toby lifted the screen back into place, Mai rushed forward pushing it away. Reaching her arms out toward her mother, little fingers stretching, groping as she leant too far out her window. Her wide eyes pleading. Elle moved quickly to take hold of her Mai's hand, her heart ached as she looked into them willing her to be fine.

Elle stood up on her toes, took Mai's face in her hands and leaned in to kiss her forehead tenderly.

"You will be happy again Mummy." Mai told her, smiling through her sadness. "I'll see you in my dreams okay."

"Okay baby girl. I'll see you in my dreams. Promise."

Mai let go. Turned away from the window and climbed up on her bed. Sitting cross legged, she silently watched as Toby put the screen in place. She waved from the shadows then lay down when he was done.

Toby put his arm around Elle and moved her from where she'd planted her feet. As soon as her eyes broke sight with Mai, her heart broke too. No, now it had split. They retreated from the yard and made their way back to the car that was gradually frosting in the cold. They sat without sound for a moment to let the night sink in.

"Thank you." Elle spoke, turning to him. "But I'll never be happy here."

"What do you mean here? I am sorry Elle, I know I haven't been the best for you." He wanted to say it before she stopped talking again.

"It's not your fault. Its this place. It's meant to do this, to push me out. I'm meant to move on."

"What are you saying Elle?" His bewildered concern obvious.

"Never mind Toby. Just thank you again for letting me see Mai once more. I know what I have to do now."

The sun was rising quickly and the light was fresh and clear. The air crisp and cool. The sky threatening a placid blue hue, not the appropriate kind of weather for abandoning children. Despite telling herself it wasn't that way, she still felt like it. She was stolen.

I had her in my arms, I could have run, hidden her but I placed her back into that woman's home. That evil woman's home. Her anger was picking up pace and she tried to fight it.

Get to Frin.

Keep your promise.

Always be there.

Chapter 21

Mrs Anders watched Elle Florence walk once again, across the black and white lino covered floor. She'd been coming to see Elanor more frequently and Mrs Anders had a deep respect for those who returned to visit the loved ones she cared for, regardless of the state they may be in. It was a kind thing to do, to think of someone in a place like this as human still.

Many families found it to be a dumping ground of sorts, where difficult things went to be lost and forgotten. Paying was easier than caring.

Not only did she respect Elle, she was beginning to like her. She was reserved, had things she didn't want to talk about. Mysterious and probably full of secrets just like her grandmother.

They looked similar Elle and Eleanor, Mrs Anders felt that talking with Elle was like a glimpse into what the animated version would have been like. What kind of perfectly healthy woman would seemingly put themselves into an endless sleeping state? She was intrigued.

The lives of those who crossed her floors was far better than reading any romance or thriller. Some patients came kicking and screaming, some quietly walked on by. She knew all their histories, what had broken them. The reasons they were to be locked away, hidden from society.

Eleanor Florence was different, with her, Mrs Anders had tried for years to figure out her background. Like she'd read a captivating snip it, then had to stare at the tempting cover because each page had been glued together. Locking the whole story inside.

She stood to greet Elle and began the walk down the hall to Eleanor's room, knowing Elle would follow. She unlocked the door and returned to her seat by the large front desk.

Elle entered the room, it was familiar to her now. The sights, the sounds, or lack of. Even the smell had grown on her. This time though, something was different. The room with the frozen woman that never changed. Had changed. She couldn't put her finger on what.

She scanned the room, taking in the tinnier details that built the bigger picture, blocking out the haphazard shapes that overlay the back ground. Closing her eyes, she took a breath, something piked her senses. A new smell. Dusty and metallic.

She looked to the wooden chest and noticed the lid ajar. She couldn't recall if she'd left it like that or not. Moving toward the dresser, the chair was a out of place, only slightly, but still, it had been moved.

Upon the dresser, Grandma's brush was pushed to the side and there were blue smudges on the creamy white surface. Ink. Elle realised. It didn't make sense, nothing appeared to be missing however, so she shrugged and took her usual seat beside her Grandmother.

Placing her hand down onto Eleanor's arm, she felt something unusual beneath the sheet. Bumpy and hard. Lifting it to see her arm, she saw tiny crystals and beads.

Surprised, Elle stood and flicked the entire sheet from Grandma's body. Revealing an elaborate gown. Vintage French lace covered in tiny hand sown crystals. It was yellowed with age but still one of the most exquisite gowns she'd ever seen.

Clearly a wedding dress, she couldn't recall ever hearing she'd married. She was baffled. Why should someone change her into something so inappropriate? She planned on questioning Mrs Anders on the way out. But right now, she wanted to say her good byes. Elle felt she'd be meeting Grandma in Frin, but in the back of her mind there was always an uncertainty. Always the hovering question of her sanity. Is Frin real? Is this real? Am I real?

"I wish we'd been able to talk Grandma. You could have told me the truth about Frin. I still don't know if I am doing the right thing." Elle took her hand feeling something inside.

A folded piece of paper, back and front covered in a swooping, slanted script. Taking it from her clutch, noticing the ink stains on Grandma's fingers, she looked over her Grandmother with a frown.

To my dearest Elle,

I am so thankful that you've come to see me even though we haven't been able to communicate. I am sorry that I missed you. I have been living in Frin so long now, that I can no longer come and go between worlds like I once could. I think this was my last trip. My body is so old now.

I am afraid to look at my reflection as I sit and write to you. I'm not even sure why it has survived so long, perhaps to keep the connection open so we could reach you. We've been trying our best to do so. Perhaps something else. I have learned there are reasons for things and most we will never know.

How do you like my dress? I almost married once, in my old life but it wasn't right. I loved another named Corrigan. I thought it would look nice to go out in, when my body finally gives up which surely isn't much longer.

I imagine the struggle you're going through. I once did myself. I made a big sacrifice leaving my old life behind. And Nessa. She could never understand why I stayed in Frin. She had wanted to once. Your mother had fallen in love with Trey and he was in no position to return her affections. Your mother grew spiteful, mad. Trey requested her leave, it was a very hard thing for him to do. She wanted me to go with her. It was difficult, saying no to my daughter.

Though she was a woman and not a child and did not need me anymore. You need to understand that there is a darkness in Frin too, and it must never be fed. Your mother fell under it's spell. It was devouring her, corrupting her. This too happened to Laura, Trey's love. Only she understood the consequences and left of her own free will.

Trey speaks of his heart break the day Laura demanded she be sent to Earth. He didn't understand completely but obeyed her wish because he loved her. Unlike Nessa, Laura could see the path ahead and knew what needed to be done.

Laura passed away on Earth as we all must someday, at the age of 26. However, she left a daughter and a note behind.

The note had directions for Trey to follow. She told him to watch over the girl, his child. She said the child must be raised on Earth, firstly to be protected but also to learn valuable lessons and strength that could never be obtained in Frin. The girl must grow old enough to bear a daughter before learning the truth and returning home. It was a cycle that needed to be implemented.

Laura told him that when the darkness within her was overcome she'd return but could only do so in the form of an Earth born woman, of Frinian blood. She was convinced this was the only way to guarantee she had a way back to Frin. She was also convinced that her power would filter on through her bloodline and the combined light of us all would some day defeat the darkness for good.

Trey in his desperate pain believed her instructions to be riddles written by the darkness. But, his hope of having her return forced him to follow them strictly.

In the beginnings Trey hadn't realised the potency of our spirit, our essence. He simply loved the motherless child but soon learned the truth. With each generation coming forth our strength grew and the darkness faded, still seething but weakening. We have such a wonderful purpose Elle. Something I'd have found comfort in knowing throughout all those hard and painful years when I felt I had nothing.

I understand this letter is but a small amount of comfort to you in this time, perhaps we can share more in person. I feel myself drowsy and do not have much time left. So, I will finish with this.

Elle you must make a choice. There is both light and dark within us all. Whichever is strongest in you will help make your ultimate decision. You are either a light one of Frin or a dark one of Earth. You cannot be both.

I know you will make the right choice.

With every ounce of my love,

Grandma.

P.s Go to Torian. He is a good Frinian man, he can give you answers. He's waiting here on Earth for you. Forever if he must.

Elle refolded the letter and sat staring at it. Her mind a buzz. She couldn't even imagine what her Grandmother had looked like sitting at the dresser in her beautiful gown hurriedly scribbling words for her. She was merely a breathing corpse. Was it all a hoax? A twisted game of torture?

Could it be true? Torian a Frinian man not a dramatized actor in her dreams?

She hugged her Grandmother, adrenaline started to pump through her veins causing her weakened body to feel energised and strong. She smiled. Looking to the mirror, she knew her appearance had completely changed. The deep sadness that screamed silently from her eyes had been beaten down, it struggled to win back its forefront place but she could see it receding.

Driving in her car she felt a giddiness growing in her tummy, like butterflies. She remembered these. Elle kept glimpsing herself in the rear-view mirror, still in awe of her transformation.

She no longer cared if it were all some crazy hoax. No longer cared if none of it were real. Her darkness had lost it's battle and she could feel. The light filtering through her window, hitting her thigh was warm and her pale skin soaked it up. The wind rushing through the windows gap, was cool, forceful puffs of it to whip her hair around.

A pink glow slid its way up over her dull skeletal version. From her smallest of toes, it smoothed its way ascending her calves, her thighs, painted her belly, chest, chin. All the way to the top of her scalp. She shivered as it reached the top, like a snake wiggling free of its dry and lifeless skin. Elle was new and fresh and warm, like someone had scoured her body clean of all it's deadness. She was alive again after such a long hibernation. And there was nothing more in the world she wanted right now than to be drunk on the man that smelled like coffee.

Chapter 22

And he was there. Standing tall behind the chrome coffee machine, steam rushing up around him creating an-other-worldly scene. Time was stand still as she stood confident, watching him. So beautiful, well- built, so rugged and strong.

Her senses peaked as she kept looking on. She felt high, soaking in the rich coffee scent that saturated the air, her eyes roamed his body, those tanned, inked arms as he reached for a small cup.

His sleeves, roughly pushed up his muscular arms like he'd shoved them there, no time for precise folding. The top three buttons undone revealing a little of his smooth chest behind black fabric. It wasn't enough, her mind began to create a vision of what was not shown.

It was a lifetime since she'd seen him and yet she'd always felt him with her. His steel blue eyes hadn't changed, she noticed when he gazed at her while he worked. His look was of relief, his jaw seemed to unclench, a breath released, the farrow of his brow softened and smile lines creased by his eyes. There was no sheepish glancing, no accidental eye catching. Both stood magnetised by the other. It had been too long.

Torian slid a take away cup across the counter toward her, as she reached for it, he placed his hand on hers. A sudden fire burned through her, ravaging her. As strong as she now felt, a pink flush rose and Elle's spine tingled.

"I'll take you to my place." His voice intoxicated her. "Will you wait for me?"

"It's the least I can do." She said.

He'd waited for her, if she believed it all. And she chose to. For over a year now he'd continued living an Earth life for her. Day in, day out praying she'd decide and one day he'd be free to go home. She could sit and wait. For the beginning of a new life. Of course, she could.

Taking the coffee and pulling up a seat in her usual spot, her, attentions turned to the other customers. A couple sat by, either new into their relationship or maybe they really were in love. She'd never much believed in true love or soul mates, not of late anyway. To Elle it seemed unrealistic and pretend, short lived and fake.

The ideas she'd formed on the matter were basic, she thought people simply found each other attractive, worked out if they liked each other and then proceeded from there. She'd never understood the concept of fate or destiny, love was just an animalistic instinct. Looking again to Torian, perhaps she was wrong.

An old woman sat alone, two hands braced around a mug as she watched the ocean. She took a sip and sighed, reached for the cardigan hung over her seat and tucked it around herself. There was a familiarity about her that Elle couldn't place. Maybe she reminded her of herself. Alone. The woman felt the curious presence and looked at Elle with a curt smile. Elle smiled back and shamefully removed her eyes from the woman.

She zoned out pondering her life, the new one ahead. Frin. It was calling her, it had been pulling her toward it from the moment she'd been conceived. Like a vortex gaining strength, dragging her in. Earth was not meant for her. She and this world, two opposing forces pressing against each other unwillingly. It didn't want her and she didn't want it. Her time had come on Earth and she was now happy to accept what may come. Allowing it to draw her in naturally.

The sound of a plate being placed down before her stirred her from thinking. Torian pushed the delicious smelling food toward her.

"I am so glad you are here." He lifted his hand, as if to touch her but changed his mind, in case he never wanted to stop. "Try to eat this. I won't be much longer."

It was a creamy fettuccini, delicately sliced mushrooms, hunks of chicken and it smelt peppery. She needed this she knew, and so did Torian. The carbs, the fat, the protein. He hadn't just prepared her a meal, he was looking after her.

She hadn't eaten properly in so long and despite feeling well of mind and soul, it was now her body she needed to care for. Mouthful after mouthful she felt even more grateful. She knew he'd look after her, provide for her, do what was best for her.

She'd made it half way through when she felt full. Clearly, she wasn't going to eat as much as before, right away. She looked to Torian then back at the meal and mouthed an 'I'm sorry'. Torian smirked, then gave her a mock stern look. Elle stuck her fork into the pasta, swirled it and put one more forkful in her mouth. Shoved the plate away and rubbed her belly dramatically while she chewed. He chuckled, shook his head and took an order to a table full of customers.

His laugh, she was in love with that sound. She was anxiously excited to have an actual conversation with this man. It wouldn't be long now and they'd be alone, at his place. Elle hadn't even thought of Torian as having a place. He was just always here. In this café. She couldn't picture it, couldn't comprehend the concept.

Finally, the stream of customers grew thinner and the ocean began once again to allow the sun to enter it. The shimmering blaze dying as it ended another life cycle. Torian locked the doors and threw Elle a cloth. Together in silence they wiped down tables and finally the counter. Torian opened the till and removed all the cash, handing it to Elle.

"What's this for?" She asked confused.

"It's for Mai. I don't need this shop anymore. It's served its purpose. Just put it in your bag and we'll talk more at home."

Home. What a nice word. And he'd said it like it was theirs. Not his. Wanting to question more, he silenced her with an arm around her waist. Her head sitting perfectly in the dip of his solid shoulder. Feeling safe and warmed by the fire that swept her insides again.

It was hard having him touch her. All she wanted to do was kiss him, every part of him. Stroke his skin and smell his faint aftershave. Get as close to him as she physically could. She no longer cared for words.

Leading Elle to the back door and out into the darkness, they stopped a moment wrapped in each-others arms to look at the sea. Dull white foam crashing onto the dark sands, the sounds repeated soothingly. Torian tucked his hand up under Elle's neck, stroking her ear between thumb and forefinger. He turned her face toward his. Looking down at her with such pride and love. Elle's heart swelled, she knew he was happy to have her. She could read it in his eyes, feel it in his body and hear it in her mind.

He leaned down and she could feel his warm breath as he brushed his lips against hers. Asking for permission. Elle pushed herself up just enough to press her lips against him. And then he kissed her.

Deeply. His lips were a tasty warmth, his tongue swept gently across her bottom lip as he softly sucked it into his mouth a little.

Elle couldn't breathe and she didn't care. Her insides were contorting and twisting and contracting and melting. This was not of this world. She held onto him tightly, feeling his thick toned body beneath her palms. She knew she'd never get enough of him. This wasn't enough, it wasn't satisfying the starvation she felt. She wanted him all over her, inside her. She wanted him everywhere all at once. Suddenly he broke away and pulled her back.

"Let's go." He said simply with lust drenched eyes.

They came to an orange door covered in amateur graffiti, only a block from the café. Torian took a key from his pocket and unlocked it. Taking Elle's hand, he led her up a long flight of stairs, reaching another door. Inside was a dull glow radiating from tiny lights strung amongst the high and exposed beams.

Elle was inspired by the very sight. Torian's home was a funky studio. A big open space with floating timber stairs leading up to a platform raised above the kitchen area. The railing that traced them was suspended from the ceiling and made of sun-bleached driftwood.

On the beach side, floor to ceiling windows perfectly framed the ocean. Modern polished concrete floors were splattered with paint and the walls were dressed in many captivating paintings. The paintings were abstract, dreamlike. Very surreal with familiar features. Peach skies and persistent blue eyes. Some were darker, clouds and gloom, rain and from the shadows, almost hidden, those same blue eyes. Only in the darker paintings, the eyes seemed sad and lost.

"Did you paint these?" She wanted to add his name but couldn't.

"I did." He said nodding his dark blonde head. His arms folded, hands tucked under his armpits while he watched her reactions and emotions as she studied them further.

"You're very talented."

"As I'm sure you are. Frinian's are natural creators and artists."

Elle looked to him. Considering. He mentioned Frin. She smiled and continued to view his work. She knew those eyes were hers, she'd been haunting him, just as long as he'd been haunting her, perhaps longer. And now here they stood only feet apart in this beautiful space. And like the surrealism of his paintings this moment was unreal. Like it was all a dream.

"Torian, why are you here? Why did you come for me?" She frowned worried it was actually a dream.

"Trey sent me. He knew you needed something to make you remember Frin. Usually Florence women come to us sooner than you had. He was concerned something had gone wrong. That Laura's path had been broken." He took her hand and led her to the lounge. The suede felt nice beneath her palms, she stroked it while listening.

"Trey was worried that Nessa was attempting to sever the connection. He knew she would never forgive him and that she'd allowed the darkness to harbour within her. Being on Earth will only fuel her choice to give in to it. She will only become worse. Trey believed it would be her revenge, to destroy generations of work. And in the long term Frin itself. We had to do something."

"So, you were sent to me? Not of your own free will?" Elle sunk a little.

"I was born to be with you Elle. For all my life I've had these dreams of a dark-haired woman with blue eyes. It was strange and confusing. I finally confided in Trey and he knew what it meant. He'd been trying to devise a way to reach you but I was the answer he'd needed. As much as Trey had followed Laura's instructions, there were forces at play that no one had control over. It was meant to be like this." He smiled at her squeezing her hand gently. "In Frin, we know that Florence women arrive. You're like goddesses brought to us. Brining light and strength but what I didn't know was where from. Trey explained to me the unknown pieces of the beginnings. How Laura's darkness had forced the connection between Frin and Earth open. As people here know nothing of Frin, Frinians know nothing of Earth. I didn't believe him, it was far too unrealistic." He chuckled and rolled his eyes, clearly now knowing differently.

"Earth is so opposite Frin. How did you cope?" Elle was so intrigued with his words, like hearing some fanciful fairy tale.

"At first I didn't. I had to learn to deal with the emotions. This place is so heavy. Everything is so negative, it is so easy to fall into it and stay there. Trey had explained this all to me, I was prepared in some way so I continued to fight. He set me up with money which I'd known nothing of before, told me how to fit in and basically just wait. And I did for so long. But the moment you walked through those doors I felt it. Just finally seeing you in the flesh for the first time gave me so much hope. You were real."

"I thought you were just a dream." Huddling closer, she understood he was still technically a stranger and yet somehow, they'd been together always. "This is all so tough to process."

"I get that. It was hard to hear when Trey told me I'd been born because of you, for you. A woman I'd never met had so much influence over the outcome of my life. However, if we'd never met, you'd never have slipped into Frin. You're strong, you'd be forever fighting the darkness within, here on Earth. Nessa would have succeeded and Laura would never have been able to return. All of Frin would eventually cease to exist just as other worlds have, if you and I had never met. It is a lot to take in."

"It really is. Maybe that's why my feelings toward you are so strong, it's hard to explain but I feel like I need you to survive. And I don't even know who you are." Elle stopped a moment, unsure she wanted to think it all factual. "If I were to believe it all, so much weighs on you and I and yet we're strangers."

She considered that these feelings may not be love after all. Some cosmic connection to save lives. But it didn't matter, she wanted him and he wanted her. Saving people, an entire world, was just a side note. "Will you tell me about the beginnings?"

"The beginnings are stories that we're raised on, like a history of when the darkness began. Folklore I guess. We learn of Trey and Laura's unbreakable love and how the darkness rose, seemingly from nowhere. It crept in and touched Laura's heart in the night. It turned her almost insane, she was such a strong and powerful being but this was too much for her to bear. You must remember being raised in Frin there is no negativity and if so, minimal. For someone who was so pure to have the darkness inside was like unending torture. I guess that's why Florence women come from Earth? To learn how to deal with it?" He pondered. "Laura knew she had to leave Frin in order to save it. The darkness was using her, trying to suffocate Frin and everyone in it. So, Trey finally allowed her to go and promised to do as she wished. We would welcome these strange and beautiful Florence women generation after generation, they'd bring so much joy. They seemed to be so uplifted and strong being with us in Frin. Their very auras pushing the darkness further and further back into its own shadows."

"My grandmother, Eleanor, wrote me a letter and spoke of the darkness, I don't understand. The little I've experienced of Frin hasn't seemed dark to me."

"You've been with me that's why." He smiled and squeezed her sensitive ribs, Elle held back a giggle. "Elle you need to understand that there can be no appreciation of the good when there is no bad. Beauty cannot exist without ugliness to define it."

"So, when do we slip?" Elle didn't feel impatient despite her question. She could have happily stayed tucked up in Torian's arms in his place for an eternity. His home was so creative, she could feel his passion hanging in the air. It was like he'd spent his time waiting for her, creating this artful cave for the two of them. Elle was content never to leave. But she wanted her baby.

She wanted Mai and it was not a possibility here. Elle now knew that Nessa had changed her schools and was moving house. Even if Elle could find out where Nessa was keeping her they'd never be able to have the life they once did. Nessa seemed determined to make sure of it.

"We need to prepare first. You won't be able to slip with those drugs in your system so we'll need to hang out until that happens. We should make arrangements for Mai. We need to ensure that she can find a path to us on her own. She can slip but she needs to be careful. We need to know that when the time is right she can stay with us and fight. You know she's the youngest to slip?" He added impressed.

"She's a special girl. I've made sure she knows not to talk about Frin."

"That's good. Nessa won't ever allow her to leave too. Not after the lengths she went to take her from you."

His words comforted her. While she knew she couldn't be physically with Mai, he had a plan. She'd be taken care of in this world. It would be a long hard life for Mai denying any knowledge of Frin while attempting to slip unnoticed. Living a life with Nessa, growing older and stronger so that some day she could also become a goddess of Frin. A Florence woman.

"Elle, there is something else you need to know." Torian spoke quieter, humbled.

"I can imagine there are a million things I need to know about this new life I am destined to lead." She replied with a smirk while staring into the red paint splatters beneath her feet.

"I have to kill your body."

Chapter 23

Oh. Elle's mind went blank. Kill. That's part of the plan? She sat silently tasting this words inside, her skin chilled. She'd wanted to die for so long and in so many ways, she didn't want to feel anymore. The pain, the sadness, the distrust of everyone around her. But here she now sat, full of feeling, full of life with a man she loved in a way she couldn't comprehend and he wanted to kill her.

"Kill me?"

If he were any other man, perhaps she'd have run in terror. Perhaps not. It was Torian, Elle's trust in him was strong and for reasons unknown to her. Or maybe she was weak, gullible. A life in some fantasy world seemed far easier to commit to than suicide however, this plan involved death too.

Elle didn't want to make eye contact with him, not yet. She looked to the painting on the wall directly ahead of her. In the back ground was a blurred village, sort of, in a warped colourful way. In the foreground the tree. The one they'd made love under. Had they made love? She still wasn't sure what it was they'd shared so long ago. The more she looked at it the stronger her arousal grew. Pink warmth rose to her cheeks, turned on by a murderer. She shifted uncomfortably, intertwined her fingers. What a strange sensation, her body and brain in turmoil.

"It's only your body Elle." He decided to speak sensing her worries, her fears.

"Only my body?" She murmured. "And without that, what's left?"

"Your soul is who you are. Your pure essence will be present in Frin. You do need to understand though that once your body dies, you can never return to it. Or Earth. Your connection will be severed."

"This is like the fine print or something? The catch to wanting a peaceful life? Will you produce a contract for me to sign too?" She was becoming sarcastic. Dying?

"Look, if your body remains alive you can be pulled back into it." He was completely serious as he spoke, ignoring her attitude.

"Who would pull me back?"

"Your mother is the clear choice. You may not want to believe the true extent of her corruption, but she's becoming unearthly on the inside. With every lie, every negative thought she feeds it. She's tried so hard to keep you here and ruin Frin's future."

"Couldn't I just slip again? Even if she did?"

"You could, if you were given a chance. We're afraid that if she successfully pulled you back, she'd kill you."

"But you want to kill me. I don't understand the difference except for the hands behind it." Elle couldn't grasp what he was telling her. "At this rate, I see death either way."

"If you die here, while your body contains your soul, your spirit, whatever you want to call it. All of you dies. Your existence everywhere, will be dead. Your essence dispersed into the atmosphere. If you've slipped into Frin, the very best parts of you are preserved and safe. It's your shell that no longer exists. This is why we need your body to die after you've slipped. To protect you Elle." He waited for her thoughts, but none came. "I don't want to lose you. I could sense how near death you've been and all I could do is make stupid coffee and wait. Do you know how hard that was? Being unable to intervene? To hold you and explain? To tell you it's all going to be okay?" Torian was angered by his helplessness, his eyes shaded with memory.

"Lucky you make great coffee. It saved my life." She smirked and gave him a playful jab with her elbow. She got it now, understood what he meant by killing. She was amazed and perplexed by her acceptance of it all.

Still, at the end of the day this could all be some strange murder plan. If she wouldn't kill herself, someone else could and she'd make it easy for them by believing all their weird and wonderful stories. A hired hitman with extremely warped methods.

"You know I love you right?" His eyes concerned. "I was once frustrated to think you were my only purpose in life. But now? That you're here with me, I don't need any other reason to breathe. You are my whole world." And he pressed his mouth on hers.

Elle gave in to him. Her muscles weakened, she slumped into his arms. His kiss exhausted her and she felt relaxed, content. He stopped as she closed her eyes. He stroked her forehead until she fell asleep, reclined back against the lounge in his safe hold.

Torian picked her up like her weight was of no burden and carried her like a baby, up the stairs. Reaching the top, he took her to the bed, it was in the centre of the space. A sprawling root system suspended above it had been wrapped with tiny lights creating a whimsical chandelier, the glow was magical. It reminded him of home.

His bed covered in pillows and a messy array of soft blankets. Gently he placed Elle down, tucking pillows around her in a nest of comfort. His eyes grazed over her while she slept, such a beautiful creature in the gentle brush of light.

"Torian?" She stirred and mumbled as he lay a blanket over her.

"I'm still here, you fell asleep. I thought you could use the rest."

"Lie with me?"

He took off his shirt and rearranged pillows to make room, laying down he slipped an arm under her neck and she moved to place her head on his bare chest. It was warm and she could hear the blood pumping, thumping through his body.

Torian stroked her forehead as she lazily traced the teasing line of hair from his belly button to his waist band. Rolling her head toward him she lightly kissed his chest, she felt his hand freeze, his breathing catch and he lay motionless.

Kissing him again she swept her fingers along the edge of his pants feeling his firm tummy beneath them. Finally, he let out a shuddering breath as her lips passed over his nipple, he hurriedly rearranged himself so he could kiss her mouth. He was more forceful now and she was wide awake. He pressed against her as if trying to melt into her but couldn't. There was something frustrated, desperate in him and Elle felt it too. No longer was she relaxed, she felt wild, unsatisfied, hungry in a lazy erotic way. Torian kept kneading her flesh firmly only feeding her wanting. She wanted him so much it hurt deep in her belly.

An ache that couldn't be hushed, he was pushing at her body and she was tearing at his. Their mouths warm, locked, their hands searching. They tried greedily to find a way into each other, become a part of the other's being. Elle wanted to feel his burning skin on hers, breaking free she sat up and tore off her top, unsnapped her bra. Torian rushed to help with her skirt and knickers. Elle fiddled with the button on Torian's pants for mere seconds before he moved her hands and undid it himself.

She pulled them down and he kicked them away. Elle climbed onto him and tried to smother him with her now slight body. Groaning and grunting like beasts they wriggled and withered together. Rubbing, pushing, but never enough.

Torian grabbed her waist and rolled her down onto the bed, looked into her eyes as he covered her with his heavy warmth. Elle sighed and pulled him closer to kiss him again. Pausing a moment to savour the kiss she could feel the hardness of him hovering, waiting to enter.

Torian stopped kissing and again searched her eyes, suddenly he thrust and was inside her. He was so thick and she so smooth. Made for each other, yes, she believed it. Elle cried out in pleasure, pressing harder against him to feel every inch.

This was good but still she had an ache inside her heart. Torian filled her in only one place and she knew they could have more. Elle craved him all over her, everywhere, right now. These sensations a mere shadow of the complete ravishment they could have together in Frin. Here, this was all she could physically take and she continued to cry out in a sad ecstasy.

Like the waves heard crashing, they moved together rhythmically, purposefully. Locking his fingers between hers he raised them above her head, sinking them into the pillows. He lent down, tenderly kissing her breasts. Sucking a nipple between his lips slowly, roaming his tongue over it. Releasing her, their eyes met and he rocked calmer. Torian withdrew and patiently, Elle waited for the delicious thud, over and over he pushed into her.

And then it happened. Bodies, hands, eyes interlocked they came. Letting go of her hands, Torian grasped Elle's bottom and pulled her in closer. They shuddered together amongst hushed moans, wave after wave until Torian relaxed on top of her. Both tingling they lay still.

Elle's breathing was laboured as she hugged him tight, arms and legs wrapped around him. This feeling of him on top of her, inside her, was divine and she never wanted him to leave.

She breathed in his manly scent, running fingers through his dark blonde hair. She could envision what they looked like lying there, naked upon the bed. Beneath the glow of lights from the roots above. A mess of blankets and pillows strewn, their clothes thrown about. Her feet spread wide at one end, her dark hair flayed about at the other. A big toned, tanned body covering hers, dressing her so she was toasty and secure. Safe and protected. Torian rolled off, leaving Elle feeling a loss. Holding her hand, Torian kissed her so softly.

"We will be together again soon. I promise."

Elle knew what he meant. In Frin, they'd physically be together. Morphing into one seething erotic creature of radiant energy and love. The sex was good. The best she'd had but now that she was aware of more, of what they could have together in Frin; a complete revitalising connection. She knew she'd never be satisfied so wholly again.

Rolling onto her soft belly, Elle leaned on her forearm and placed her chin onto his chest. It was moist and she traced the tiny translucent beads of sweat prickling his skin. Like condensation on a cool glass, his hot flesh meeting with a chilled atmosphere, she drew circles, connecting them.

"I trust you. I'll let you kill my body."

"I bet you say that to all the men." He winked and pulled her up onto his chest feeling her breasts pressed against him. He continued to speak as he brushed his hand up and down her naked back. "I just want you safe. It was hard to tell you, Trey believed it was best not to let you know. In case you were afraid or couldn't handle it. He was worried you'd be truly lost to us if you knew. But I refused. You need to know the truth. Have a choice."

"I'm glad you told me. I mean, I wasn't expecting it, being told I had to die? But I'd rather know now than after it had been done, without my permission."

"You deserve the truth. Deserve making your own decisions." He frowned thinking. "If you'd decided to stay, not come with me to Frin. I'd have accepted it. I would have lived a life of destitution without you though."

"I bet you say that to all the women!" Elle smirked, attempting to light the shadow that fell upon him.

In fact, she didn't know how to respond to him seriously. To state so plainly that he'd live a life of destitution without her was overwhelming. She'd never been wanted like that, loved, needed like that before. To have someone understand her, complexities and all, was so unnerving. And she liked it.

Chapter 24

Toby sat in his car at the top most level of the carpark, central in town. He'd brought Elle here once in the height of a dark night. He'd brought along a bottle of red wine. A fancy expensive one, he wanted to impress this woman. She wasn't as easy to entice with elaborate dinners in pricey restaurants like other women he'd known. She didn't care for meals that were served for people with stomachs the size of a sparrows no matter how pretty they looked. She couldn't understand why they'd pay so much to leave still hungry.

She would then request they stop at the ice cream shop in the main street and Toby always tried to act unimpressed about it. He'd deny the cheap treat for himself.

Truthfully, he looked forward to this part of the night the most. She'd take a delicate spoonful from the small tub and swirl it about her mouth as it melted. She said she liked the cold creaminess.

They'd stroll the street together and she'd take off her shoes and carry them in the hand that held her spoon. Her nude feet on the dirty sidewalk made him cringe but she didn't care one bit. He envied her lightness, her freedom to do as she pleased, say what she wanted and be who she was.

Together they'd sat in his car that night long ago, listening to his favourite music, looking over the light speckled town. Surprising her, he pulled two crystal flutes and the bottle of wine from under the passenger's seat. She held a glass out for him to fill with a smile.

She'd moved a little and some wine found itself dribbling down the crystal, dripping onto her leg. Toby had watched the blood red drop slide silkily down between her thighs. Suddenly he asked her to get out of the car. Elle did as he asked and stood watching him through the open door. Taking a napkin from the glove compartment, quickly he dabbed at the wine on his lambskin seat cover.

Then she laughed. Standing in the cold, atop the empty car park she laughed at him. He was so angry, going on and on about how the stain would never come out, not understanding why she didn't see it was a big deal. She'd zoned him out and wandered to the ledge, sipping the wine, looking out over the black city. Dark haphazard shapes sprinkled with glistening street lights.

Sternly he called to Elle. Told her they were leaving. She turned to him and laughed more, questioning his seriousness. Her laughter infuriated him, he poured the remainder of the costly wine onto the concrete, told her to get in, driving away leaving the empty bottle on the ground.

He touched the stain now, he'd made such a drama over it. He was now glad it was there. They'd made a memory that night and now he wished it were different.

Toby was panicked. He had no idea where Elle was. Comatose in a back alley for all he knew. He was worried that without care she'd die of starvation or dehydration or simply because of the earthly elements. Depending on where she was. His mind was forming the worst scenarios and he cried. He never cried but he couldn't even combat the tears that fell the moment he realised she was gone.

He'd already searched the very few places he knew she used to visit. And nothing, no indication of where she was. He found it astonishing how easy it was for her to disappear, the fact that she went nowhere, saw no one, had made it so simple for her to vanish.

He now regretted bring Mai home to her. And couldn't believe he ever thought it was a good idea. He was no longer even sure if he'd done it for her. Maybe it was for him.

Wake her so she could go back to taking care of him? Cleaning, washing. Elle was in such a state and he'd been so desperate, but perhaps it had broken her further. Tempted her, teased her, reminded her of the life she'd never have. Perhaps she'd finally done it. Committed suicide. He pictured her deceased in some quiet space, her lifeless body hidden, waiting. He knew she'd do it like that. She never was one for attention.

He'd assumed she was getting better. After Mai's visit at least she was awake more, eating when she needed to, drinking. He no longer had to force her to do anything, not even take the pills. He thought his life was returning to normal and began going to work again. He'd leave and come home and Elle would be there. Until she wasn't.

For a week now, Toby had been searching and it had become desperate, roaming shopping centres just in case he glimpsed her. He feared for her life so intensely like a sharp razor blade held to his throat, the pressure growing. With each day passing he felt his chance to save her was less and less. And he feared he couldn't live without her.

Elle had put him through so much turmoil and sometimes he'd been angry with her for it. He'd made so many sacrifices that he'd never thought he'd make for anyone but he had done it for her. Elle had such dark demons but an alluring light too. After it all he couldn't give up, not now.

"Nessa, Elle is missing. Clearly, I'm desperate calling you. It's my last resort. Have you got any ideas?" He spoke blankly into the phone. Knowing Elle would never have gone to Nessa.

He was torn, he'd wanted to hide Elle's disappearance from Nessa, from everyone. Thinking he could find her soon enough and no one would have further reason to withhold Mai. Though now, he didn't care. He just wanted to find her.

"When did she go missing?" Nessa asked concerned.

"Eight days now, I've looked everywhere. I've got nothing left." His pain cracked his voice but he held back the tears.

"We need to find her immediately."

"I agree. But how? And please don't tell Mai. I don't want her to worry especially when we don't know anything."

"I should tell Mai. Tell her to be careful." Nessa said absently, not really to him.

"What are you saying? Be careful of what? Do not tell her Nessa!" Toby's mind clicked. "Are you seriously worried Elle's lurking around?"

"How do I know this isn't some plan you've both been working on? Is Elle really missing?"

"You've got to be kidding me! Of course, she's missing. You are the last person I want to be talking to right now but I wanted to call you, as her mother, to see if you knew anything before I called the police." Now he was strong and booming.

"Why would you call the police?"

"Because Elle is missing! You've destroyed her! For all I know she's dead somewhere."

"Toby she's not dead." Nessa laughed with malice. "You'll never see her again. She's in Frin. Or will be soon."

He hung up. Threw his phone smashing it. He spent the rest of the day pacing between his room and Mai's, rubbing his forehead. Looking over Elle's and Mai's belongings. Everything so physical, still in its allotted space despite their owners stolen from him.

The child in his life taken, his woman gone. It had all fallen, his whole life like a sacred stained-glass window. In one shuddering explosion his whole world fell into rainbow destruction.

Chapter 25

The days they spent together blurred into weeks, Elle and Torian spent many nights in deep conversation pouring over ideas. They'd worked hard together on making solid plans.

Torian had taken Elle to make a will. Still the idea of helping to plan her own death was unreal. What little she did own, she left to Mai. The money Torian had given her along with the remainder of her own accounts were stowed away into a trust. She also planted some belongings into a safety deposit box. Eleanor's diary, the shell Mai had given her on the beach, the letter Grandma wrote along with one she'd written herself. They'd be released to her at sixteen. These things they decided would help Mai find her way to Frin should Nessa succeed. Should she find out Mai could already slip and find a way to stop her.

Elle wasn't sure what kind of life Mai would live with Nessa and wanted to ensure that should Nessa somehow keep Mai from them, that there was another way. A plan B. Especially now, once her body had died, there was no returning. Elle thought maybe Nessa would never talk to Mai about Frin, hoping to keep it from her. Or perhaps she'd mention little things, fishing for information.

Not knowing how Mai would be treated plagued Elle's mind. The one thing she did know was that Nessa would have her ears and eyes open watching, waiting for any hints Mai may give up. Mai had promised not to say a word and hopefully never did. Eventually Nessa would assume her blissfully ignorant grandchild knew nothing. She'd believe she was successful. Broken the chain if not via Elle then through Mai.

She would live out her life in some kind of satisfied spite, haunted by memories of a beautiful life missed. Hating Trey, Laura, Elle. Perhaps expressing to Mai how horrible her mother had been to leave her behind. Eventually she'd die, like any other person of earth would and Mai would be free. To stay or go. To decide.

Once their plans seemed secure, well thought out and thorough. They relaxed and it was heavenly. Talking about a life in Frin, making love and eating food seemed to fill most of their time. Elle began to envision a life with Torian in Frin, she could feel how it would be already. Safe, happy and loving. She could feel his love and knew he wanted nothing more from her than her mere presence in his. He made her feel confident and beautiful, she felt desirable.

Lazy mornings in bed tracing freckled constellations on naked bodies. Picking out individual coloured flecks in each-other's eyes as the sun brightened them. Touching, kissing every part they could. Memorising scars, marks, finger prints.

Torian would cook her delicious meals and they'd lay on their tummy's naked on the concrete eating together. It was chilly but refreshing, they'd spent days without clothes, no need, she felt free and natural. She had no fear of him, no desire to shy away or hide herself from him, he looked her over as a captivating whole.

She was addicted to his ways, and her complexion glowed. She was beginning to remember who she was or Torian was reminding her. They painted, ordered coffee and walked the beach, sat in the sand numerous times and watched sunsets together.

Her days merging into one long golden haze, she could handle this. Spending all her time with a beautiful, masculine man, who took care of her and knew exactly what to do and say to make her happy.

Her nights however hurt. She thought of Mai every evening as she lay quietly waiting for sleep to take her. Torian would hold her, give the back of her neck a firm loving squeeze and press his forehead to hers. He'd look into her eyes and tell her everything would be okay. They would lie there and he would stroke her bare spine up and down until her heaving chest calmed. He would kiss her mouth until her sobs ebbed. He would kiss her salty tear-soaked cheeks until they dried.

Elle missed her girl. She had come from her, they'd shared one body. Mai was her baby and as much as she loved Torian, she'd never be whole without her child. Torian promised to never let her go and finally Elle would fall asleep in his arms, curled up and warm like an abandoned kitten found.

Elle was walking along the shoreline, her nude feet sinking softly into the dark wet sand leaving a long path of prints. The ocean was mean and angry, growling and thrashing toward her. Despite it looking like it wanted to attack her, she felt calm.

She watched a bird swoop down into the violent sea, it splashed into the seething waters and rose again abruptly. A glimmering, slithering fish tossed about in its beak. She heard a giggle. Elle turned back toward the beach and ahead of her was Mai. Walking away from her. Elle called.

"Mai, wait for me!"

Elle tried to run but she couldn't. The glugging sand sucking at her feet, slowing her down horridly. Mai kept giggling and began to run. Elle's heart started to race, pounding aggressively against her bones. All she wanted to do was lift her feet and run but all she could manage was a heavy sloppy jog. She looked to the sea and it roared at her, sickly turquoise threatening to smash her.

"Mai please wait for me!"

Suddenly the sand dried. Her feet came free and she could run. She felt elated and light as she bolted faster and faster towards

Mai. The wind in her hair, the sun on her face she was happy and smiled.

She reached Mai and went to scoop her up into her arms but she was snatched away. Sucked down into the dry powdery sand leaving only a dry puff where she once stood. Elle fell to the ground and began to dig at the course gritty sand, harder and faster but she couldn't find Mai. Her tears hot and sad, her chest felt hollow and afraid. She gasped for breath between sobs. Finally, she stopped, sinking back onto her heels, looking at her bleeding finger tips. The ocean screamed at her again and she screamed back. Only she couldn't hear herself. She screamed and screamed in silence.

"Wake up!" Torian's voice demanded.

Elle sat up sobbing. Torian wiped her tears and held her.

"It's okay. This is a good thing Elle." He soothed.

"It was a horrible dream."

"It was a dream though. We've been waiting for this." He smiled.

Through her tears she smiled back. He was right, they'd been waiting for this moment. Regardless of good or bad, it was still a dream. Her mind had finally cleared the drugged fog. It meant she could slip, it meant she'd soon see Mai.

Calmed, she curled back down into his embrace and fell back into disturbed sleep. Visions of Mai, the waves, sucking sands and wriggling dead fish passed in and out of blackness.

She woke feeling flustered and hurried.

"We can leave. Maybe tonight?" Elle was keen to move on and see her child, and now she knew she could slip again, her impatience was strong.

"Let's give it a couple days to be sure." He watched Elle's face fall. He knew she wanted to leave as soon as possible and he wanted to go home too but it needed to be right. If she didn't slip and her body was gone, they'd both be lost. He wouldn't live without her.

"Then let's pass that time quickly." She said with a sly grin and he felt himself stirring at the invitation.

"Come with me beautiful."

His voice ripped delicious shreds off her. He took her hand, leading her to the base of the stairs, inclined his head gentlemanly and indicated she go first. Giving a slight bow Elle went ahead. Torian followed.

He began to slide his hands up the back of her thighs to cup her backside and back down again to stroke the back of her knees. She slowed. He watched her round bottom moving with each step, watched her calves tighten and release. Her hair silky, falling to her sweet, tucked in waist.

She wasn't sure she'd make it to the top before her legs became shaky and collapsed beneath her. She stopped. Two steps from the summit, looking up at his beautiful bed beneath his one of-a-kind chandelier.

Flashes of the things they'd done together in it, twisted her insides with knowing. She turned to him. Wrapped her arms around his neck, fingers threaded into his hair and pulled him close. His firm jawline pressed between her breasts, she threw her head back and allowed a slight moan to escape as he nuzzled into them.

With his arms wrapped around her, Torian began to knead her soft bottom firmly. Closing her eyes, she kissed and nibbled at his neck allowing his touch to become harder, wanting. Torian slid his hands down from her bottom grasping at her thighs. He reefed them apart and picked her up. Her feet left the step she balanced upon and she wrapped her legs around him for support. She knew he wouldn't stumble, falter. He'd keep her safe, he always would.

Crossing her ankles around him she could feel how hard he was against her knickers and wished they weren't there.

He carried her. Throwing Elle against the bed he stood looking down at her with a dark playful grin and began to unzip his pants, sliding them down awfully slow. Elle sat up clawing at his arms pulling him down toward her belly. He kissed it, stroked her thighs, teasingly pulled down her underwear watching her the entire time.

Torian paused a moment, "I love you." He said before kissing, licking and enjoying her most womanly parts like he never tasted anything so divine.

With her back arched and her fingers tangled in his hair she came, it was hard and scrumptiously violent. She pulled him up to kiss her mouth, he plunged into as he did so. She cried out as another set of waves flowed over her, slower, deeper waves this time.

Elle pulled him over and Torian happily swung her up on top. Tucking her feet under his calves to secure herself in place she leaned back and he lifted to meet her. One hand squeezing her breast teasing a nipple, the other tugging gently at her hair. She lay down onto his chest, she could taste herself as he kissed her deeply. Elle felt him shudder within her as he came. Laced in a light sweat they lay in an intimate glow for the rest of the afternoon, entwined like they never wanted to be apart.

Elle was happy. Amazing conversations, laughs, sex. It was good and yet she still wanted more. They'd have more. In Frin, they'd melt, have that special love making that was far more satisfying, far more loving. Not just good, otherworldly. But for this moment, in his arms. All was good. And good was enough.

Chapter 25

The time had come. Torian felt they'd waited long enough for everything to go ahead smoothly. Elle was excited to finally leave, go to Frin, see Mai. But she was also terrified. It was the day she had to die. The day her body would cease to exist on Earth. Removed for good.

Together they'd discussed what steps they'd take but Torian would not tell her exactly how he would kill her. She had wanted to know but he had refused. He didn't want her to remember that part, didn't want that burden on her shoulders.

Her life here would end and her new one in Frin would begin, all he wanted for her was to seamlessly flow from one to the other. Devoid of thoughts about her own death to shadow her.

But it would shadow him. She'd asked if she could do it herself. Suicide wasn't an option either, she wouldn't make it to Frin. She couldn't even take pills or poison her mind would shut down, she'd never get there. Elle didn't push it, she understood what he said and honestly didn't think she wanted to know anyway.

All kinds of emotions and thoughts raced through her system. Her mind turned to Toby and still those pangs of guilt hit her hard. She had left him, abandoned him.

God only knew what he was doing or thinking right now. He would never have allowed her to leave if she'd sat and tried to talk it out with him. She knew that.

Having convinced herself he would be okay, perhaps even already was. She told herself that what she'd done, was the only way she'd ever escape him.

"Let's have something to eat." Torian suggested breaking her concentrated thoughts.

"I'd prefer to have it over and done with." Elle really didn't want to drag out the anxiety or the anticipation over the situation.

"I know. But this is hard for me, harder than I thought it would be. I just want another happy moment with you first." He seemed tired, stressed.

"Please don't make it sound like it'll be my last meal. Ever." Her trust in him was absolute, he'd be her murderer and she was fine with that but she didn't want doubts seeded. Not even tiny ones. Especially right now.

"It won't, not at all. I just, I'm just paranoid that's all. I mean, if you don't slip? And you're actually gone." He rubbed his forehead. "Look I know you don't need to be hearing this right now. I'm sorry."

"You're right, I don't. But I want you to talk to me. About anything. And yes, it's a huge scary thing but I'm in. I made my decision and I'll follow through regardless the outcome. I was never meant for this world. And to be honest if it does all go wrong, I've had the best time of my entire life with you. I'd be okay to go. So just in case; I wanted you to know that." Elle lifted his chin, smiled and kissed him. "But it won't go wrong. We've waited plenty of time, my systems clear, I've been dreaming. We're all good to go."

She tried to sound upbeat. And completely okay. But she was scared and now only realising she'd been totally ignorant to how Torian felt about it all. It was something that had to be done but she now knew, it wasn't something he actually wanted to do.

She couldn't imagine exactly how hard. Though she considered the idea of herself having to kill him. And immediately rejected the idea from her mind. She would never be able to do it. Never.

Torian cooked for her. Fluffy scrambled eggs, sprinkled with a little feta and shallots. It smelled good. It looked good, wisps of steam swirling languidly from it. They ate together in silence. Torian lost in his own thoughts, Elle could see it in his eyes. He didn't want to make eye contact with her. He looked closed, like he didn't want to talk. For once, it was he doing the overthinking.

Elle reached out to him, taking his hand. "What is it?"

"Even though I loved you, before I even knew who you were..." He paused gripped her hand tighter and looked up to meet her eyes. "I never would have been able to comprehend how much I feel for you now. I had no idea what this Earth place would be like but I managed through all the heavy dark feelings. Through all the falsities and people trying to pretend every single day of their lives; it was exhausting. I didn't think I could stay here and wait for you. It was hard. But when I finally knew you were real, you existed. I knew that no matter what, I'd see it through. I just knew that someday you would be mine and we'd return to Frin together." He repositioned his grip on her hand, clinging as if he thought it would slip and he'd never get it back. "You are everything to me Elle. Be it here or in Frin, I will love you anywhere. Having to physically kill your body? I'm now not sure if I'm strong enough to do that."

Elle didn't know what to say. She looked him over, his dark blonde head hung as he stared at the table, his shoulders slumped forward, his top half naked. His muscular arms outstretched to hold her hand.

She ran hers over his tattoos, all swirling in blacks and greens and blues. They suited him, like he'd been born with them. Her heart ached for him, this beautiful man that loved her. She'd do anything to take his pain from him, strip him bare of it. If she could.

"Torian I love you so much. I've never had anything like this before. There is only one love that is just as strong though. The love I have for Mai." She stood and rounded the table to lean over him and hug his neck. "I know it won't be easy but I have to slip into Frin so I can be with you both. There is a reason why us Florence women are connected with Frin. I think it is the right path for me and I need to know why. I need to be there for Mai too, so she can find her way. I miss her so much. And I will never see her again if I stay here. I would always have you and love you but I'd never be complete."

Nodding his head, finally he stood. "It is time then."

Together they lay down in his bed for the last time. Torian held her, made love to her. Slowly, lazily like he never wanted it over. Finally, Elle fell asleep. Unaware of his tears leaking into her sweetly scented hair. He stroked her face, memorised it. Gently kissed her softly parted lips. Holding her, he didn't want to let go.

Waiting he watched the sun rise and spill its golden magic across the room, he watched the light fade again as night crept in. Still Elle slept. He checked her pulse and it had slowed. He held a hand to her lips and felt her ever so slight breath. She had slipped. He was finally very sure.

Torian scooped up his love and still, his tears fell as he carried her lifeless body down the timber stairs. Earth, he hated in this moment. Hated the way it made him feel. So dark and cruel. Horrible things occurred and most people were immune to it, deaf to it. Used to it.

All they wanted to do was smile and pretend it's all perfectly fine. And perhaps their own tiny world it was, but the entirety wasn't. And no one wanted to correct it, no one wanted it better. Everyone out for themselves. A confusing place full of secrets, lies and ignorance.

He couldn't stop the dark and emotional onslaught. Perhaps he'd been here too long and now with what he had to do, he'd succumb. He took his beautiful Elle into the kitchen and lay her down upon the concrete floor where they'd lay and laughed and eaten so many times before. Only now there was no animation from the only woman he'd ever love. He returned to his bed, taking a pillow and made his way back to Elle.

Torian opened the large chest freezer remembering the night Elle had questioned why it was so big and yet so empty when she'd gone in search of ice cream. He took the pillow and placed it inside then turned and picked up Elle. He hesitated and held her close, taking deep sobbing breaths to soak up her scent. Her essence into him.

He felt her warmth against his chest and for a moment thought perhaps he'd just place her back into bed. He could lock this place up and no one would ever know what it hid inside. He'd waited his entire life to find her and here, right now, he had her. The tormenting pain crushed his insides. But this was not about him. Selfishness. Another aspect of this Earth he hated right now.

Taking a deep breath, he began to lower Elle into the freezer. His tears hitting her body as he leaned in, tears that would freeze like little diamonds with her forever. He tucked her legs up and positioned her arms so she would be comfortable. He knew she couldn't, wouldn't feel anything but he was here and very aware. Her body was with him, in his complete trust and he couldn't just treat it like she was nothing.

He wanted to do it right for her but also for himself. Show her and her body the respect it deserved. He smoothed her hair back neatly and stroked her soft cheeks. His arms were becoming chilled and his body quivered. It wouldn't take long, once he was brave enough to close the lid and walk away. Her body would slow down, as the crackling cold crystalized her from the inside out, her organs would stop working. She'd gradually drift off into a frozen sleep. Forever, her body would be dead.

Finally, Torian stepped back, looking down on his beautiful, peaceful woman as the icy moist air whipped and whirled around her body, fading her out. He closed the lid. His heart pounding, his chest heaving. Pain slashed at him, paranoia screamed in his ears. What if she hadn't slipped?

He tortured himself as he slid down against the freezer, his bare back skin dealing with the harsh cold as he leaned against it. He didn't care. It made him feel something. He knew now, that Elle would be gone and his last remaining days on Earth would be consumed with an evil nothingness.

He pulled his knees into his chest and strapped them there with his big arms. He placed his head down and began to cry. He'd not cried before this day, not because he'd never felt pain but because nothing had hurt him so savagely. He continued to cry, there beside his frozen love until eventually, he fell into a horrific sleep there on the floor. By the freezer.

Torian woke and still his pain was deep and present. Strong enough to mask the physical pains he had after sleeping on the hard concrete. His eyes were swollen and sore.

He stood in front of the freezer for a long time, too afraid to see what he had done. Finally, he opened it and peered in. Elle was there. All icy and surreal. Her skin pale and blue, her lips a macabre shade of purple. Her hair held micro snowflakes. He leaned closer and his chest convulsed, tears spewed again and he had to look away. He looked out the windows to the beach outside. It was all golden, colourful and vivid and here he was in devastation with his dead monochromatic beauty.

Devastated, chest rattling with a heart beating too fast. Praying to god, any god that he hadn't just murdered the love of his life. Murdered his life. He knew what he had to do now. He looked one last time at Elle and decided to kiss her, gently he brushed his warm moist lips against her hard, cold ones. Closed the lid and took his studio key from the hook by the door. He walked down the flight of stairs and out into the late afternoon sunshine. Briefly it blinded him. He locked the door behind him and threw the key as hard and as far as he could into the powdery sand.

The golden afternoon light was soaking into his skin as he walked the dry sands. Wind whirred the sand by him as if he were trying to cross a harsh dry river. He reached the waters edge and walked in. He kept walking out into the sea as the waves crashed into his body, slamming him and abusing him and he felt he deserved it all. With his pants soaked and the water up around his armpits he felt heavy, the salty water stinging his already tender eyes. His tears still fell only now, mingled with the oceans spray he didn't notice them.

A wave came, lifted him and he lost his footing until it passed, another came and took his feet from under him again. Torian began to swim, heading straight towards the horizon, chasing the sinking sun. The waves slowed into a swell becoming lethargic and lucid. The gentle motions sucked him further out, sliding him up and over and on more. He continued to swim until his arms burned as badly as his eyes. He stopped. Turned to see the shore but couldn't.

All he could see was ocean and sky. He lay back and floated. A suspended being, crushed between two worlds. The up. The down. It was quiet besides the water that lapped at him. His wet hair now darker flaying about his head rippling with the water, his face and stomach soaked in the suns residual heat. His drenched black pants trying to suck him into the depths. The waters around him were jaded green. He felt a calm now, an acceptance. He knew what he'd done and what needed to happen now.

Torian closed his eyes. A reminiscent smile came over his lips as he thought about Elle waiting for him beneath the weeping willow. She was framed in sunlight against a peach sky. She was laughing and swinging her daughter high up into the air. He just watched her. Loving her, waiting for his painful drowning to begin.

Chapter 26

It was the day before Mai's fifteenth birthday when the police arrived at the door. Nessa wasn't home. 'Brunch' with some guy. Mai was used to it. Nana had always been like that, personally Mai thought she was a bit old to be still getting around but she liked being left alone so she didn't say anything.

"Is something wrong?" Mai had had run ins with the police every now and again, she practically knew all the local cops first names now. But these guys she didn't know.

"Are you Mai Florence? Living with Vanessa Florence?" The chunky one formally asked.

"She likes Nessa, but yeah that's us."

"Your mother's body has been found."

"Wow." Was all she could manage. She knew her mother was gone but never really thought about where her body was. The last thing she expected was that someone would coming knocking on the door to tell her it had been found. Weird.

Totally weird. So, they've found her body. Her dead body. It just clicked. Mum wasn't left in an unknown hospital with an unknown name, somewhere in a coma. She was actually dead. She'd never thought about it before. She wanted to act shocked but it wasn't that shocking to her.

"Um, come in? Cup of tea?"

"Yes thanks. Is your grandmother home?"

The cop was very sensitive, well his tone was Mai thought. Maybe he genuinely feels sorry for me. He was a big guy, round though and kind of reminded her of a teddy bear, surely no crim would be afraid of him.

"No, she's out having brunch with a friend." She said as she placed the tea cups on the table. She couldn't be bothered to offer milk, sugar.

She flicked her long hair over her shoulder, Nessa had once mumbled that her mum used to do that too. Mai liked the idea of being similar to her mum in some small way so she continued to do it. Plus, it pissed off Nessa she was sure.

Her hair was the same colour as Elle's only she went for a grungy, rebel type style and shaved up under one side. A rave shave, it was pretty popular but she made it look good.

"There seems to be some interesting circumstances surrounding your mother's disappearance." He kind of kept glancing around the room, as if not sure how much the kid could take. It bugged her. "Do you want to wait for your grandmother?"

"No, it's fine. Really. My mother disappeared when I was only six and I'm kind of over being treated like a sad lost kid. I want to now. Just tell me okay."

"I understand. Your grandmother would have just relayed the information to you anyway."

Not likely, but continue chubby man, she felt like saying. Instead she nodded in agreement.

"Your mother was found in a chest freezer in a studio apartment. The lease on the place had finally run out and when the money stopped and no one turned up to resign the owner went in. It appears to have been abandoned years ago and no one had noticed."

"Okay. Wow. That's a lot to take in. I never expected Mum to be found, I thought she'd just disappeared and after so long? I don't know what I thought. So, she's been frozen all this time?"

"Yes, and we believe we know who is responsible for her murder. A man by the name of Torian Amos, he was the tenant of that studio, we think he may have been stalking your mother for quite some time. He had paintings and all sorts of things that belonged to your mother. The whole place is like a shrine dedicated to Elle Florence."

Mai thought it sounded beautiful. Torian that old romantic. She'd never seen his place but she imagined it now to be some amazing place. Like he'd specially created it with all his love, as a kind of modern-day tomb for her mother's preserved frozen body.

The cop sounded intrigued too, wrong but intrigued. He probably was telling her too much but the details were curious. Probably a bit of excitement in his life.

"So, this Torian Amos killed my mother and put her into a freezer. What a sicko. Do you know where he is?" She chose to play along, holding back an eye roll.

"Mai, he did not kill your mother first. See this is the strange part. She was alive when she was put into the freezer. And stranger yet, there are no signs of struggle. You would imagine if someone was put into a freezer against their will, there would be a great deal of struggling. I know I would. The freezer wasn't bolted or chained. The tox screens came back clean too."

"Tox screens?" Finally, something curious.

"Toxicology report, it showed that she didn't have any kind of substance in her system. So, we are baffled. She wasn't drugged or bound. It was like she allowed this stalker to just lay her down in that freezer." Now he was amazed. "It's almost like she wanted him to, asked him to. We need to find this guy and question him. It's the only way we'll know."

Yeah sure, it would all seem so baffling to this guy. She had to admit, it was a pretty baffling scenario.

She remembered the first month or so, after Toby and her mum had put her back into the bedroom window in the fresh hours of morning. She would never forget it. She was so sad and so lonely.

As much as Nessa had tried to fake a loving grandmother role, she never mastered it. It was nothing like that raw, loving honesty she could feel around her mother. Mai had desperately missed her, just wanted a hug. Most nights she tossed and turned, she'd try so hard to stay awake in case Toby decided to come steal her away again.

Finally, she'd fall asleep, slip into Frin. As happy as she was there with the others that loved her, Trey knew there was more. An underlying emotion that wasn't welcome in Frin but he'd never turn her away, instead he'd spend time with her. He'd let her know plans were being worked on and soon enough she'd have her Mummy back. This isn't a forever thing, he'd say, just a little while thing.

As mature as Mai had to be at that age, she still was after all, only six when her mother 'went missing.' Of course, after Toby's phone call to the police Mai's whole world changed. Police would turn up whenever they felt like it to ask questions of Nessa and her. They were hard to answer especially when she'd promised never to speak of Frin to anyone, especially Nessa.

She couldn't tell them that she'd seen her Mum before she went missing, she couldn't tell them Toby had taken her from her bedroom in the night. Nessa still had no idea they'd had one last good bye. School was different too. Her teachers became even more coddling toward her. As far as the world knew, she was already a messed-up kid, having to live with her grandmother because her Mum was insane. And now missing?

Newspapers, evening news reports, posters, bulletin boards all showed pictures of Elle's smiling face. Toby had chosen a picture of her before the depression had settled in, before sadness made a home within her. She looked beautiful in that picture. Not the kind of woman who'd run away. Mai was only two when it had been taken but she did remember her mother like that. Vaguely.

Elle's disappearance was a big deal to everyone and she had to pretend she cared. Pretend like she was sad and lost and afraid. Even though she knew there was a plan, even though she knew the secrets. Even though knowing not seeing her mum was only a little while thing. So much attention, so much pretending.

And now it will happen all over again. Thankfully I dropped out when I did. Not too hard to isolate myself while it all blows over. Mum will be brandished all over the place, all over again. It wasn't the clear cut, quiet path out of this world that they had planned after all. Damn Toby calling the cops.

Mai feigned tears, asked the cops to leave. They obliged mentioning they'd return to question her grandmother perhaps when Mai was at school, so they didn't upset her further. Mai nodded hurrying them out the door.

Nessa didn't know Mai wasn't going to school yet and she really didn't care to tell her either. For a while she did care, between moving in with Nessa and around eleven years old. Nessa was her Nana after all and she was a kid and had no one else. She cared until she was old enough to realise that Nessa didn't. Most things she said weren't true, just words created to get her own way, manipulate or gain her benefits of a sorts.

Every now and again she saw Toby. After twelve months and still no luck finding Elle, Toby began to turn to Nessa. He'd been a mess and he'd never gotten over losing Elle completely. He'd changed that's for sure.

Mai didn't know what kind of comfort he gained from Nessa, a verbal back and forth or the physical kind. She really wasn't interested.

Mai didn't like him much. She decided long ago that Toby had been mostly to blame for her mother's depression and misery and that she had deserved better. Even though Earth would never have provided the happiness she searched for. Her mum had deserved to be treated better by the man she'd devoted everything to. His loss.

Toby still tried to talk to Mai, perhaps out of pity or maybe guilt or maybe he really did care. He knew the void Elle had left in his own life, maybe he knew Mai would feel it too, most likely worse than he. Occasionally he tried to be all fatherly, she brushed it off, told him to get lost. Go have kids of your own if you want someone to boss around.

As far as Mai could tell, in this world she was alone. Living a lie with Nessa, waiting for the day she could slip and stay. Escape this stupid, crappy world and never come back. Mai knew she had to wait until she was old enough to have a baby, it was kind of her key to unlocking Frin's door.

She didn't really want a baby and couldn't even picture herself with one. Though she knew it was essential, for Laura's spirit to have a gateway back to help Trey fight the impending war between the darkness and light. So, for the sake of saving a world, she'd wait. Wait for some dreamy guy to come along and get her all knocked up.

Mai thought it kind of sucked knowing all the details. She knew her own mother had grown up with none. She knew she had the upper hand of knowing what was planned out for her. She knew her destiny. But it was boring. It really did take away the surprise, the mystery of life.

It was like her choices were taken from her and she had no say. But she found a way to be herself, rebelling was pretty fun. She did try however, to go out of her way to find this man who'd be the father of her child. The sooner he came along the better.

She'd go out with friends and get drunk and some cute guy would want to make out with her, being drunk she'd decide yes, this must be it. Might be him. Only she'd wake up with a huge headache and some random groping at her. She'd kick him out of the bed and go find something to eat from the fridge feeling like a huge idiot the whole time.

Mai had no patience she admitted. If she had to spend this waking life in waiting then she thought she may as well make the most of it. Make the waiting room a little less sterile, a little more fun.

She partied, drank and smoked sometimes, she thought it made her look older and sexier. She would sneak out of Nessa's house at all hours of the night to meet friends and boys or just roam the streets. She really didn't have any rules. Well she had plenty of rules. Millions of them handed out by Nessa and even Toby threw in a few. She just didn't follow them.

Nessa had lost control over Mai long ago and there wasn't much besides physical restraint that Nessa could do about it. As long as Frin wasn't a part of Mai's life, Nessa backed off despite clearly taking it as a weakness. She just drank more, met more people. Brought them home. And Mai continued to act out. If she were honest, she enjoyed tormenting Nessa.

Nessa had come home one night and found Mai straddled on top of some young man. Nessa had pulled her barely matured body from his and threw pants in the kids face. Screaming at him to leave or she'd call the cops. The kid begged her not to, as he shamefully dressed in a hurry while Nessa shoved at him screeching. Just as Nessa turned to Mai and began to yell, a man stumbled from Nessa's room wondering what the yelling was all about.

Mai burst out laughing. "At least the guy I was banging was cute!"

In all reality Mai was quite angry she'd been left on Earth, had to wait. She knew her own behaviour wasn't appropriate. She was intelligent and she was proud of the woman she knew she'd someday become.

One of the Florence women, it was almost the equivalent of being a celebrity on Earth, only she wouldn't be considered 'better' than anyone else. It wasn't their way but still everyone wanted to know the Florence women in Frin. They were beautiful, their big blue eyes and long dark hair, curvy bodies, they seemed to be so special to the Frinians.

Suddenly they'd just appear and bring a light and joy that was a benefit to all. Each one helping fend off the darkness in Frin, each one adding to their strength. Whenever a Florence woman returned home it was an event like an angel returning to heaven. And Mai couldn't wait until it was her turn.

Everything on Earth seemed so staged, she was tired of being a little kid playing house. People did what they thought they were meant to, not what they wanted to. Not Mai. People were bossed around, at home, at work, into things they didn't agree with or accept but did it all anyway. Not Mai.

Only she wished the negativity at her freedom to choose, wasn't so vicious. She hated being labelled a bad person when all she wanted was a right to decide. Mai couldn't wait for the day to come when she could shed her body for the last time and just slip peacefully. She wanted nothing more than to just be with her Mum and Torian in the only place were she actually felt unconditional love and acceptance. She just wanted to leave this world behind already. She just wanted to go home.

Chapter 27

Mai was out. Nessa didn't know where but she'd pretend to care if anyone asked. She had no control over that brat, it frustrated the hell out of her but she did like having her out of the house, so let it go. Sometimes she wondered if she did the right thing taking her away from Elle the way she did. Perhaps it had been irrational and not well thought out, just spontaneous spite. And then she'd been the one stuck with this unruly kid after her plans completely backfired anyway.

She had truly thought Elle would have stayed and begged like the weakling Nessa had assumed she was. She thought she'd eventually give Mai back, once Elle knew who was boss and not to mess with her. Then she'd forever have the perfect bargaining chip to bribe, blackmail and hold over Elle.

Nessa had wanted to show Elle she had power over her, that she was in control and Elle had better heed her words and do as she was told. She did not expect Elle to just up and leave. Especially without Mai. But she did, she hated herself for underestimating her. Hated that she ended up stuck raising Mai. Even though she was tired of her rebellious grandchild, she knew taking Mai from Elle would have wounded her very deeply. She took it as a consolation prize.

Toby was coming over to have dinner with her. They'd decided to move on from their original differences. With Elle's disappearance and Nessa's feigned shock and sadness at the loss of her one and only daughter, Toby ended up with a misguided soft spot for her.

Toby had changed over the years Nessa noticed. His arrogance had slackened and he had toned down his attempted superiority. She didn't think he'd done it on purpose, just one of those naturally evolving things that happens when you lose the best thing you ever had. It humbled him.

Now that Elle's body had been found and an investigation was underway Toby asked to catch up and go over their thoughts. Nessa agreed, feeling the need to keep up her faked interest. She knew what her daughter was doing and where she was, it angered her, infuriated her. Nessa hadn't gotten her own way. But how could you explain emotions like that to all other clueless souls.

She was a mother, her child disappeared years ago and now had been recovered, dead. It was sad, any mother should be sad so Nessa played sad.

She placed a large plate of spaghetti Bolognese down in front of Toby. He said a polite thank you, even though he knew he wouldn't finish the meal, just eat enough not to be rude. Nessa might be good in the bedroom but her kitchen skills were lacking. Toby wondered if that was why she stayed single. So she didn't have to look after a man or maybe it was the other way around, they tried her food and left.

He took a mouthful, chewed, swallowed. He put his fork down ready to begin their conversation.

"So, this Torian Amos is the number one suspect." He opened and shut his mouth a few times wanting to say more but stopped.

"He is. Reality is, I don't think they will find him Toby." She wanted to appear sensitive. She could see his angered look, thinking of this man who took her, made love to her, killed her. Her, his Elle. She poured two glasses of red and slid one across the table to Toby. He skulled it down, shoved the glass back requesting more.

"Why won't they find him Nessa. I want to meet this man. Look him in the eyes." He wanted to punch something, anything.

"Look at the facts Toby. He literally closed up his café the day Elle went missing. The money was missing, he'd only ever paid for things in cash, so he had no trail. Even the rent and utilities on that studio were paid upfront for ten years. I mean who does that? I'd waiver references and identification checks too, if someone turned up wanting to pay extra and for a decade in advance. What a pile a cash that've been. Who would say no to that?" He didn't respond. Just frowned at his wine. "No one has ever heard of him, he had little to do on a personal level with his customers. It's like he found Elle, lured her in, killed her and disappeared as well."

"He touched her, hurt her." Toby glared at Nessa.

She realised that he wouldn't get passed the idea of another man with Elle, the part where she was dead, he seemed to be blocking out.

Nessa tried laying out the information, the unlikely event of Torian being found. He never would she knew. But resigned, there'd be no point putting so much effort into his lost cause. Toby wouldn't give up no matter what she said. He loved Elle, despite their physical affair. He'd always love Elle. Not Nessa.

Once Toby had decided that he had actually loved Elle it was far too late. She was already lost to him. Elle had once loved him, very much and he knew it but he'd been to full of himself to genuinely return her feelings. Instead he tried to act too cool, too collected, almost as if he was too good for her. And finally, when she felt rejected, unloved and no good about herself, he began to regret everything he'd done. Toby completely blamed himself for Elle's slow and painful slide from woman in red to the woman now dead.

He lived with the guilt over his actions and never had been able to love another woman the way he loved her in the years since she left. He had placed her on a pedestal and no one had ever come close to being like her, replacing her. Toby knew he would grow into an old and very lonely man and for the first time in his life he took full responsibility for it. It was his fault and he accepted it. He had a woman who was so far out of his league, he should have been worshipping her not rubbishing her. If only he'd made her feel precious and wanted not insecure and sad, she'd have stayed, been his and he'd have been happy.

Lifting his third glass to his lips he stopped. "Nessa, I hear what you're saying. It's unlikely this man, this monster will be found after all this time. He's probably moved country, changed his name. Who knows? But I'm not going to tell the cops to halt their search. If he is out there he'll be found. One day, just like Elle was."

"I'm not asking you to stop. I just want you to accept the possibility. It's just been so long now Toby, you haven't let it go. I worry about you. I just think you need a different focus in your life." Nessa reached across the table to stroke the back of his hand.

He pulled his hand from hers frowning. "I don't think we can carry on like this anymore. It's not healthy." He took another almost cold mouthful and chewed in silence. She remained silent too, seething. "Let's just take a break and see how it goes once the investigations over with."

"Why Toby?" She didn't give a damn about Toby but she didn't like losing. Nessa's anger rose. "I don't understand, we aren't doing anything wrong."

"I don't feel right about it. With Elle finally being found, it's brought on a whole new wave of thoughts and feelings. I still love her you know that." He nodded to affirm his own statement. "Maybe in some way I felt closer to her being with you."

"That's just weird. I never said you couldn't love her. In fact, I'm the one who gave you permission to love her in the first place!"

"Don't say it like that Nessa, I had a choice in the matter."

"No, you didn't. If it weren't for me, you'd never have met Elle. You followed her around like a little puppy, waiting for her to give you a pat. So pathetic." She spat it like venom. "And then to top it off, once you finally made her believe your crap you treated her like nothing."

"Nessa, I think I should go. I'm not in my right mind, clearly neither are you. I think coming here was a mistake, you're being mean again. You're just trying to hurt me. Trust me, I hurt everyday because of my own actions. I just thought we could talk, maybe gain some closure. I'm not going to listen to this." He stood picking up his plate to take to the kitchen.

Nessa stood too, she swung her hand down knocking Toby's plate to the floor shattering it. Spaghetti slipped and slithered all over his polished shoes, pieces of lumpy red meat plopped from his pants. But Toby refused to fight back. She was flying into another rage, the kind she had when she didn't get her own way. He wasn't going to give her any material to convince her that her irrational onslaught was deserving.

Right now, Nessa hated him. She hated rejection. Again, someone was being chosen over her. Laura, Elle. And both of them weren't even there for their men. Why did they deserve so much love? What made them better than her? Nothing. Nessa wanted to hurt Toby physically, mentally, emotionally in every way she could.

Spite prickled at her tongue as she spewed her words. "You want to know something about Elle? She was fucking Torian." She gave it a minute to sink in. "Because she wanted to. She loved him."

"What are you saying? Why would you say that? You're an evil woman Nessa. Elle was your daughter how could you say that! She was taken, murdered. You just want to hurt me further is that it? Make me cry?" He started for the door and she followed.

"If you're going to, at least wait until your home, cuddled up in your bed, alone. I don't want to deal with that shit. You wanted answers Toby so there they are. Elle was no angel." Nessa began to shove against Toby's back and he stumbled out the door onto the small front patio. "Your Elle loved Torian Amos and he loved her. More than you ever did. And you will never find him Toby because he is fucking dead. Just like Elle. How is that for fucking closure?" She began to laugh hysterically.

Toby was too shocked by her words to know which way was up. He didn't want to believe her, but perhaps it was true. Was this man loving her in a way she deserved, in a way he was too pig headed to? But still why would he kill her? He was confused, sad. He stumbled back and tripped over the single step that led onto the patio. He fell hard against the cool dewy lawn. His head pounding, vision sent spinning. He scrambled his way up onto his feet and made it to his car. He climbed in and locked the doors attempting to drown out Nessa's menacing, crazy laugh.

He took a moment. Watching her stand there in her mad insanity beneath the dull glow of the patio light, swirling with insects. Something had snapped inside that woman. She reached for a potted plant and drew back ready to throw it toward him. Toby sucked in a breath and started the car, reversed out quickly.

Halfway down the block his anger suddenly began to rise as the thoughts processed in his mind. He pulled over, begun smashing his fists against the steering wheel over and over again, allowing a hollow furious roar to rip up and out of his throat. Abruptly his mind was filled with images of Elle and Torian. Cops had shown him pictures, he was god like. If she was sleeping with him because she wanted to? It made Toby all the more insecure.

His hands all over her body, her naked skin pressed against his, crying out in ecstasy, crying out with love. She had wanted him, of course she did. Toby's stomach turned, his nostrils flared as his breathing increased. It was like there was red hot fire inside his bones and he was about to implode. All he could do was grip the steering wheel as his knuckles went white.

Of course, she wanted him, of course she did. I have fucking loved that woman for years and she'd been screwing some guy behind my back. Of course. How dare she treat me like that! I'm glad she's dead that stupid bitch.

Nessa watched him drive away. Watched his brake lights come on and sat on the step for a moment waiting to hear his faint yelling. She smiled, stood slowly and returned to the wine. Smug with herself she finished the bottle off and reached for another pondering her latest renewed efforts. This could work she thought. She'd planted some seeds and they had certainly germinated quickly. Soon they'll take hold and smother that barren space. Toby's fragile and now mad, she'd accomplished that. It hadn't been her intention but the night had turned sour and she always hated to be reminded that she wasn't wanted. Some one had to pay for that.

Elle thinks she's smarter than me? Thinks she escaped? I'll show her. Nessa took a deep drink from the bottle she held. Toby and I will both show you that you can't just run off without my permission. She thinks she's happy and everything's fine, suppose she would after all this time. Well it will end horribly and abruptly. Torian, Trey and all those Florence women, I can not wait to see them all smothered in the darkness. She guzzled the bottle, grabbed another and giggled to herself the entire time.

Chapter 28

Her eyelids fluttered open. She knew what she'd see, peach skies that no longer seemed abnormal. It was home. This is home, she took a breath a deep, calming, rejuvenating breath. Her essence had been poured back in the mould that was Elle. She was full and light.

The constriction she'd always felt in her waking life on Earth was lifted. It was like the noose around her neck had been removed at the very split second she was about to hang. Finally, the life she was destined to live had begun. Reborn.

Elle sat for a while to take it all in, her surroundings were so unlike Earth's. There was a lack of hard and cold all in one tone. A lack of man-made things. No grey roads, lacing the environment like ribbons flicked out and allowed to land where they may, framed by pale grey sidewalks. No geometric buildings in yet another shade of grey crammed against each other providing cages people voluntarily chose to be confined in. No men in suits, no women in heels.

Torian had tried to tell her this world would take some getting used to. Elle agreed that the land and environment itself would take time until her awe subsided but the people? No, Frin was a simplistic natural world. Utopian. Filled with beings whom knew how precious their land was, how essential to their survival it was. They nourished it and cared for it, for they knew it would provide abundantly everything they'd ever need to live and survive.

The tree under which she sat seemed to be a slightly higher point in the landscape. The ground gently fell away from the old tree in all directions. Sweeping down onto an open plain to her left, the long waving grasses rippled. She could hear the soft rattling of the seed heads tagging one another. It was scattered with skeletal trees sprinkled with fresh curled up buds.

To Elle's distant right was the ocean. The shoreline curved out away from her in a crescent moon shape. The ethereal peach skies were reflected in the waters, making it look like a bay of sparkling rose champagne, the clouds fairy floss, melting into the liquid.

Directly ahead of her was a high mountain range, it reached up to tickle the golden smeared vapour. She couldn't tell if the peaks had splintered and spliced up to meet them or if the clouds had sunken to shroud the inquisitive tops. Beneath the impressive mountains was a deep forest, its volume spilling out toward her. Even from this great distance she could see their majesty. Huge and ancient trees. She didn't think even ten grown men hand in hand would be able to embrace their trunks.

Elle's heart felt light and buoyant, she was excited, curious. Such a beautiful new world and she was eager to explore. A lifetime, Torian had said. We have a lifetime. I have forever to get used to this new world. In the beginning she hadn't understood exactly what Torian was implying. Elle assumed forever meaning the span of her life. Until she died. But like all things in Frin, beings were given the option to choose.

The more he explained to her, the Florence women she soon came to realise, he spoke of at least eight generations of women in the present tense. She'd been confused, how could they all possibly still be alive? They were not immortal he'd said. And people did die. The people of Frin were not immune to injuries nor illness, they were treated by powerful spiritual healers who used rituals and expansive knowledge of medicinal herbs. However sometimes terminal illness would take hold or an injury far too beyond the repair of anyone, let alone the healers. There was a place, that all knew of, that could end pain and suffering.

The shadow caves they were called. A place where those who'd chosen to leave this plain of existence could go and surrender to the shards of light within. There were many reasons people chose to leave. Though not everyone always understood the reasons why another decided to enter the shadow caves. Still they allowed the individual the choice. Respected it and said appropriate farewells.

Torian had went on to explain that the shadow caves were deeply regarded as sacred. They were worshipped and not to be messed with. Those wishing to do evil could quite easily turn this haven of peaceful departure into a weapon. In awe of such a thought Elle decided she'd rather not see them let alone know where they were. Though couldn't help wondering if they were hidden among the mountains before her.

She shivered as if shimmying the last of her old self from her bones. Like she was a treasure found in the dry sands, the last of the salt falling away. She stood, rounding the willow with its curtains of green. She pondered why it was this spot she always awoke. She recalled it featured in the bedtime stories Nessa had once thought was a good idea to tell her. Perhaps she'd awoken here to? Maybe all the Florence women did?

Her rambling thoughts turned to Torian, how far behind me would he be? There was a considerable time lapse between worlds, would she be waiting moments or days? What seemed like a single afternoon in Frin was in fact days on Earth. A brief flash of concerned entered her mind and left just as abruptly. Bad feelings and ideas came and went like the breeze here, they were allowed to exist, felt, accepted and left. Unlike Earth where the smallest negativity took root, flourished and destroyed its host.

Peering off toward the horizon, Elle found the worn path through the soft grass. It headed toward the suns. The suns she considered. Strange and beautiful. If she followed the path it would lead her through the plains and up the hillside beyond. She knew that she would reach the small village, Torian's home. No, my home.

Her feet swept her along, the powdery dust beneath them, the sweet smell of fresh foliage swirled her down the path. The temptation to follow the path, follow the suns was luring her further along. She heard a feigned cough. And her heart stopped.

Elle spun around, her eyes meeting with the most glorious sight of all. Torian, causally leaning against the tree, wore his trademark look. Hands in his pockets, a slight slouch curved his broad shoulders and his head tilted just enough to make him look like he wanted to play. Devilish and utterly irresistible. His steel eyes examining her as if he wanted to make sure she was okay. His smile radiating relief. She was here, she was okay. Now I can be okay.

Elle ran to him and flung her body against his knowing he could take it. He picked her up and hugged her so tightly. "Elle." He breathed into her ear as if he was breathing her into reality. "I love you so much. You'll never understand. I'm so thankful we're here now. The first day of our new life together and all I want for you is happiness. I plan to make you feel it everyday of my life. This is my oath to you."

She pulled back and frowned, looking into his eyes, she saw the traces of a deep pain. She knew that home in Frin the wounds Earth had inflicted upon him would fade but he'd always have the scars. She didn't know what he'd experienced in the days since she'd fallen asleep in his arms. The newfound desperation in his love told her it had been changing.

In the depths of her soul she knew she'd never have been as brave as Torian had to be. She'd never go through with killing his body no matter what the reasons. But he had done it. Not because he wanted to but because he loved her and wanted her safe from Earth's growing evil. From Nessa. He had wanted Elle to be happy and to be with Mai. He had done it for her, putting aside all his own feelings and emotions, his wants and needs.

It had to be done, it was part of the plan. He knew it all. But still he'd wanted to back out, find another way. He went through with it all because Elle had requested him to. Knowing he'd suffer with his actions, still, he did it for her.

"Torian. I am so grateful to have you. I'll never let you go." She squeezed him harder.

Suddenly a cold shudder racked her body. Panic began to rise up into her chest as if her heart were becoming frosted, icing over.

Her eyes wide and scared. "What's happening to me Torian?" She started to cough.

It was uncontrollable. There was pain, so much pain and cold. Her mind sent spinning, this isn't how I'm meant to feel here. Her breaths coming randomly and raggedly, it felt like ice was slicing at her esophagus. Her hands flew to her throat, groping and grabbing trying to defrost her dry, freezing windpipe.

"Keep calm, relax. Slow your breathing. It won't last long okay?" Torian hushed trying to soothe her hair away from her petrified face. His own tears melting away, he held his cheek against her head so she wouldn't see, they were one now in Frin, connected, he could feel her pain. He knew he caused it. He couldn't soothe himself. Nothing could. He focused on her.

Still holding Elle, he moved to sit down, leaning against the familiar old tree. He pulled Elle up onto his lap and held her like a night terrorised child as she fought the panic. He cried softly and continued to hush her as the death of her body finally reverberated through space and time. He was thankful he'd reached her on time to ease her through it.

Finally, gradually she began to feel warm light well up inside her chest and her throat relax. The fear sliding down off of her seeping into the dirt. Once her vocal chords shook the last of the chill she asked. "What was that?"

"All your ties to Earth have now been severed. You can never go back now. And I promise you, you will never feel anything like that again in your life." He kissed her forehead as if in apology.

Closing her eyes and laying her head against his warm chest. "As long as we are together, then I'll never want to go back."

They stayed, with Elle curled up on Torian's lap for some time, just being alone, being together. Both lost in their own world of thoughts about this new life they'd live.

Elle's thoughts were broken when Torian rose, picking her up and placing her on her feet beside him. "Let's go."

Smiling she slipped her feminine hand into his masculine one. She'd follow him to the ends of the world and back again. To the moon, the stars, to the deepest depths of the deepest seas. Anywhere he went, she knew she must go. Wanted to go. He led her again to the path she'd started alone, heading toward the giant forest that had lured her earlier.

She watched him from beneath her lashes, the way his muscles bunched and released, so smooth, so firm. Each one defined yet all working together to animate, create this magnificent man. Salacious feelings heated her body. Her thoughts turning to those times spent in his bed that smelt faintly of aftershave and them. Torian glanced at her. He could feel her sneaky gaze, feel the vibes radiating around her.

"Should we stop a moment?" Elle asked innocently.

His smile broadened. "As hard as you are to resist my beautiful, there are people waiting for us." He kissed her. "We have to keep going, there will be time."

"Fine." Elle pouted playfully.

Torian chuckled at her faked distaste of the idea. He knew what she wanted, what they both wanted. After the last tormenting days, he wanted something special for Elle, wanted perfection for her. She had no idea what he'd had to do to her body and never wanted her too. The residue of his horrific deeds had left him with a burden he wanted to shrug off. Seeing her utterly happy, perhaps would do just that.

Elle continued to watch him, slowly, seductively and Torian did the same, her dress, the one he'd given her. Matched perfectly to her rosy flesh beneath it, far more appealing than the sickly blue shade he couldn't shake from his mind. It was an ivory colour, embroidered with flowers of yellows and oranges. It was sleeveless leaving her arms to feel the brush of warmed air, it scooped low around her plump breasts. Fitted perfectly against her waist and fell of her hips naturally, it was light and flowy and swished just above her knees as she moved. He found it so womanly, so appealing.

Her excited childlike curiosity at the new landscape amused him but he knew how she felt. He'd been like that too when he'd arrived in Earth. He'd never experienced anything like it. Cars, the roads they followed along. People pressuring, bustling, selling things, mostly useless things in exchange for plastic and metals.

Without Trey's guidance he'd never have survived. Even the simple task of making coffee, he'd never done in his life, he'd been a farmer in Frin. He worked the land with his friend Senlangi, long and hard days to provide his community with fresh produce. He enjoyed it, it was satisfying work. A world away from being a barista, collecting coins per cup.

Frin was a wholesome place, where work was always available. There was so much for all to do and anyone could choose their path. Farmers, hunters, cooks, builders, artists, musicians and teachers. Everyone was a teacher. All knowledge was shared. Everything was shared. Even feelings. Thoughts.

He focused back on Elle and knew she'd feel him do so. It was how things were communicated. He'd heard people on Earth say that their ears were burning and therefore someone was talking about them. He thought it may be similar. At first, he thought that people of Earth had the same abilities as those in Frin but soon found, it was only an expression. If he thought of Elle in a particular way she'd know. If he felt love, she'd sense it. The same way she would sense someone watching her from across a room. If he wanted, he could look her in the eyes and pass direct and simple messages to her.

She'd also sense if someone felt badly toward her, sometimes it would cause pain depending on the strength of those emotions. This was how those affected by the darkness were recognised. Those who allowed the darkness in, were cast out, some even sent to the shadow caves. Laura had been the first victim of the darkness. And since then it had claimed more and more Frinians.

It was becoming less rare in recent times, for the darkness to find a foothold within a Frinian person. When it did occur, everything imaginable was done to wipe it out. The darkness had become a disease in Frin and they did all they could to prevent it becoming an epidemic. Healers would smudge affected beings, pray, worship and make offerings to the light, anything possibly to destroy it. Affected children were more often than not the only ones to be saved. Adults, once infected over time became evil, hollow monster like versions of who they once were. Torian hoped Elle would be the strength, love and light they needed to keep the darkness back, send it further into retreat. He knew she would.

Chapter 29

Torian was taking her to a very special place. A place he visited regularly from the very first morning he'd dreamed of Elle and realised he loved this imaginary woman. He made offerings to the essence every chance he had, seeking knowledge and understanding. Searching for answers about this woman he'd never met. He'd thought of this day for years and now it was finally here.

Elle watched a flock of unusual birds, her emotions playing out across her face and Torian couldn't help but laugh aloud. She was fascinated by the tall gangly birds. They looked similar to the birds she knew of as ostriches only these were bigger and brighter. An amazing creature with long scrawny legs in shades of orange, their bodies a purple hue that continued to fade up their feathers reaching a small head. A short stumpy beak in dark blue.

"They're called quaints." He began to explain. "They feed at sunset, hence their colouring. They lay low in the grasses of the plateau until it's the perfect time of day when the beetles and insects rise to meet the last of the light. See there, that's the male, they have darker legs. We hunt them sometimes too. They are delicious. Taste like chicken." Torian laughed.

"Amazing." Elle was breathless, speechless. She didn't even respond to his joking, she was far to enraptured to acknowledge it.

Elle was calm and relaxed. He could sense it. All her stresses and worries, the crippling anxiety had been washed away. All those heavy, smothering emotions that had taken up residence inside her had been flushed. Elle was clean and fresh, now that she was home.

His beautiful woman he pondered, she was far more beautiful here. No, she'd become ethereal in this peach, glowing atmosphere of Frin. Despite Earths' harsh light and dragging gravity, to Torian she'd still seemed magical.

Angelic even, but here now, her appearance surpassed that of Laura Florence. And anyone who still retained memories of her still told of her beauty. She'd been Mother Nature incarnate, exotic and intoxicating, powerful, intelligent and incredibly kind and yet here is this woman. My woman, he thought. She is more than everything. She'll become everything to everyone. Such great responsibilities lay ahead for her and she will handle it with bravery and grace. And I will be there with her always. She is my all.

Continuing on down the slope hand in hand they headed toward the ancient forest. Torian lead her into the line of trees, they started to thicken around them immediately as they followed a well-worn dusty path through.

The canopy above curled over them forming a tunnel of green shadows. Branches and leaves intertwining into gnarled webs of nature, embracing them. Knives of light sliced down to lightly pierce the bare earth. It flickered about them as they walked on through, minute bugs stirred and swirled around them so close but not so close to touch their skin. The light reflecting from their metallic wings created a gentle glittering tornado. The bugs parted and allowed them through, settling back down to the ground, ahead of a light mist. It became thicker and thicker, Elle looked to Torian with curiosity but he kept on and she did too. There was a radiating energy within the mist, a magic she could feel it.

Torian stopped within in the thick mist and faced her. Elle could only faintly see him beaming at her, a safe ghostly form in the moisture, swelling around them like it had a pulse.

A wave of feeling rushed over her, his love. Radiating, thumping around them. He winked and she heard him in her mind. After you, he thought. Elle released his hand and wandered deeper. A buzz of tiny blue flames, fairies, howled and hovered in front of her face, little arms beckoned her to follow and flew off quickly into the fog. Her overpowering curiosity enticed her to run, chasing the blue flames through. Abruptly the fog receded, like someone had lifted a sheet of silk from her face.

And then she saw. The community. Her community. Her happiness almost brought her to tears. She could sense the overwhelming joy these people felt toward her. Elle had been found, saved.

These people cared, they wanted her and she was safe. Her whole life she'd been constantly homesick for a home she didn't know she had. Her previous life, a dirty cloud of melancholia. This moment, right now was like her insides had been dipped in gold. Home.

Torian stood back, gave her space. He felt every emotion they way she did. She was his lover, his life, she'd become a part of his essence and these emotions were new to him too. He'd never had a stronger connection with anyone in his life, everything she felt was reverberating through his system. And this was different. Very different to what he'd experienced before, stronger more vibrant and moving.

Tears streamed down his cheeks as he watched the community welcome her from the edge of the mist. Her hair streaming lightly in the river of air about them, like it was lighter than it should be. Skin glistening with the moisture beading upon it, her eyes wide and smiling as she embraced people who were now her family.

They loved her, he felt it, the aura surrounding this mass of people directed toward her. He was so proud of her his heart constricted. I will protect this woman for all my life, he promised himself.

The woman he'd dreamed of and loved was home and she was better. Happy finally, a way of life she deserved. Torian's happiness for her overwhelmed him. Eventually she backed away, retreating with a beaming smile to Torian's side. Taking in the community from his perspective was breathing taking. Serene.

They'd gathered in a huge clearing, a rough circular shape. Beyond the gathering a sheer rockface shot up, exceeding even the height of the trees. No top in sight, it was covered in moss and lichen, colourful fungi. Among the rocks, openings with carvings decorating their entrance. Narrow paths weaving back and forth providing access, perhaps they were lived in.

Torian raised an arm in the air. The community cheered as Elle looked at him confused. "I'm signalling that we're leaving now. I have something else to show you."

Elle waved good bye as she again followed Torian, down another path to their left. He explained that everyone would now most likely remain behind to celebrate her arrival.

"Shouldn't we stay?" Elle enquired.

"No, everyone understands you need time. They're just happy you're here for good." He smiled. "As am I."

Leaving the forest, they came out upon an open space, she again could see the ocean far beyond. She saw houses, small cottages. They were simplistic but so pretty, rustic picket fences surrounded them. Overgrown flowers and greenery abundantly grew along them. Vines covered in fresh blossoms about to unfurl tangled together, creeping up the cottage walls. Thatched rooves, some with lawn like plants covering them.

Birds had nested among the beams that supported the roofs in triangular shapes above the carved front doors. Lanterns hung from posts that lined the paths between homes, the dark must be magical Elle thought. Whimsical, romantic, comfortable.

Many families must live here she decided. Opposite the dwellings an open clearing, grassy and central to the expansive space.

Long tables were set out, decorated with flowers and foliage, large candles of varying sizes strewn long the centre, were melted out onto the timber table. Beyond those, big stone lined fire pits, spits for roasting meats and benches bearing vegetable laden baskets.

"This one is for you." Torian stopped her in front of the last cottage, pointing.

"For me?" She'd not considered where she'd actually reside.

"Well for both of us, if you'll have me."

Elle elbowed him in the ribs playfully. Of course, she would and he knew it.

Suddenly tears burst forth. Torian took Elle in his arms smiling, her tears were joyous and he kissed them lightly away. "You're so beautiful and you feel so beautiful. Your emotions are almost too hard for me to handle, I've never felt anything like this in my entire life. Thank you for allowing me to experience them with you."

Elle peered up into his face overrun with happiness and love. He couldn't help it. He had to kiss her, pressing his lips against hers he groaned, like he was releasing a pain he'd held onto for too long. Elle kissed him back, her arms wound around him. She felt his warm moist tongue against her lips asking for permission to come home. Parting her lips, she tasted his tangy citrus and wanted more of him. Torian pulled away and she took forever to open her eyes, lingering in the moment, savouring the tingling fizz thrumming through her body.

"Do you want to see inside?" Torian asked when her eyes met his.

She simply took his hand in response. Torian opened the door and nodded for Elle to go ahead, immediately she was ambushed by the pure charm. Torian's art hung here too, decorated by nature creeping in through the ceiling beams. Vines and blooms swept to the floor, large candles stood on timber slices in the corners. The furniture incredibly rustic and covered with cushions of velvet and silks.

Her eyes moved to the left where she saw an arch into another room. The bed was there. Animal furs, feather pillows. She could no longer absorb her surroundings now that she'd found the place that they would share each night embraced together. Elle looked to Torian and smiled, stroked his arm and took his hand again. He nodded and let her lead him.

Torian lit the candles that sat on small tables by the bed as Elle removed her clothes. He watched her take the straps off her shoulders and slide them down, she reached back for the buttons on her dress and he went to her and helped. Gently brushing her hair aside and sweeping it over her shoulder as it shimmered in the candle light, he undid them one by one, revealing her smooth back.

Elle wiggled and the dress fell from her hips to the floor and she kicked it aside. Torian took the sides of her lace trimmed under wear between his fingers and tormentingly slid them slowly, getting down onto his knees taking them with him. He lifted each foot in turn to step her out of them.

Torian brushed her toes and swept his hands up her calves, thighs and caressed her round bottom. Her skin a burning glow. He hugged her swollen hips feeling her soft backside against his chest, his face placed on her back. His arms wrapped around her, he stroked her tummy. Elle closed her eyes and enjoyed his loving cuddle, she turned around and held his cheek against her breast, running her fingers through his hair loving him in return.

Torian lifted his face to take her nipple between his lips, gently sucked before releasing to take the other. He kissed her sternum, her belly button, tracing a path between each stop with his tongue. He could sense Elle's wanting, her fingers tugging now at his hair she pulled him harder against her. With his arms still around her legs, his hands took her inner thighs and pulled them a little further apart. And traced a moist line lower.

Finally, he kissed Elle in the place she felt desperate need and she involuntary moaned. Elle massaged his muscular shoulders as his tongue firmly stroked her back and forth. With her knees feeling weak she pulled at him to rise. He kissed her again deeply and the taste of herself on his lush lips drove her insides mad. Torian lifted her from her feet, cradling her, kissing her, he carried Elle to the bed and lay her down. From behind her thick lashes she languidly watched her man.

But he was more. As he removed his clothing, one button at a time he revealed a god. The flickering light transformed his body. Inch by inch he became more, his flesh inviting and hard. Large and safe. He took down his pants watching her gaze all the while. Her vision lingered, curiously, passionately for too long on the part of him that made him a man, the part of him that allowed them to become one. The part of him she allowed into her very being.

He came to her and lay down beside her on the furs. Embraced innocently, they felt natural and raw, naked and alive. Elle could feel his skin heating her while she moved her hands over his muscled body and she could no longer resist, she climbed upon him. Torian held her hips, so she hovered over him. Elle struggled against him, pushing down toward him, but he was too strong. She lent forward and bit at his chest playfully.

"I liked that." He smirked seductively and she felt him release the strength that held her poised above him.

Grateful, she pressed against his tip and rolled her hips in a circular motion to position his large size perfectly. Then pressed down against him. Elle's eyes flew open she could hear a distant erotic cry as she felt his thickness fill her.

She realised it was her own sound. Like she was outside herself. She could hear him and herself in her mind, crying out in delicious agony. Torian rose to embrace Elle chest to chest as they rocked against one another.

And then they felt it, looking into each-other's eyes they knew it was coming. As Elle threw her head back in pleasure, they became translucent, ghosting into one another. Through the misty version they were transforming into, their veins pulsated gold, in rhythm to their climax. Elle could feel Torian throbbing inside her entire body and their golden blood pumped as one. Their hearts met, pressed and blended into one. A single thump and an intense light lit the room. Glittering shock waves radiated from them again and again like they were the core of an atomic blast.

The people of the community continued their gleeful partying in the glade among the ancient trees, beneath the infinite stars. Drinking, dancing and playing when suddenly the waves hit. Shimmering gold washed through the trees, over them, lighting the glade magically before fading off into the darkness. Silence befell them all as the glimmer came again and again.

Finally, the last radiated through, they waited to be sure it was over. A buzzing murmur picked up quickly as they looked to one another with smiles and smirks. Whispering and muttering good things. Someone cheered loudly enticing the others to join in and the glade became an echoing chant of joy. The energy of the party had increased tenfold, drinking and dancing resumed with new found vigour.

They all knew what had transpired, but this was different, this was powerful, passionate. Like nothing they'd witnessed before. This was special, two rare souls finally found each other among the universe and reunited. Oh yes, tonight they'd party.

Elle and Torian lazily woke late and lay in bed together. Elle looked at Torian and broke out in a glorious smile, she couldn't help it. She giggled and put her hands to her face. Torian took them and held them so he could soak in her gorgeous smile.

"I've never felt so refreshed and satisfied." Elle said wriggling her body. "I've got not a want for anything."

"For nothing? At all?" His playful look returned.

"Actually, I am hungry." She winked at him.

"Ok, time we got up I suppose. I've got places I want to show you and people I want you to meet." He beamed with pride. He'd been desperate for her to meet the people he cared for.

The moment they stepped outside their cottage door there was an energy to be felt. A jovial hum of people going about their day. She could feel their positivity fizzing through her, giving her a buoyancy about her movement. There was a calming constant sound she couldn't quite place, Torian sensed her slight confusion, nudged her and pointed to the waterfalls.

High above them in the cliffs was a large pool. It overflowed, spilling down like liquid crystal into a swirling blue pool below. It was filled with children squealing with delight, splashing each other and showering under the waterfalls gentle pressure. The pool continued on into a stream that babbled over rocks that had been smoothed over many years. Little timber bridges arched over it in places, in others stepping stones. Large bowl-shaped flowers bobbed against the little rapids, babies groped for them as their mothers held them in the shallows.

"This is just heaven." Elle stated to Torian who simply smirked and nodded.

"Here come with me." He took her hand, twisting his fingers between hers.

As they moved through the people, they stopped their work to pause and smile, nodding to them both as they passed. Some came to shake Torian's hand and hug Elle, welcoming her. Children came running, peering at Elle from behind bushes, rocks and from behind the legs of the adults who stood by. The braver older children threw flowers at her feet. One child came to hand Elle a floral wreath, indicating she should put it on her head.

"Like this?" She asked arranging it down over her hair.

The boy nodded his large horned head as Elle knelt down beside him. He's a minotaur her mind acknowledged.

"Thank you kindly. It's beautiful."

"My dad said I should make it for you." The boy spoke shyly.

"Oh, did he now?" Torian laughed as he turned to find the boys father and hugged him. "Elle, I want you to meet my good friend Senlangi and his son Ocran."

Elle stood to meet him, extending her arm to shake the impressive bull-like man's hand.

"We work together." Torian explained.

"Nice to meet you Senlangi. I'm sorry, I didn't pronounce that right." Elle blushed slightly.

It was a tough name to say, the 'lang' part of his name was almost guttural. It sounded like a strong masculine name when Torian said it correctly. She'd made it sound feminine. Senlangi was a big man and well built. His chest was bare of clothing but he had a fine thick hair covering his head and broad muscular shoulders. His head was distinctly that of a bull featuring a heavy set of shiny black horns. And his eyes, like his sons were soft and gentle, the colour of rich Baltic amber.

Elle could feel his good intentions around him almost like the very physical handshake. He was a kind and caring man, liked to joke around. She could tell why he and Torian were friends. They had a lot in common.

"You are lucky you are one of the Florence women." Senlangi chuckled. "They all pronounce my name that way. You will have to meet my promised woman. No one laughs harder than she when a Florence woman says my name in such a pretty way."

His accent was nice, kind of Jamaican she thought. Elle blushed a little again, but laughed along with Torian and Senlangi.

"You'll have to bring the family by soon for drinks." Torian patted Senlangi firmly on the back, hugged him like a brother then took

Elle's hand again to lead her further on. She waved to Ocran as they left. He beamed at her like she'd pronounced him king.

"Where are we going?" Elle finally asked him as they reached the outskirts of the busy community.

"I'm taking you to the temple of love." He smiled at her after a momentary pause, he seemed hesitant to tell, as if it were meant to be a surprise. "We were headed there yesterday. Before we got distracted."

"Oh." She smiled. "Temple of love. That sounds interesting, it's a religious place?"

"I suppose so but not like those of Earth were people believe in entities to guide them. Here we make offers to the essence of our emotions. Love for example, we pray it will embrace us and bless us with its presence. The temples provide us with more of a place to be grateful of how we feel." Torian seemed to struggle a little with his explanation. It was a place to feel rather than know. "There are temples all over Frin, each for their own purpose. Many Frinians will make a pilgrimage to visit specific ones for many different reasons."

"I look forward to seeing it." She smiled at him in awe of his passion toward the topic.

"You will like it. The temples over the many years have become alive with the emotion with which they focus. How could they not? With so many beings coming and going for centuries with their auras so focused. The energy has slathered the place, soaked it all up."

"And they are all like that? I find it fascinating."

"They are. I've always dreamed of travelling to visit them all. Make offerings to each." His dreamy gaze turned to the mid-morning sky imagining it.

"I'd like to come with you someday." Elle squeezed his hand and he laughed.

"I was hoping you would. We'd be gone for many years though. Perhaps when our life here is settled in, we can discuss joining a travelling party. We'd head toward the sea and make our way up the coast visiting other villages and communities on our way. We'd then turn inland once we reached the point where the three suns meet."

Elle remained quiet as he spoke, she loved to hear him talk like this. She could hear his passion and desire. His ambition. Clearly this was something he'd considered many times and Elle was intrigued. An amazing chance to spend time with this inspirational man, seeing even more of her own new world by his side.

As they continued along their path, the trees began to thicken, hugging them, the path narrower and narrower, becoming more and more littered with petals and flowers. Soon she felt only the velvety petals beneath her toes, a beautiful pastel carpet in shades her mind couldn't even start to comprehend. She'd never seen anything like it.

Ahead of them was a building, the temple of love she assumed. It had been hand built of stone obviously ages ago. So old and mossy, like some lost Mayan ruin. Tucked in amongst tropical type plants, exotic flowers and creatures she'd never seen before.

It was a spiritual place, Elle could feel it in the way her senses responded. An ancient strength and knowing smothered her with wonder. A magical wisdom shrouded in mysterious fog, everything coated in a sultry moisture. Her heart's rhythm changed, slowed and calmed, her eyes devouring the incredible sight.

Torian patiently allowed her to soak it in before leading her to the curved, crumbling entrance and walked her through into the heart of the building. The floor was stone too, worn smooth by many bare feet being placed where hers were now. There was a buzzing pulse to be felt. The energy, the very essence of millions of prayers, pleas and people, absorbed deep into the pores of the stone.

The golden dusted clouds could be seen through the ceiling where bare beams offered nothing but support anymore. There were many windows that were merely openings left in the creation of the walls. The building itself hadn't been created to be magnificent or extravagant as those on Earth usually were. Its magnificence lay in its basic construction, designed to soak and ferment in the potent emotions of those who came.

There was however a statue standing before her. It was large and interesting, bathed luxuriously in focused light. Finally, she moved toward it, leaving Torian behind. Carved of stone, she noted as she circled it. Like the path leading to the statue, it too had been rubbed smooth with thousands of years of touch.

"I know what this is." She turned to face Torian once her initial inspection was complete, her eyes wide with certainty.

"Tell me Elle. What do you think?"

"It is us." She trailed soft fingertips over it, running them through each crevice and over every curve, following the lines.

The statue was of a couple, intertwined intensely. It was abstract yet clear they were in the heat of making love. The artist made it appear that they were melded into one. Her hair, long and swirling, melting into his chest. Her breasts melting into his embrace. His arms melting around her, his hands disappearing into the small of her back as he held her tight, their legs tangled.

Torian observed her caressing the statue, considering. She may have been right. She seemed so sure. Perhaps it had been created in their image a long time ago, prior to either of them existing. Life was unpredictable and astonishing. Especially of late. He hadn't even known there was another world besides his own. He decided that he could not disagree with her. He had no grounds to state that it was not of he and Elle.

Elle continued to look on in awe and she looked beautiful. She was bright. Being bright in Frin was a very special thing, a powerful thing. Elle had the ability to draw people in, surround them with the brightness of her-self. She unknowingly could embrace them within her own aura of radiating goodness. The goodness was protection. She was a natural magnet always pulling others in. Keeping them safe.

She also was a powerful repellent not that she understood it yet. The darkness, if she faced it, would recede in her presence like she was its Queen. It feared her and would shrink before her.

Elle had no idea how integral she truly was in the coming peak of their Frinian world. Soon, either Frin would overcome the darkness, quenching it for good or the darkness would overcome them. Plunging their entire world into a seething horrific and violent endless night. Their Utopian ways would cease and hell would begin.

In this knowledge the darkness had been able to seed further. People were afraid, and fought it daily, those who couldn't remain calm and patient with fate sometimes were swallowed whole by the evil.

There was a general knowing that Laura would return, she'd promised them that. And her return would signal the beginning of a war between good and bad. Light and dark. However, there was an underlying hum, would she return at all? And this was where the darkness fed. In uncertainty.

Torian shook his head, placed a palm to his aching heart. My Elle, the fight you must face. His throat restricted a moment and he swallowed hard. He'd never leave her, she was his soul.

"Elle?" She turned and smiled, the kind that sent warmth through him. "Can I ask you something?"

"Yeah sure." She came to stand by him taking his out stretched hands.

"Will you join me?" He asked with all sincerity.

She paused, smirked. Looked left then right and back to Torian. "I have joined you...."

"No, no..." Torian laughed. "I mean, will you promise to spend your life with me?"

"I have done that too. And I mean it. I love you Torian."

"I don't think you understand what I am asking." He laughed at her adorable bewilderment. "This is like a marriage proposal."

"You want me to marry you?" Elle's heart jumped and her smile was involuntary.

"Well join me. Will you join me?"

"Yes. I totally will." She had no doubt.

Torian took her hands and placed them on his chest, his steel eyes sparkled boring into her. His intensity grew and Elle closed her eyes. Visions whirred in her mind. Elle could see herself walk into the café, felt her heart leap and freeze as she saw herself move closer. The woman of my dreams she thought. This was strange, Torian was showing her his memory, his emotions. She now felt the love he had for her from his very own perspective.

He'd wanted to run to her. He'd wanted to kiss her, tell her he loved her. He wanted to scoop her up, run out into the warm rain, take her hands and ask her to join him that very second.

She felt his conflict in knowing he couldn't possibly do that. She felt him calm himself, remind himself he had time and had to be patient. He kept reminding himself to just make her the best god damned coffee he could. Over and over he repeated it like a chant to keep him focused. He'd looked to her occasionally as she sat alone staring out at the rainy seas. He'd wanted to make an excuse to come sit with her but there was none he found reasonable. She'd been deep in thought and he chose to leave her to it.

Elle watched herself get up, push in her chair and leave the café. His heart slumped, she could feel his loss. His uncertainty at when he'd ever see her again. His persistent and nagging thoughts of 'please come back.'

He had a plan, a part to play and patience was a huge part of it. Elle had to come to him. So regardless of how much his heart pounded, no matter how tight his chest squeezed he had no choice but to leave her be. Just let her go out into the painful world alone.

Elle frowned and suddenly her eyes darted back and forth as if she were reading something across the stones beneath her feet. Something, only she could see. They stopped. And she looked up into Torain's honest eyes and began to cry tears of happiness.

To feel his emotions and relive his experience was incredible and touching. Humbling. He'd spent over a year in an isolated distance from her and all he'd wanted was to make her smile. Pull her from her depression, tell her there was more. Stroke her hair, kiss her brow and let her know everything would be okay. But he couldn't. His pain had been intense. Like watching a loved one be tortured and being helpless to stop it.

He broke his gaze and hugged her tight. Elle could feel his aura of love intensify, grow and encircle her too. It was a bliss, a peace she'd never known.

"I will promise to share my life with you Torian." Elle murmured into his warm chest.

Slowly, yellow petals flitted down through the non-existent ceiling. One by one, then more and more. Swirling and sweeping, flicks and sparks shooting off when they drifted into the suns rays. The temple became filled, yellow, orange and tiny glints wafted, riding gentle waves. Suddenly, they were sucked out. And the temple was still. Torian and Elle stood in amazement looking at each other for just a moment, then burst out laughing.

"I believe we've made sufficient offerings to the temple of love this day." He laughed, he swept Elle off her feet and spun her around. "Love has blessed us."

It was the best day of his entire life. Thus far.

Chapter 30

A knock at the door stirred Elle and Torian from their lounging and idle chatter. Torian went to answer it.

"Come in, come in." Elle could hear him say. "Elle, we have a special visitor."

"Hello Elle." Trey was standing in the doorway. He was an impressive and gentle vision. "I wanted to welcome you home. I'd have come sooner but didn't want to overwhelm you. I wanted you to settle in a little first."

"Hello, and I thank you. I've never felt better or more at ease in my life. I'm glad to be home." She smiled and accepted his held out hand. He lifted hers to his lips and kissed it.

"We had actually planned to come see you later this evening." Torian mentioned.

"And I already know why. Which is my second reason for being here." Trey beamed and wrapped an arm around him. "I congratulate you both on your impending promise."

"Thank you again." Elle smiled blushing.

"We'll complete the arrangements." Trey confirmed.

"Complete?" Torian questioned.

"Oh Torian, I have long known you two would be joined. It will be an event that will bring much hope and happiness to far more beings than just yourselves. It is exactly what we need at the present." Trey smoothed his dark green robes and held his hand for Torian to shake.

"Well I too, thank you. We are very grateful and honoured you've thought so deeply on this." Torian said as he shook his hand. "I am looking forward to it, to say the least." He took his hand from Trey's and placed his arm around Elle's waist giving her a squeeze.

Trey stood for a moment in his regal manner, looking over Torian and Elle with pride. As if they were his very own children. He gave his head a slight nod, he'd completed his studying and turned toward the door.

"I shall keep you no longer. You will be joined on the eve of the next day should that suit you both?"

Torian took the door handle and opened it for Trey, he turned to Elle with a questioning look. Mentally asking if she was okay with Trey's suggestion.

"Of course, tomorrow would be wonderful." Elle answered for them both. She had no idea what needed to be organised for a marriage in Frin but had no concern. She didn't care as long as she and Torian were officially and formally recognised as in love and together.

Trey left and Torian closed the door behind him. He slumped back against it. He looked at Elle and smirked. Elle squealed and rushed to hug him. Torian lifted her from her feet and kissed her. They both felt like school kids, full of excitement. Tomorrow couldn't come soon enough. They chattered pointlessly about this and that, about how the time would seem to stretch until their ceremony.

"Let's go fill the time?" Torian suggested and Elle agreed.

They left their home in search of a meal and company. They joined many of the others in the open field where the long timber tables lay out in the open, laden with fruits, vegetables and breads. The mouth-watering aroma of freshly hunted meat wafted through the air making their tummies growl.

"There they are. Finally left the bed I see." Senlangi laughed in his exotic accent as he approached with his wife and son.

"Senlangi." Torian's smile grew. "Good to see you."

"And you." He replied. "Elle please meet my magnificent woman, Clearah."

"It is nice to meet you Clearah. And good to see you again Senlangi." Elle winked.

Clearah laughed as Elle had previously been informed that she would. Clearah was a fascinating woman, she too like Senlangi and Ocran was a minotaur. Her coat was white, a shimmering white in this late light. Her eyes like her families, were of a deep amber, laced with thick dark lashes. Her horns were of an ivory shade. She was gorgeous Elle determined.

Senlangi rolled his eyes at her knowing she'd said his name on purpose. He put an arm around Ocran and pulled him forward from his reserved position.

"Ocran has told me a lot about you." Clearah said moving in to give Elle a welcoming hug.

"Has he now? How are you Orcan?" Elle knelt to face him.

"I am good thank you." He twisted his hands together and couldn't make eye contact.

"I think you have competition Torian." Senlangi leaned in to murmur into Torian's ear with a chuckle.

"No, he does not!" Orcan protested overhearing his father, he was annoyed.

"I would be happy to be your friend too Orcan." Elle smiled as she rose to her feet.

"That would be swell." This time it was he who rolled his eyes, a characteristic inherited from his father no doubt. "May I go find my friends Mother?"

"Yes, go ahead." He'd already run off as Clearah called after him. "Make sure to eat well, don't get distracted." She turned to Elle laughing. "He will most certainly get distracted and request fruit at bed time."

"I know what that's like. My little Mai would do the same." Elle's giggling slowly wanned, her cheerful face becoming frowned with concentration. Mai, she'd barely had a thought of her since arriving.

"Oh love, let us go find a drink." Clearah nodded to the men and put an arm around Elle. Torian, worried, moved to accompany them but Clearh held up her hand to stop him. "This is woman's talk. We'll be okay. Come Elle."

Clearah led Elle to a grouping of large rocks, covered in a pale blue moss and offered her a seat. Leaving Elle staring at the ground, deep in thought for a moment. She returned with two carved horn cups and handed one to Elle.

"Here you need this. You'll like it."

Elle took a sip and immediately pepped up. Cherry, honey perhaps? There was a potency about it and Elle assumed it was alcoholic, or infused with something intoxicating in the least. She took another refreshing mouthful before finally looking up into Clearah's warm open face.

"What's your girl like?" Clearah asked.

"Well she's my world. I'm finding it difficult to understand how I'd almost forgotten her. How could I?" She frowned again and Clearah could sense the obvious shift in aura. "Even now I feel her fading from my mind again."

"It's okay. It isn't you. And you're not a bad mother, let's just get that said. You're in Frin now, you haven't completely adjusted as of yet. Here, the very atmosphere can strip you of pain and heartache." Clearah took Elle's hand. "Perhaps you needed a breather? A moment to not worry."

"Torian and I will be joined tomorrow and it's all I've thought of. And Mai won't even be present?" Elle looked off toward the fires where the meat still cooked. "It's a big deal."

"Oh, it certainly is. A special day. But don't forget. Mai too is a Florence woman. She will return home just as you have. She is a strong and smart child, she has already come many times. It is a rare thing for a Florence child to visit so regularly. When the time is right, she'll be here with us all. And for good."

"I know. Just in this moment I miss her incredibly." She managed a weak smile.

"Of course you do. It will be your burden but do not let it become your weakness." Clearah waved her hand around to show the community and its people. "This is your home, your family now. And if you embrace it and enjoy it, before you know it Mai will be here and a part of it too."

Elle nodded and remained silent as she finished her drink. It really was calming. Her body had relaxed and her mind slowly regained its ease. Mai was okay. Elle reminded herself that time worked differently too, while she'd been here in Frin a few days Mai had only lived half a day or so. Elle knew the time she'd spend waiting for Mai would be considerable but it would be much less for Mai.

It comforted her knowing Mai would be here someday. This was their path. Their destiny. As much as it didn't seem so in this moment, they were important and things neither of them understood, were unfolding. She looked to Clearah after her contemplation and smiled. She could do this.

"Thank you." Elle hugged Clearah, feeling like she'd found a life long friend within her, another relationship she'd never really experienced. "I think I need more of this yummy drink."

"Oh, I totally agree. It's the herbal infusion, very relaxing." Clearah laughed and stood, motioning for Elle to accompany her this time.

They scooped the red liquid from large stone bowls and moved closer to the fires as they sipped and chatted about their kids only in a lighter way now. Music began to play, rhythmic and hypnotic. Elle's body could feel each tribal-like thud in its pulse, string instruments joined.

A few people took to the open grassy space by the fire to dance and sway. Clearah took Elle by the elbow and pulled her over. Together with drink in hand they danced and laughed. Eventually, the men joined them. Torian wrapped an arm around Elle's waist to pull her in closer and spun her. Elle's drink almost spilled and Torian reached for it and took a swig.

"What's this you've got my woman drinking?" He laughed heartily in Clearah's direction as Senlangi took her by the hips and lifted her high into the air.

"She's a terrible influence I swear to you." Senlangi laughed back at Torian over the music.

"I love this stuff." Elle giggled taking another sip. "Thanks to you Clearah."

The song faded and they all slowed. They'd worked up a slight sweat and went for more drinks. Elle was feeling light and joyous, surrounded by good, kind people and having fun. They decided to eat before dancing more.

The meal was delicious, rustic and homey. Fire roasted vegetables and meats still moist and succulent. The cherry herb drink and a tummy full of wholesome food put any worries Elle had to rest.

"Have you mentioned the nymphs to Elle yet?" Clearah asked Torian after finishing her last bite.

"No. I haven't."

"You perhaps should. The Florence women usually are a little weary of them." Clearah almost scolded.

"What are the nymphs?" Elle looked to Torian curiously.

"They live in the woods. They help with the joining ceremony. I think Senlangi and I will help with those hides. Clearah it's probably better you explain." Torian and Senlangi rose and made their way over to stretching racks where hides had been curing. Elle suspected they didn't necessarily require taking down and putting away right in this moment but she was interested in what Clearah had to say.

"The nymphs are wonderful." Clearah began with. "But they're handsy. They'll prepare you for your joining, cleanse you, make you feel more relaxed than ever. They'll bring out your already exceptional glow."

"Okay." Elle wasn't sure what she was meant to understand. "You said handsy?"

"They'll strip you down. You'll be touched." She laughed.

"In a good way I am assuming."

"I don't want to explain in too much detail or you'll lose the experience. But I didn't want you to be completely unaware. I think perhaps it was your great grand-mother who was a little startled by their ways." She giggled again. "It is actually quite nice, if you're prepared."

"Okay..." Elle still didn't quite know what Clearah meant but decided she soon would. "You mentioned my great grand-mother. Like Mai, my family slipped my mind. I haven't seen any yet. Why is that?"

"It's kind of tradition to give new Florence women time to settle and adjust before overwhelming them. It can be an emotional time and too many emotions can overwhelm us all." Clearah giggled and turned away blushing.

"What?...." Elle questioned the unsaid.

"I imagine your reunion will be felt by all. Just as your union with Torian was." Clearah was now beaming.

"Oh. Right." Now Elle too was laughing.

"Come, let's find these bashful boys and head home. Tomorrow is a big day for us all, we need our sleep."

Chapter 31

Together Torian and Elle woke wrapped in each other's arms, snuggled among their furs. The sun lazily wavered, pushing through their sheer curtains to lay down upon them. Tiny particles floated and danced, glittered suspended in the light.

"Hello." Torian smiled at Elle.

"Hello to you."

"It's our day. I've waited for this for so long Elle." He cuddled her tighter.

Torian got up, leaving Elle relaxed sleepily on the bed. He returned with arms full of fruit, the smell was sweet, Elle's taste buds twanged immediately. Most of what Torian carried toward her she'd never seen before. He placed the fruit down on the end of the bed and climbed back in.

"Offerings left for us." He said happily reaching for a round fruit the colour of jungle green. He held it out to Elle and she took a bite, wiping sticky juice from her chin as she closed her eyes to savour. A little spicy. It was exquisite.

"You fill your tummy and I'll make us coffee."

"Coffee?" Elle asked wide eyed around a mouthful.

"Yeah, Trey allowed me to bring a plant back." He winked. "I couldn't allow you to live without it. We'll grow and roast our own. It'll be the best you've ever had."

"Everything here, with you, is the best I've ever had." Elle got up naked from the bed and stood proud before him making her point obvious.

"Don't tempt me so wonderfully woman. I'm making coffee." Torian turned away and went to heat water listening to Elle giggling after him. She'd witnessed the uncontrollable response his body gave as she teased him.

He'd been right. The coffee was the best she'd ever had. The cherry on top Elle thought to herself. What a life. What a perfect life.

When they'd finished and dressed, Torian with his heart melting smile announced it was time to leave. As they walked from their home into the forest Elle noticed that everyone else was adorned with flowers and interesting, dressier than usual clothes. Some followed them on their way.

At a fork in the path, Torian and Elle turned to the right and everyone else continued on their way down the left. Eventually they came to a pretty little clearing.

"It's time for me to go." Torian said as he stopped walking and faced her.

"You're leaving?" Elle frowned looking to the ground.

"We'll see each other soon enough. This is your time now. To get prepared."

He lifted her chin to meet her eyes. His lips full and soft pressed down on hers and he hugged her.

"I love you Elle."

"I love you too."

Torian left Elle standing alone wondering what she was expected to do. She looked around the clearing, she could hear running water and birds calling. Soon she could hear voices in a pretty language she'd never heard, coming from the trees.

Suddenly the forest nymphs emerged from the green shadows all around her. They were salacious creatures, largely voluptuous and clearly very comfortable in their own nakedness despite only revealing themselves to women.

The nymphs had lived in the ancient forests for centuries enticing women into their depths for love making and pleasures. They were considered teachers of a sort allowing women to learn how to love themselves, their bodies and become more empowered and in control.

The nymphs had good intentions at heart, they could sense needs and wants of others. They catered to each woman as an individual and helped her grow into her whole being, embracing her very basic primal instincts.

They were alluring and beautiful and Elle went with them willingly as they took her gently by the arms. Walking further into the forest, the nymphs stroked her, cooing at her pretty hair and skin. The running water became louder and the smell of burning spice, like pine needles came to her.

They came upon a small fire and the nymphs indicated Elle to stand by it. A large shell sitting precariously atop a stone, held water taken from the spring a short distance away. One fair haired nymph took burnt wooden tongs, picked up a big round stone from the flames and placed it into the water. It sizzled and spit as she slowly dipped it into the cool water. She continued adding more, unlocking all their retained heat.

Another nymph, this one with red hair that hung in voluminous waves all the way down to her large round bottom, offered Elle a smaller shell. Elle thanked her. It was filled with small round berries of red and yellow. Elle stood holding the bowl unaware of what she should be doing with them.

The biggest softest nymph took one and held it to her lips, motioning to eat them. The nymph then took another and squeezed it until a drop of juice fell into her palm. It was a blood red liquid. She then wiped it away after a moment showing Elle the stain it had left on her pale skin.

Elle took a few and gingerly put them into her mouth. She liked the flavour and decided these where what the previous nights drink had been brewed from. She knew they'd calm her and she now knew too, that they'd stain her lips a deep seductive red.

When she'd finished them, the nymph took the bowl back and swept a finger over Elle's lips seemingly satisfied. The five nymphs now took to Elle's clothing. They moved cautiously to begin with, assessing Elle's limits but she obliged happily as they removed her dress. They removed her bra and knickers, leaving Elle to stand nude by the fire as she watched them study her unusual items. The nymphs were not accustomed to clothes but the kinds the Florence women arrived in, always peaked their curiosity. They pulled the fabric, stroked it, smelt it, utterly fascinated.

Once they'd filled their interest, they turned their attentions back to Elle who stood naked, patiently waiting on the soft grass beneath the peach skies. They hovered over her body, looking at it, every inch. They began to stroke it as if working her out. Then they began to fondle her.

One squeezed Elle's nipple and appeared pleased with the response, another smoothed cool palms over her bottom, while another played with her hair and began to loosely braid it.

Elle closed her eyes, not exactly knowing how many hands were on her skin but it was comforting and relaxing and she allowed the sensation to take hold of her. She felt warm water trickled over her shoulder, sliding down her back, a soft finger chased the waters path. More water was poured over her shoulder this time it trickled soothingly over her collar bone and down between her breasts, this too was pursued sending a lethargic shiver down her spine. More and more warming water was poured over her until she was wet. Before the slight breeze could cool her, many hands were washing her skin with a soapy, floral scented oil.

Every inch of her body was washed and massaged, her shoulders, her neck, the small of her back and her stomach. Both breasts held, squeezed and stimulated. Each limb, every muscle kneaded and teased, releasing the entire world from her soul.

With her eyes still closed she felt the massaging hands moving further up her calves, then her thighs, as her inner thighs relaxed apart, another hand moved in to cup her intimately.

A brief wonder as to if she'd have been startled should Clearah not spoken to her, came and went like it was a feather in the wind. The hand began to sensually wash her as others gently supported the weight of her body and others massaged her scalp. Stoke after stroke she fell further into relaxation until suddenly her body shuddered deliciously. The nymphs took her full weight as Elle's knees went weak and a lazy smile spread across her face.

When they'd finished washing her, they used an exquisitely soft fabric to pat down her entire body. Elle opened her eyes and looked at each pretty and mischievous face in turn, she smiled at them. She felt like she'd awoken from the most rejuvenating sleep and was grateful. Any vague memory of tension had been washed away with those warm waters, absorbed into the earth beneath her nude toes.

Together the nymphs took a large piece of sheer white fabric draping it over Elle's head. They proceeded to tug and pull carefully, adjusting it around her. One left and returned with a wide woven leather belt and tucked it up under Elle's breasts tying it securely. Taking the remaining lengths, she criss-crossed them around Elle's waist, hugging it tightly all the way down to her hips.

The garment was loose around her shoulders, falling apart to drape her shoulders, leaving her collar bones bare. The sleeves were long almost covering her hands, the fabric hovered around her knees tickling the backs of them. One side was scalloped and hooked up to tastefully reveal a thigh. The overall outfit was comfortable and light. Simple, yet allowed Elle's femininity to be displayed, the sheer material revealing just enough of her nudity to confirm it completely.

They nymphs directed her to swirl and she did, they ran off into the forest as she admired the soft flow by the spring. She could hear the strange melodic voices of the nymphs as they returned arms laden with flowers. They dumped the blooms before her feet and started to pick out the daintiest, most unique flowers in shades of coral, pinks, and yellows.

They all took turns to place them in Elle's hair and once completed they took a step back to study her again. They squealed in delight and giggled, their thick white bodies bouncing along with their joy. They all kissed Elle then began to drag her softly into the woods. The three distant suns where now low in the sky, casting a magical atmosphere as they sashayed on.

Finally, the promiscuous forest nymphs stopped. Pushing Elle to continue on without them. She thanked them thoroughly and they nodded with knowing as they ran off into the hidden places of the forest, Elle catching flashes of red hair, blonde hair and white flesh as their mysterious voices faded away.

Elle walked on toward the growing sounds of a large gathering, her feelings began to alter as the combined emotion of the crowd filtered through the trees reaching her. Joy and an over powering sense of love.

As she came closer, she could see the crowd despite still being hidden within the tree line. There appeared to be a translucent, slightly iridescent cloud swarmed around the people. An emotion she could see, not only feel. This would be the happiest day of her life, she was home and she was in love.

After one last deep breath Elle stepped from the trees. Heads turned and all became silent. Every set of eyes on Elle. Abruptly, the crowd roared a happy cheer and Elle stood in awe of the shimmery cloud now swirling in pink around them all.

A female fawn stepped forward from the crowd, she wore a delicate yellow fabric shrugged around her shoulders, it fell on the bias to her waist where her body became a thick and sleek coat of hair. Her knees were reversed to Elle's and when she lifted her polished hooves to move closer, they bent backward.

"My name is Tiarnah. And these are for you Elle Florence." She handed Elle a bouquet of wild flowers tied in a quaint bundle.

"Thank you, these are really pretty." She pulled them to her nose to smell.

"You're most welcome, now you should probably go to Torian before he bursts. We all feel it." She laughed and stepped back.

The interesting assortment of beings started to shuffle aside, bowing to Elle as they created a path for her toward the temple. Well built, statuesque people, with large white wings neatly tucked down their backs, stood out prominently. Smaller fox-like people stood closer, their curious eyes bouncing back and forth, their ears twitching to catch barely detectable sounds. Bird headed women perched bare breasted and proud, like guardians by the entrance. Their yellow feathers shone.

Slowly a hollow thumping song faded in as she walked on. She was showered with petals as the blue flamed fairies swarmed in from every direction to guide her. The music continued, rhythmic and entrancing, it seemed to reach in and touch her soul, mingling with her pulse until it felt to be her life source.

Still the haunting song pulled her along, the crowd seemed to fade from the edges of her vision until it was only her and the sounds inside her body. She held the bouquet and watched her feet, lift and fall, lift and fall against the floral littered earth. She reached the temple and peered in through the crumbling arch as the fairies filed in ahead of her.

In the darkening light, a soft flickering blue shone down from the rafters where the fairies had taken their places. It was like the heavens had been dragged down and strung up just for them. Each beam held masses of fairies giving off a pleasant crackling hum, with their combined flaming auras radiating warmth. The open ceiling displayed actual stars, splattered, glistening quietly against the early champagne night.

Garlands of flowers and foliage had been looped and wrapped, swooping down from the rafters and sparkling insects buzzed on rapidly beating wings. The stone floor had been carpeted in velvety petals which stirred as if alive when the warm breeze came and went. The space was utterly magic, the beauty of it caught in Elle's throat.

And then she saw him. Standing there beneath the lover's statue, slathered in the blue glowing light. Her heart began to pound in her ears and her breath quickened. The butterflies in her tummy tormented her.

He stood in his way. Hands in his pockets, which were brown and worn low. How could he look so devilishly sexy and playful, yet innocent all at once? Her eyes hovered over his defined muscles, her gaze sliding down. His chest was bare and Elle loved the contrast of his colourful tattoos against his clear stomach skin.

Finally, she met with his eyes, his wide steel eyes. And still she remained, despite wanting to put her hands on his cheeks and feel his strong jaw against her palms. Kiss his ever so slight dimple that lived on his chin. Kiss his thick soft lips, the ones that could leave burning trails on her body.

Torian's smile grew as he watched her mind gently wander. He flicked his dark blonde hair back, indicating her to get in there with him. He couldn't wait any longer, he'd saw her make her way down the path, up to the temple's entrance. This was it, him and her.

Her hair was beautifully and loosely braided, it swept away from her face to reveal her pink flushed cheekbones. Her chin coming to a delicate soft point, her brow defined but not harsh, framing those mesmerising jewel-like eyes. They were lined with thick lashes just calling him into their depths and those lips stained in a succulent red.

He'd never seen Elle like this before. She seemed to be the very air of light. Always beautiful but this was something more, indescribable. The way she moved in that dress was ethereal. Time around her was slower and gravity didn't seem to acknowledge her. Her bare feet seemed to hardly touch the ground, everything about her was glowing. Her aura had changed, he was now aware. A pale lining of pure white encompassing her whole. She is special this one, Torian thought to himself. Elle reached him, smiling in that breathtaking way as she slipped her hand into his.

Chapter 32

The ceremony itself was simple and heartfelt. The atmosphere and perhaps the berries, had given the whole event an otherworldly feel. It was surreal and mystical and felt like the whole world belonged to only the two of them in that moment. Everyone and everything faded away as they made their promise to one another. Their trance had only been broken once the crowd gathered roared with happiness at the completion of the ritual. They both beamed with joy as they turned to face the people.

Children were brought forward to receive their blessing as was a Frinian tradition. New promises of love offered hope and it was customary to allow the future generations to absorb some of those vibes, bathe in the thick aura. They were given more flowers and little hand carved trinkets. The people took turns to rub over the lover's statue for good luck and well wishes, then slowly the crowds dissipated. Everyone heading off toward the feasting tables back in the community for drinks, meals, music and good company.

The sky had become a dark indigo by the time Torian and Elle were the last remaining people in the temple. Torian waved at the inquisitive fairies who still lined the beams above them. The fairies flared their flaming auras in aggravation, then took flight into the darkening sky.

It was spectacular to watch, the large swarm a blazing blue, flying high up into the endless purple. Suddenly they began to part, zipping off into a million directions leaving burning white trails streaming across the sky. Like a thousand shooting stars fled into the darkness. Torian watched Elle's open-mouthed wonderment and knew he'd never tire of her curious nature.

"Elle, it has occurred to me that perhaps you're a seer." He took a seat with his back rested against the lover's statue reaching his arms out to Elle.

"A seer?" She questioned, taking her place on his lap. "Is it more interesting than being bright?"

"I think both are interesting." He smirked and kissed her forehead. "You see so much more than there actually is. You see the wonder in the most mundane things."

"Well. Thank you?" She raised her eyebrows. "And those fairies are hardly mundane."

"It is a compliment. And I suppose fairies are as exciting to me, as cow is to you. Though even on Earth you could see the magic of things you witnessed every day." He laughed. "Many Frinians seek to become seers, it takes time and learning. But you just can. You have a unique perspective and that's special."

"I am glad I guess but I don't understand the significance. What does it mean?"

"Well for one, you'd be a suitable teacher if you wished to be." He smiled with pride at her.

"A teacher? That would be great, but I can't teach." Elle stated plainly.

"Yes, you can. You've come from a whole other world Elle, the way you see ours is amazing. Our teachings are not the same as Earth's, we learn about our world and our people and how to treat each other. I know many a parent who'd love for you to spend a morning with their children. Just show them your world, explain what you see and feel, allow them to tap into your way of viewing the world."

Elle smiled at his passion, she felt his pride pouring over her and she felt calm and safe. Perhaps teaching would be nice she considered.

"Just open their eyes that's all. Like you've done to me without even knowing it." He kissed her forehead again.

"It's getting late. Shall we go join the celebrations?" Elle asked him.

"So soon? There is one remaining part of the ceremony Elle."

"There is?" Elle gave Torian's sly grin a questioning look.

"We're here in the temple of love. We've been joined and now we give an offering to the essence."

"Oh." Elle now understood. Her insides couldn't help but give a lazy, tasty crunch deep in her belly.

Torian looked into her smiling eyes as he repositioned her on his lap, her legs now spread, straddling his outstretched ones. He leaned back against the cool stone of the lover's statue to admire her. Placing his hands on her backside he pulled her hips toward him, tucking her firmly in place. His hands traced up her spine and Elle's muscles released their tightness beneath his firm strokes. With his fingers tucked into her hair behind her head, he leant up to pash her mouth fiercely.

Elle felt his desperate want. The energy he gave was of wanting to make her feel good, he wanted so badly to make her feel beautiful and desirable. He wanted to be a part of her. This only made Elle want him so much more. She could feel him grow bigger and harder against her nakedness as she sat over his thighs, she tucked further against him and kissed him back.

As Torian slipped the light material from her shoulders Elle shivered at the slight touch, her eyes closed and she gave up completely. The fabric fell around her waist, held only in place by the belt, her breasts bare to the sultry air. He took his lips to her shoulder softly, nibbling at her skin, pressing his warm chest against her sensitive breasts.

The delicate burning tingle had begun, feeding the sparks within. Elle lunged at his neck, taking teasing little nips at his throat. She could stand it no longer lifted her hips just a little. Torian unbuttoned his pants and immediately she felt him. He was so hot and hard against her belly. Elle repositioned herself and Torian took her by the hips to help guide himself into her body. Elle moaning softly as he slipped slowly into her.

The fairies had returned, flying in and around them curiously watching their love making. Eerie flickering blue lights glowing and flashing over their hot moist flesh.

Elle and Torian oblivious to anything that was separate of them. Their distinct scents mingling, their endless love and their passion for one another created a dome of bliss and nothing would tear them apart now. There was no world for them right now, they were the entire universe.

Elle's eyes connected with Torian's and he pulled her ever closer to him. She could feel the belt wrapped around her waist, gripping and tearing at her skin but she didn't care.

Abruptly she felt it. Torian was fading before her eyes, he was opening, swallowing her whole. Devouring her essence and absorbing Elle into himself to coat her in his being. She could feel her skin warming as he melted over her. She could feel his touch caressing and stroking every inch of her body. He was inside her and smothering her. Her heart started to thud and she was vaguely aware that she now shared his heart. His pulse was now her pulse. From the depths of them both an animalistic roar tore up sending the fairies fleeing out into the night again.

Finally, exhaustingly her body shuddered. Utterly beautiful pain ripped through her belly, through her limbs, wave after wave. The sensation had built up into such a desperate ache and then it tore away at her. Releasing her lushly, allowing some relief as the feelings began to recede. It felt like a lifetime of drunken bliss before Torian's body melted off her, the heaviness she felt of his being shrouding hers began to fade. A slight sense of loss as their hearts separated.

Torian took her in his arms and hugged her to his chest and Elle stroked it. The silence was delightful and full. Their emotions thick in the air of the temple of love as they lay beneath the lover's statue. Their statue.

"How was that for an offering?" Elle finally opened the space.

"I imagine there's never been an offering that good. Ever." He smiled broadly down at her.

She nodded and watched the little blue beings peek back in, gradually they returned to zip about the garlands. She thought about how much she loved him and said it within her mind.

"I love you too." He replied aloud.

"You heard me?"

Torian nodded but remained silent. Slight concern cornered him for a moment as he thoughtlessly played with Elle's hair. This beautiful woman, with no need to hone her telepathy, a seer with a vibrant white aura. She really was special, but this often indicated a legendary destiny lay in wait for her. A destiny which often meant sacrifice, danger and sometimes death.

He pushed aside his darker thoughts, he knew Elle was more than he or perhaps anyone would understand. She had a purpose that he couldn't even begin to imagine. He also knew how clueless she was to it all. To how beautiful, how unique, how important she was. And while on this day they'd made a promise to each other, to always belong to each other. Torian knew that a woman like her with a destiny so divine would never truly would belong to him. She'd always belong to something greater than he.

Finally, they got up and hugged once more and left toward home. Even from a distance, they could see the glow from the fires and hear the people as their jovial chatter mingled with the air. There was a cheer sent out as Torian and Elle walked into the field hand in hand.

There was a large central bonfire and smaller ones scattered around. The smell of tasty meats, roasting on rustic spits over open flames was mouth-watering. Elle couldn't recognise the beasts being cooked but her taste buds didn't care. The meat was browning and she could see fat dripping and rolling across it as it lazily turned, keeping it moist and juicy. Other fire pits held different kinds of birds skewered above them on branches.

There were women busy with cooking bowls and pots, chatting contentedly among themselves as they took stones from the hot embers and placed them into the liquids. They had root vegetables prepared ready to boil and bake.

Torian put his hands onto Elle's shoulders and carefully turned her to face the dark edge of the field. An impressive figure emerged from the purple night, walking into the fire lit circle.

It was Trey, magnificent and tall. Elle's heart couldn't resist a slight flutter as the glowing fire light drew him in and engulfed him. As he reached Elle and Torian he held out his open palms and Elle placed hers on his and smiled.

Trey's inquisitive emerald eyes peered into hers as if he could read her soul. His strong build seemed larger than any man she'd ever seen, despite Torian standing by his side, a tiny bit taller.

It was a difficult concept to take one's aura into consideration. It was his vibrant, thick aura that gave him such a large and magnetic presence. His dark long hair hung sleek and straight, strapped in the same way as when they'd first met. A simple leather band, decorated with a golden emblem in the centre of his forehead.

A crown perhaps, one that was humble and simplistic, symbolic of his nature.

He was a king of sorts and once had ruled in a far away place. Torian had told her of glorious castle's carved into enormous trees. Trey and Laura had lived there together.

However, when she'd explained to Trey that the darkness had taken her and that it would come again to destroy them all. He'd left it all, to abide by the instructions Laura had left behind.

Some of the community who lived here now had felt compelled to join him in search of the returning place of Laura's line. Maybe one day he'd return but not until Laura returned and Frin was safe. Until then he was the leader of this community, keeper of the Florence woman.

"I congratulate you both. You have a wonderful life ahead of you." He said as he gave Elle's hands a squeeze before releasing them to pat Torian on the shoulder.

"Thank you, I'm sure we will." Elle replied as she beamed at Torian.

"We all felt your great joy and immense light. It is a relief to know it is so strong." He smiled with shadows in his eyes.

"Why is that Trey?" Torian's brow knotting as he read further into the comment, he'd hoped they'd indeed have a long happy life, before Elle was needed for their cause.

"I have felt Laura's presence. I do not completely understand it at present. There have been no recent births." He took a sobering breath and lightened before turning to Elle. "Perhaps it is just your arrival confusing my perceptions. It is still quite strange to look upon your face and see such a resemblance to my beloved Laura."

Elle didn't know what to say. She could feel his love for Laura swirled in his aura like a haunting ghost. She felt the slight morose and she felt compelled to say something to make him feel okay.

"You do not need to say anything my dear Elle. Just having you finally arrive is enough. Do not mind me I am just a very old, lost soul." He winked at her. "Enough heavy talk. Let's enjoy this evening!"

The aroma in the air, the sounds, the atmosphere, put Elle at ease immediately. They made their way to Senlangi and Clearah. Elle complimented Clearah on her appearance, she was such a lovely minotaur. Her creamy white coat had a pale brown swooping pattern trailing down her thick neck and her large bovine eyes were amazing. This night she wore a single gold ring in her shiny black nose.

"My promise does look particularly beautiful tonight I agree." Senlangi added. "Congratulations on having a promise of your own Torian."

"Well thank you my friend. I am quite pleased myself." He kissed Elle sweetly.

As the men continued their back and forth banter, Clearah took Elle to meet Tiarnah the fawn who'd given her the bouquet, properly.

"A lovely ceremony." Tiarnah stated.

"You know what? Forget the formalities, let's get ourselves a drink." Clearah smirked. "It's really the only way we'll get to know each other truly."

"Sure, I'd love some of that sweet wine." Elle said.

"Oh, I have something better. Senlangi has a special brew of his own. Come on." Clearah hooked and arm around Elle and Tiarnah's elbows and dragged them off to find the men.

"I know what you want." Senlangi laughed as he saw them approach. He took wooden cups from the table nearby and poured generous amounts from a water tight hide that hung at his waist.

He handed one to each, inclined his large bulls head toward Elle suggesting she take a sip. Elle took a mouthful and swallowed it down, her eyes opening wide. It was strong and almost took her breath away, the others laughed.

"Just wait a moment, the flavours will hit." Senlangi instructed in his unique voice.

Suddenly the flavour did hit, there was a sweetness and a tartness all at once, almost like raspberries or maybe pineapple. It was tropical and fruity and messing with her mind. Attempting to place familiar flavours to something so exquisitely different to anything she'd had before, was difficult. Elle liked the drink and thanked him.

Torian took Elle, moving toward the tables. The candles of random sizes in various stages of melt, were all lit and flickering over old mossy branches that dressed the tables. Jars filled with strange mushrooms and fungi stood intermingled with it all. Elle wasn't sure if they were edible or purely aesthetic.

There were piles of food, meats dripping still uncarved, steaming bowls of roasted vegetables and heaped fruits. Some looked like huge figs, others like small dried dates, yellow things similar to persimmons, orange grape like berries. Leafy green salads with thin wooden sticks placed across them, had big caterpillar looking creatures skewered onto them. As her eyes feasted on the delicious abundance, her ears heard something familiar that broke her greedy gazing. A happy laugh.

She spun and before she knew what she was doing, she'd flung her body at a woman and hugged her.

"I can't believe it!" She exclaimed.

"Believe it Honey. I'm right here. We all are." Eleanor Florence released Elle and spun her to face a small gathering of women who all vaguely, looked like different aspects of Elle herself. It was like looking into the mirror of her life at different points. Seeing herself as a middle-aged woman, an elderly woman and everything in between. The Florence women. Her family.

As she looked over them, she overwhelmingly counted seven. All the Florence women were here, besides of course Laura who'd begun it all, Nessa who was no longer welcome and her little Mai. Little Mai her precious baby, still too young to join them. Eleven generations of women if she included herself. Such a surreal sensation shimmied down her spine.

"There are eight of us here." Elle stated astonished. "I can't wait to get to know you all."

"No, you're wrong my girl." Eleanor said with that memorable twinkle in her eye. She looked beyond Elle and pointed. "See? There are nine of us." She chuckled.

Before Elle could even turn to see, her heart stopped beating. She drew a deep breath and held it. As she moved to look, time slowed and became frozen.

There across the field a girl stood proud. In super slow motion she started to run toward Elle. Big blue eyes shone, squeezed with a smile at the corners. Her thick long hair streaming back away from her matured face as she tore through the atmosphere. The white ankle length gown she wore, rippling about bare feet that pounded the Earth.

Elle felt the wooden cup she held, gradually slide beneath her fingers as she lost her grip. The cup fell slowly like it were suspended in mud, yet faster than the drink it held. The liquid a deep red floating pool, drips wavered hovering in the fire light.

Suddenly time sucked back into itself and the cup clattered to the dirt. The wine sloshed like spilt blood, droplets covering her feet, spots staining her dress.

Elle's breath caught up and her heart swelled. Her chest heaved in a painfully joyous sob, tears burst forth as she watched Mai running. Her muscle's tensed as she pushed away from the ground, taking off toward her daughter. Her arms outstretched, her smile beaming she ran as fast as her body would allow. The air around her was sucked up, whipping at her as she pushed through it, tears swept back to streak her hair. All she could see was Mai and she ached to hold her.

This was all she'd ever wanted, the illicitly pure emotions threatening to collapse her heart. She was loved, she was home and here was her baby girl.

Chapter 33

It was all black. An empty void of nothing stood disturbingly before her. In the depths of her mind she heard a small voice, echoing like a distant memory.

"Mummy, I want you back." It said, shyly, hollowly.

It peaked her interest and her heart beat harder. Thudding. She tried to move her fingers, her toes but it was all solid stone. She moved her eyes back and forth but nothing could be seen. Trapped. She felt trapped in a world, a universe of immense black. Darkness.

"Come, let's go. She can't hear you dear." Another ghostly voice reverberated through the endless nothing.

No don't go, she thought insanely. I hear you, I hear you. I am here. Don't leave me. Please stay. I want you to stay. The desperation feeding a buzzing energy, her pulse becoming rapid and intense with panic.

The light crept in, through the crack of eyelids. Exhaustion followed the effort of creating a slight split. Blinding white consumed it all and feeling returned to her limbs. Still, she could not move a muscle, she could not say a word. Though through her paralysis she became aware of tight bindings at her wrists. They squeezed and it ached and she tried to moan. It hurt so much.

Weakened, her eyelids closed and the darkness returned. Enveloping her being, her mind, her soul in a pitiful hole. She screamed inside but there was not a sound, no worldly indication that she'd ever really existed. So, she screamed and screamed.

"Elle!" Torian's voice broke through.

She woke startled, cradled in his arms, relief washed over her whole. She was safe, she was loved and she was at home in Frin. Everything she'd ever wanted was right before her eyes.

"Don't worry Elle." He said. "It wasn't real. None of it. It was all just a dream."

www.ingramcontent.com/pod-product-compliance
Lightning Source LLC
Chambersburg PA
CBHW071901290426
44110CB00013B/1233